A Symbolic and Connectionist Approach to Legal Information Retrieval

A Symbolic and Connectionist Approach to Legal Information Retrieval

Daniel E. Rose

Advanced Technology Group
Apple Computer, Inc.

 LAWRENCE ERLBAUM ASSOCIATES, PUBLISHERS
1994   Hillsdale, New Jersey   Hove, UK

Lawrence Erlbaum Associates, Inc., Publishers
365 Broadway
Hillsdale, New Jersey 07642

Cover design by Mairav Salomon

Library of Congress Cataloging-in-Publication Data

Rose, Daniel E.
A symbolic and connectionist approach to legal information retrieval / Daniel E. Rose
p. cm.
Originally presented as the author's thesis (doctoral—University of California, San Diego, 1991).
Includes bibliographical references and indexes.
ISBN 0-8058-1388-8
1. SCALIR (Information retrieval system) 2. Information storage and retrieval systems—Law—United States. Artificial intelligence—Data processing I. Title.
KF242.A1R67 1994
343.73099'9—dc20
[347.303999]   93-38963
                                                           CIP

Books published by Lawrence Erlbaum Associates are printed on acid-free paper, and their bindings are chosen for strength and durability.

Printed in the United States of America
10 9 8 7 6 5 4 3 2 1

Contents

List of Figures

List of Tables

Preface

This book was originally written as a doctoral dissertation at the University of California, San Diego, in 1991. When I began the research a few years earlier, the world of artificial intelligence (AI) was sharply divided into those who defended the dominant symbolic approach and those who saw a revolution in the rebirth of connectionist models. During much of the time I worked on SCALIR, the kinds of symbolic-connectionist hybrids I advocated were viewed by both camps as inherently flawed. Over time, this perception has begun to change. Today, hybrid systems are the focus of workshops, books, and journals. It is especially appropriate that this book be published now, as research on hybrid systems flourishes.

The changes in legal information retrieval (IR) are slower, but they are coming as well. Last year, West Publishing Co. released a new on-line search system based directly on techniques developed in the IR research community. I would like to believe that experiments such as SCALIR (which West facilitated) played a small part in encouraging the acceptance of new approaches in commercial IR systems.

Overall, however, the messages of the book are still timely. In fact, more people need to access more textual data in more complex ways than ever. The interweaving of AI, IR, and human-computer interaction will be increasingly important in addressing this problem. Ultimately, that's what SCALIR is about.

Acknowledgments

This research could literally never have been done without the support of West Publishing Co. and Shepard's/McGraw-Hill. At West, I would like to thank Michael Fix, Steve Haynes, Eileen Knabe, John Niemeyer, and, especially, Andy Desmond for their invaluable assistance. At Shepard's, I would like to thank Teresa Browne, Allan Markolf, Mary Ostgren, and especially Myrna Bennett and Ron Berg. Apple Computer, Inc. also provided support during the final stages of the project.

I would like to thank Annette Feldman, formerly of the University of San Diego (USD) law library, for introducing me to the world of computer-assisted legal research, and Paul Horton, of the USD law faculty, for letting me join his class on intellectual property. I would also like to thank the lawyers and students who participated in the evaluation of SCALIR; the confidentiality of the experiment prevents my listing their names.

My advisor, Rik Belew, has been teacher, supervisor, colleague, and friend over the past few years. Rik deserves a lot of the credit for the existence of SCALIR, because it dates back to the time I brought his thesis home for a little light vacation reading and returned transformed by the idea of adaptive information retrieval. Rik put more time and effort into helping me with SCALIR than I could have imagined; he deserves my thanks for this, and his family and other students deserve my apology.

The rest of my dissertation committee — Gary Cottrell, Jeff Elman, Don Norman, and Walt Savitch — all influenced my work more than they probably realize. Many of my ideas were shaped by the issues discussed in their diverse seminars. Norman Anderson and Jeff Miller of the psychology department at UCSD deserve special thanks for their advice on my experimental design. I would also like to thank my fellow students in the Cognitive Computer Science Research Group, who provided a source of useful criticisms and discussions about SCALIR over the years, and who suffered through an unending series of "practice talks" for conferences, oral exams, and ultimately one thesis defense.

My extended family has been a source of support throughout this project. I must have absorbed the tricks of the academic trade from my parents, Hedy and Peter Rose, who demonstrated two different ways to get a doctorate. They have always encouraged me, even when they didn't understand exactly what I was doing. Carolyn, Robert, and Claire Gruber also played an important role in the final stages of this work, providing legal, statistical, and culinary input, respectively.

I would like to thank my son, Jordy, for remembering me even after I'd been in the lab for days, and for starting to sleep through the night when he was 2 months old.

Most of all, I would like to thank my wife, Susan. As a computer scientist with an extremely healthy skepticism, Susan was the finest editor any writer could wish for. Her pursuit of quality is evident in everything she does. Most of all, though, Susan showed me that there's more to life than work.

– Daniel E. Rose

Chapter 1

Introduction

Last year, the United States Supreme Court wrote over 5,000 pages of opinions, published in 5 volumes. Federal Courts of Appeal accounted for another 40,000 pages reported in 27 volumes. District Courts added about the same amount. In addition to a smaller body of statutes and regulations, these documents *together with the thousands of volumes that preceded them*, constitute much of the law in this country. Moreover, every attorney is expected to be able to "find the law" (usually court decisions) that applies to the situation of his or her client. This research task is difficult and time consuming. Yet this is just one example of a widespread problem: how to find information in large bodies of text. It is faced by scientists looking for research articles, historians looking for newspaper stories, and managers looking for corporate documents.

Many of the documents in these diverse fields have recently become available on-line. Some of these documents, such as office memoranda or business correspondence, are created using word processors and continue to exist in electronic form long after their paper copies have been printed out. Others, like books or journals, are converted to electronic form (often through manual rekeying) by publishers, even if the initial manuscripts were produced with ordinary typewriters. Still other documents are being added to on-line databases through the use of scanners and character-recognition software. In short, the volume of text available on-line is already huge, and will only get larger as the use of computers continues to grow.

There are clear advantages for having text corpora available on-line. Physical access to the text is significantly easier; in some cases the researcher may be able to find the desired document without leaving his or her desk. If the text is easily accessible on-line, the user may not

1

require bound copies, thus reducing unnecessary duplication. On-line documents may be passed across large distances from one person to another in minutes. Computerized indexing methods allow rapid access to nearly any part of the text corpus, eliminating the need for hunting through library stacks, scanning microfiche cards, or flipping through journal pages.

What the availability of on-line text does not change, however, is the difficulty of *finding the desired information*. Many lawyers, for example, continue to prefer manual research methods when given the choice. This suggests two conclusions: First, existing on-line search methods are not meeting the needs of users. Second, manual search methods may have strengths unnoticed by designers of on-line text retrieval systems. To address this problem, new approaches to finding information on-line are needed. The research described in this book is one such approach.

1.1   An Interdisciplinary Approach to Finding Information

Suppose one wanted to design a computer system to assist the research process in a certain domain. Ideally, the system should be able to search huge databases of text rapidly, and be able to differentiate between documents that seem more relevant to the user's problem and those that seem less so. It should have some information or "knowledge" about the problem being researched, about the domain generally, and about the context of the search — for example, what the user has previously considered relevant, what has already been found, and so on. Finally, it should be designed in such a way that it facilitates the original research task.

Each of these three goals is a major research problem in its own right, drawing on the techniques and tools of three different subfields of computer science and cognitive science: information retrieval (IR), artificial intelligence (AI), and human-computer interaction (HCI). A system designed to meet only one of these goals is likely to have difficulty satisfying the others. In contrast, a combination of approaches from the three disciplines may offer a collective solution not available to any one in isolation.

This book describes an attempt to bring the tools of IR, AI, and HCI to bear on the information-finding problem. The attempt takes the form of a system called SCALIR, for *S*ymbolic and *C*onnectionist *A*pproach to *L*egal *I*nformation *R*etrieval, which is designed to assist research on copyright law. Although SCALIR represents only one way to address the problem, I believe it demonstrates the value and feasibility of an interdisciplinary approach.

Like any partnership, the union of AI, IR, and HCI requires some compromises. Although IR has contributed statistical text indexing techniques to the SCALIR system, the SCALIR research rejects many of the traditional IR assumptions about retrieval, relevance, and evaluation. AI has supplied the basic structures and mechanisms from which SCALIR is constructed (in particular, spreading activation search in semantic and connectionist networks), but they are applied to an "industrial grade" problem and thus are less theoretically pure than most AI researchers advocate. HCI has informed the design of SCALIR's methods for interacting with users; the user/system interface has evolved in response to users' suggestions. Yet many in HCI may find SCALIR's design process to be rather ad hoc and its interface compromised by the system's other goals. If SCALIR has broken any new ground, it probably has not done so without disturbing its neighbors.

1.2 Central Themes

Several important issues recur throughout this research. This section briefly highlights these central themes.

1.2.1 Law as a Problem Domain

Law is a fascinating institution. Its principles emerge from its large body of natural language text — court decisions — and evolve over time. Trying to get a system to represent this text is a major undertaking. The legal[1] reasoning process is also complex, relying heavily on analogies between previous cases and the current situation. Thus legal research (and hence legal information retrieval) itself plays a role in legal reasoning. In short, law serves as an ideal laboratory for AI. It is a tightly constrained and decomposable domain, yet it involves many of AI's hardest problems.

Widespread research on applying AI techniques to the law is fairly recent, at least relative to a domain like medicine. The first ACM-sponsored International Conference on AI and Law (ICAIL) was not until 1987, and the first journal for the field is due out this year. In some ways this is surprising, because there are so many ways in which law could benefit from intelligent computer systems. It may be due to the unavailability of data for research. It may also reflect the reluctance of an old and

---

[1]This is the first of many potentially ambiguous uses of the word *legal*. I always use the term to mean "pertaining to the law" and not "permitted by law."

somewhat conservative profession to embrace new technologies. In any case, the result is a fairly wide-open field with much work to be done, an inviting prospect for any AI researcher.

1.2.2   Connectionist/Symbolic Hybrids

Connectionism — the use of neurally inspired, massively parallel networks of primitive processing units, and the attendant implications for modeling human cognition — had a major rebirth in the mid-1980s. Connectionist techniques have since been applied to many problems previously thought amenable only to traditional, "symbolic" AI. This has led some researchers to conclude that connectionism is the correct approach to most problems, whereas others still believe that only symbolic techniques are correct.

I believe that both approaches have a continuing role to play in AI, and that further gains can be achieved by combining the two to create new *hybrid* systems. In the information retrieval domain in particular, connectionist models facilitate learning and the gradual combination of evidence, which are helpful in overcoming some of the brittleness of traditional IR systems. Symbolic techniques allow us to encode a priori knowledge of the domain, such as constraints representing the "physics" of the world in question. A hybrid system may thus be capable of performing a task more effectively (perhaps more efficiently, or more perspicuously, or more robustly) than a system using only a single paradigm.

There is an additional reason why this hybrid methodology is particularly useful in SCALIR: The legal system itself has some characteristics of both symbolic and connectionist models, making each approach especially appropriate for representing different aspects of the problem.

1.2.3   Text as Knowledge Representation

Text has traditionally played a central role in IR systems — their goal is to retrieve text documents — but not in AI. AI researchers who have attempted to capture knowledge extant in text often constructed formal representations of the knowledge and then threw away the text itself. The resulting representations necessarily lost some of the information initially present in the text. Thus the systems constructed were limited to the features of the text considered important by the programmer.

In a *text-based intelligent system*, the text itself may be viewed as the knowledge base. Text has many virtues as a representation, not the least of which is that, in many cases, it already exists on-line. It is capable of conveying vast amounts of information, some of which gradually emerges through continual reinterpretation. It is also easily comprehended by humans, which is not the case for many formal AI representations. The difficulty, of course, is accessing the knowledge in the text.

Rather than explicitly trying to extract the textual knowledge, SCALIR begins with intelligent tools for letting users access the text directly, bringing them documents of interest. By changing its representation of these documents in response to user feedback, the system eventually provides its users with a shared repository of knowledge about the text.

1.2.4 The Role of the User

A great deal of information retrieval research has focused on improving performance of IR systems, where "performance" is defined as a score on some measure of accuracy or completeness of retrieval. Actual user satisfaction with these systems is difficult to quantify and is rarely measured. In fact, AI techniques are often viewed as a way to eliminate more of the user's "burden," without consideration of whether the user would prefer to maintain tighter control over the search process.

Other research, often from schools of library and information science, has examined the problems library patrons have locating information, both in traditional media and with on-line catalogs. Furthermore, human–computer interaction studies have looked at the kinds of problems users have with a variety of computer systems.

Yet there have been relatively few attempts to combine the results of performance-oriented and user-oriented research. In other words, few people have asked how what we know about users' search behavior can be used to design more effective IR systems. SCALIR represents an attempt to do just that; it is based on a premise of keeping users "in the loop" at all times and improving its performance by observing its users' behavior.

1.3 Goals of the Research

The SCALIR project began with three goals:

Improving Legal Information Retrieval. The first goal was simply to construct an IR system for the legal research task that, by using an unusual combination of techniques from artificial intelligence, could overcome many of the problems facing more traditional systems.

Feasibility of Hybrid AI Systems. The second goal was to demonstrate that there were problems for which the approaches of connectionist and traditional AI could be usefully combined. In particular, I claimed that learning was possible in a hybrid system, and that such a system would constitute a whole greater than the sum of its parts.

IR for Natural Language. Finally, the SCALIR research was intended to show how information retrieval systems might provide an "end-run" around the problem of natural language processing, and the symbol grounding problem in particular.

During the course of the research, the focus expanded somewhat to include an analysis of the role of human-computer interaction in the IR task. At the same time, the third initial goal became a perspective from which to view the research rather than a concrete research program. Though the concept of IR for natural language processing is discussed in chapter 3, one will not find specific results or experiments pertaining to it. Chapter 12 summarizes the results presented throughout the book, and tries to assess how well each goal was satisfied.

1.4   A Sketch of the SCALIR Approach

The goal of an information retrieval system is to find documents relevant to a user's search request, documents that are said to satisfy the user's "information need." This requires performing some sort of matching operation between the request and the documents in the corpus, and (preferably) ordering the responses from most to least relevant. The most obvious way to do this is simply to search through every document looking for words included in the request, but there are far more efficient and effective techniques that have emerged from the past thirty years of IR research.

There are many complications that make this an extremely difficult task. First, many different words have the same meaning, and the same word often has different meanings. So if the user's search request is expressed using one set of words and the documents of interest use another, it will be hard to locate them. Second, concepts like *relevance* and *information need* are very difficult to quantify. A system may be designed to meet the needs of a mythical average user, and yet may not satisfy any real users. Chapter 4 discusses these problems in detail.

A *legal* information retrieval system (often called a computer-assisted legal research — CALR — system), is simply an IR system for law. That is, the user wants to find some sort of legal documents (usually court decisions) of interest. The notion of relevance in legal IR is often more complex than for general IR: A case that seems related to the search topic may not be relevant simply because it is no longer "good law"

— for example, because it has since been overturned on appeal. These issues are covered in chapter 5.

Let us consider a simple example of the type of research question a user might have, and how SCALIR would answer it. Suppose Jane Doe is an entrepreneur trying to "clone" a well-known computer system by reverse engineering the programs stored in the system's read-only memory (ROM) chips. She wants to know whether her product will infringe the copyright on the existing system. Her lawyer, Richard Roe, is familiar with some of the best-known cases involving ROM copyrights, but he wants to see what else has been decided.

If Roe had access to SCALIR, he might enter some terms of interest, such as ROM and chip, as well as one or more cases, such as *Apple v. Franklin*. After a few seconds of processing, the system would begin to display its response. SCALIR would find not only other cases like *Apple v. Franklin* and those concerned with copyrights on ROMs, but also other terms descriptive of the cases' contents, which Roe might use for further searches, and perhaps portions of the relevant Federal statutes concerning copyrights on semiconductor chips. In addition to simply finding the retrieved items, SCALIR would show the relationships among them. For example, some cases might have been cited by other cases; these would be shown with dashed lines. Roe could also examine the text of each retrieved document (statutes as well as cases) by selecting it with a mouse. This situation is shown in Figure 1.1. At this point, Roe could indicate which of the responses he would like to pursue further and which should be abandoned. This results in a new search; SCALIR also slightly alters its representation of the documents so that the useful items are more likely to be retrieved in the future. In fact, Roe may already be getting the benefit of the system's improved performance resulting from its use by other members of his firm.

How is this type of retrieval performed? The short answer is that SCALIR uses spreading activation in interleaved connectionist and semantic networks. Connectionist links, such as those between terms and cases, indicate statistical regularities discovered by IR indexing techniques; their weights are then altered in response to user feedback. Symbolic links, like those connecting citing and cited cases, represent a priori knowledge available from existing legal research tools, themselves produced by a kind of knowledge engineering by human experts. The details about how the links are originally constructed, how activity propagation is achieved in the hybrid network, and how the system learns, are covered in chapters 7–10, as are the motivations for and evaluation of the type of user/system interaction supported by SCALIR.

Although SCALIR represents a new approach to the legal IR problem,

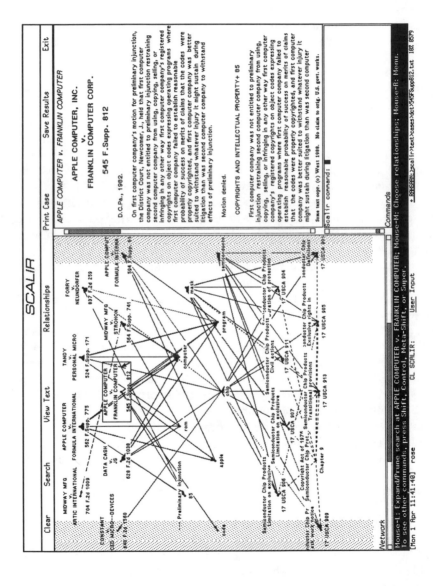

Figure 1.1: SCALIR's response to the query consisting of the terms *ROM* and *chip*, and the case *Apple v. Franklin.*

it was not created in a vacuum. In particular, it was largely inspired by the ideas represented by Belew's AIR system [Bel86]. In some cases, AIR's design principles were borrowed directly; in others they were expanded or otherwise altered. But even where it diverges from AIR, SCALIR has benefited from the AIR experience.

1.5 A Preview of Things to Come

The following is a brief description of the remaining chapters:

- *Chapter 2* is concerned with the interaction between people and the knowledge embedded in collections of text. It describes various approaches to this interaction, and concludes by proposing a set of design principles for information retrieval systems.

- *Chapter 3* is about some problems and issues in artificial intelligence (AI) that pertain to the SCALIR project. In part, the chapter defines some of the AI concepts that will be used later on and puts them in context. It also raises questions about the validity of some approaches to knowledge representation, and suggests how information retrieval may provide alternatives.

- *Chapter 4* describes the information retrieval task in detail, presents some traditional approaches to the problem, and highlights their limitations. It then describes a variety of techniques that have been used to try to overcome these limitations, many of which have inspired the design of SCALIR.

- *Chapter 5* discusses SCALIR's domain, law — how our legal system is organized, the role of text in law, the particular problems faced by a legal IR system, and how AI techniques may be (and have been) used to address them.

- *Chapter 6* presents a theory of hybrid (connectionist and symbolic) AI systems. Formal definitions of these concepts are given, and motivations for using hybrids (as SCALIR does) are presented.

- *Chapter 7* describes the static structure of SCALIR — what the network contains, how it is constructed, and so on.

- *Chapter 8* explains how SCALIR (internally) performs the retrieval task, highlighting in particular a technique used to support spreading activation search in the hybrid network.

- *Chapter 9* is concerned with long-term adaptation in SCALIR. It discusses the derivation of the learning algorithm, and demonstrates its efficacy on some test problems.

- *Chapter 10* gives a play-by-play look at SCALIR's user/system interface, and then compares it to some of the design principles outlined earlier.

- *Chapter 11* describes the experiments performed as part of the evaluation of SCALIR.

- *Chapter 12* is a look back and ahead, summarizing the work described throughout and suggesting ways to extend it.

Readers interested primarily in SCALIR's approach to artificial intelligence (including connectionism) will be most interested in chapters 3 and 6. Those focusing on the interaction issues will find chapters 2 and 10 most useful, whereas IR-oriented readers will additionally want to read chapters 4, 5, and 11. The system's internal implementation details are given in chapters 7, 8, and 9. Despite these differences of orientation, SCALIR can best be understood by examining the issues from all three perspectives.

Chapter 2

Humans, Computers, and Finding Information

In recent years, the term *user interface* has come to mean that part of the system responsible for interacting with users. This usage tempts the designer of the system to treat the user interface like just another module to be engineered, along with, say, the file input/output routines.

The original (and primary, at least among those unfamiliar with computers) meaning of the word *interface* is a boundary or edge; thus the *user interface* is not a part of the system; it is not a *thing* at all. Rather, it is simply the point where the system ends and the user begins, or vice versa; it is the place where the two come into contact. In fact, it really makes more sense to talk about the user/system interface, because an interface must lie between two entities.

Many people (including the author [RB91b]) have written about what sort of interfaces information retrieval systems should have. This is a reasonable question, but it is stated in a way that might suggest the interface-as-module view. The question thus could be phrased more accurately as:

> How should people and information retrieval systems interact? At what points and in what ways will the user and the system come into contact?

The answer depends on what task the IR system user is trying to accomplish and what priority he or she places on such considerations as efficiency, ease of use, accuracy, and so on.

This chapter is about the IR task, broadly conceived. I discuss the origins of storing, organizing, and retrieving information, and some different ways one might interact with a system for aiding these processes. These thoughts have influenced SCALIR's various ways of interacting with the user — its user/system interface — described later in chapter 10.

2.1   Archives, Libraries, and IR Systems

Before there were books, records were kept on clay tablets. The storerooms for tablets were the first archives and, in a sense, the first libraries. Books allowed authors to collect and organize knowledge in various ways of their own choosing; this organization affected the way others had to find the knowledge, and therefore how they believed it to be organized in the world. For example, Aristotle's *Metaphysics* gets its name from its position in early editions of his collected works — it came after (*meta*) his *Physics*.

Once books (or scrolls) became widespread, collections of books were inevitable. Many libraries existed in ancient times, the most famous commissioned by Ptolemy I at Alexandria [JH76]. By the Renaissance there were libraries kept by monasteries, universities, cities, and various noble patrons. As libraries grew larger and more complex, they required catalogues listing the books that were available, and classification schemes for organizing the catalogues.

There was no consistency in classification schemes, and even alphabetization was a relatively late invention. As Tenner noted:

> Most library catalogues before the nineteenth century were not the uniform alphabetical variety with which we are familiar. Libraries were divided into classes, and to find a book, one needed an idea of how it fit into the classifier's categories. If you wanted to find the biography of a churchman in one eighteenth-century catalogue, for example, you would have to learn by trial and error that the proper rubric was *Historia* — *Historia Ecclesiastica* and then read through 25 pages until you found the book. [Ten90]

The library catalogues were intended to be fixed permanent records; they were themselves books. When the French scientist Rozier suggested in 1775 the idea of cards that could be used to multiply index a book, he assumed that the "card catalogue" would then be copied to the "real" printed catalogue [Ten90]. When librarians couldn't update the printed catalogues fast enough, they gradually started letting readers look directly at the cards.

Gradually, standardized classification schemes were developed for arranging books and catalogue entries. Though such systems (such as the one used by the Library of Congress) are often intended simply for classifying books, they are essentially taxonomies of knowledge ("ontologies," in current AI parlance). As with the case of the works of Aristotle, the classification scheme affects how a reader locates a book and how she or he perceives its relation to others. As a simple example, because libraries use a one-dimensional storage system (ordered by their catalog number), a book can only have "left" and "right" neighbors. So (in the Library of Congress system), one interested in Alan Turing will find his works next to other books on calculating machine pioneers, but not books on cryptography or automata theory or artificial intelligence, all of which he wrote about. Of course, the other subject headings in the catalog may also point to the book of Turing essays, but the user has to know what those headings are to see the "neighborhoods" in other dimensions. One cannot simultaneously examine the book and scan its neighbors in all indexing directions.

Computerized information retrieval systems have sometimes been heralded as a solution to the indexing dilemma. By a variety of methods (described in chapter 4), we can index books or other documents in such a way that there are many "neighbors" along a potentially unbounded number of dimensions. The similarities are extracted automatically from properties of the text itself. Furthermore, the dimension of similarity to be searched is user-specified.

Unfortunately, the primary benefit of this approach — that there is no a priori taxonomy by which a different person has classified the book — is also a serious source of problems. Books that might previously have been found under the same subject heading may now appear far apart, particularly if the authors used different terminology to describe the same thing. It is up to the user to figure out the relevant dimension of similarity, and he or she no longer has a list of subject headings from which to choose.

2.2 A Baseline for IR Interaction

Many of the themes in this chapter and chapter 10 have to do with alternatives to the "traditional" way of interacting with an on-line information retrieval system. Of course, *traditional* is a relative term. Early IR systems used batch processing, so there was little direct interaction between the user and the system. There are also differences between styles of interaction among IR systems designed for different purposes; an on-line public-access catalog (OPAC) for a library may be designed to interact quite differently with users than a computer-assisted legal research (CALR) system.

Nevertheless, there are some properties that seem to hold for the majority of commercial IR systems in use during the 1970s and 1980s and today. These properties are:

1. A command paradigm in which the user issues a single command (sometimes chosen from a menu) and the system executes it.

2. Simple text displays on a 23-line by 80-character video terminal, often showing only upper-case letters.

3. The use of Boolean connectives and positional restrictions for query terms.

4. Command entry by typing at a keyboard.

Some of these properties (such as the last one) are so widespread as to be almost unnoticed; it is only when one considers alternatives such as automatic text completion, "DWIM" (for "do what I mean") [TM81], or pointing at menu selections with a mouse, that these properties can be seen as design choices.

In addition, many standard IR systems have an important additional property:

5. No history mechanism (i.e., current actions are not affected by previous actions).

A simple example of this involves refinements of previous searches. On some systems (such as DIALOG[1]), the sets of retrieved items are saved and given names, so the user can refer back to them and perform set manipulation operations on them later (e.g. ask to see items found both in set 1 and in set 2). On others (such as MELVYL[2]) — those that have the "no history" property — once a user initiates a new search, the previous response set is no longer accessible for further operations.

I consider systems with the five properties listed above to be a baseline for studying user/system interaction in information retrieval. To demonstrate what this baseline interaction is like, I use the example of

---

[1]DIALOG is a registered trademark of Dialog Information Systems, Inc.

[2]MELVYL is a registered trademark of the Regents of the University of California.

the WESTLAW[3] Computer-Assisted Legal Research system. WESTLAW has many attributes that make it an excellent tool for legal research. It also has others (as does its competitor, LEXIS[4]) that limit its effectiveness; these are discussed in chapter 5. In addition, WESTLAW has capabilities beyond those that will be demonstrated. For now, however, we are concerned only with how one interacts with a "standard" IR system. WESTLAW should be taken as simply an *example* of the current level of IR technology as applied to computer-assisted legal research.

Note: Because this chapter is concerned with user/system interaction, I will often defer discussion of other issues that arise, pointing the reader toward later chapters in which they are discussed.

There are three distinct steps in using WESTLAW, each of which requires a different type of interaction.

Selecting a Database. After logging on to the system and entering client information (used to assist in billing), the WESTLAW user is presented with a table-of-contents-like directory screen listing databases that can be searched and other services that can be accessed. The user enters the "page number" and the system responds by displaying the "enter query" screen for that database, as shown in Figure 2.1.

Entering a Query. To enter a query, the user types a list of terms separated by Boolean and positional connectives. For example, dog & cat would retrieve any case containing both the word *dog* and the word *cat*, whereas dog /s cat would retrieve only those cases in which the two terms occurred in the same sentence, and dog % cat would retrieve cases in which *dog* occurred but *cat* did not.

Displaying Results. In response to the query, the system generally responds with the first screenful of text from the first case in the retrieval set. This is shown in Figure 2.2. By default, the first case means the most recent case decided by the highest court, though the user can set an alternate mode in which the cases are in descending order of query term matches. The user can then view the text a screen at a time, or jump to each occurrence of the search terms in the case. He can also ask for a listing of all cases found (see Figure 2.3), and view the text of another case by entering its number in the listing.

Query formulation is a skill often taught to law students by law librarians. The *WESTLAW Reference Manual* also gives hints on strategies for forming queries:

The most common approach to researching a legal issue is

---

[3]WESTLAW is a registered trademark of West Publishing Company, which has graciously allowed use of their data for this research.

[4]LEXIS is a registered trademark of Mead Data Central, Inc.

Please enter your query.

Your database is ALLFEDS

To search for federal decisions from 1789 to 1945, use OLD as the database
identifier, e.g., SDB OLD, QDB OLD, or DB OLD.

If you wish to:
  Enter your query, type it as desired and press ENTER
  View a list of available fields, type F and press ENTER
  View detailed information about this database, type SCOPE and press ENTER
COPR. (C) WEST 1991 NO CLAIM TO ORIG. U.S. GOVT. WORKS

Figure 2.1: WESTLAW's "enter query" screen. The underscore at the upper left corner indicates the cursor where the user
would type in the query.

COPR. (C) WEST 1991 NO CLAIM TO ORIG. U.S. GOVT. WORKS

Citation   Rank(R)   Page(P)   Database   Mode
841 F.2d 742   R 1 OF 26   P 1 OF 40   ALLFEDS   T
(CITE AS: 841 F.2D 742)

James PATTON, R.L. Hildebrand, Burns Harbor Plaza, Inc., and R.L. Hildebrand
            Enterprises, Inc., Plaintiffs-Appellees,
                              v.
        MID-CONTINENT SYSTEMS, INC., Defendant-Appellant.
                        No. 87-1579.
            United States Court of Appeals,
                    Seventh Circuit.
                  Argued Jan. 8, 1988.
                 Decided March 8, 1988.
        Rehearing and Rehearing En Banc Denied April 18, 1988.

Truck stop franchisees sued franchisor for breach of franchise agreement. The
United States District Court for the Northern District of Indiana, Michael S.
Kanne, J., entered judgment on jury verdict awarding franchisees compensatory
damages, as well as punitive damages in reduced amount. On appeal, the Court
of Appeals, Posner, Circuit Judge, held that: (1) under Indiana law,
franchisee could introduce evidence of mistaken omission from agreement of his
place of business which had led to initial breach through franchising of
competitor; (2) jury could find that franchisor failed to give franchisee
sufficient time to provide additional coverage in territory, but compensatory
damage awards were so excessive in relation to proof of harm that new trial on

Figure 2.2: The first screen of the first retrieved document. The synopsis of the case, which fills most of the screen, continues.
It is followed by several screens of headnotes, which are followed by the actual opinion.

17

CITATIONS LIST (Page 1)   COPR. (C) WEST 1991 NO CLAIM TO ORIG. U.S. GOVT. WORKS
Database: ALLFEDS   Total Documents: 26

1. C.A.7 (Ind.) 1988.   Patton v. MidContinent Systems, Inc.
841 F.2d 742

2. C.A.D.C. 1984.   Stancill v. Potomac Elec. Power Co.
744 F.2d 861, 240 U.S.App.D.C. 237

3. C.A.Fla. 1981.   Byrd v. Reederei   638 F.2d 1300

4. C.A.Colo. 1976.   Hartzell v. U. S.,   539 F.2d 65

5. C.A.Ga. 1975.   Mitchell v. Young Refining Corp.,   517 F.2d 1036

6. C.A.Okl. 1973.   Stonsifer v. Courtney's Furniture Co., Inc.,
474 F.2d 113

7. C.A.Tex. 1972.   Pope v. Holiday Inns, Inc.,   464 F.2d 1303

8. C.A.D.C. 1968.   Kanelos v. Kettler,
406 F.2d 951, 132 U.S.App.D.C. 133

Figure 2.3: Listing retrieved documents in WESTLAW. Most recent cases are shown first.

combining a basic legal theory with the broad factual circumstances surrounding the case. For example, the query

```
assum! /5 risk /p ic* snow*** snowfall /s
            slip! fell fall***
```
retrieves cases that discuss the legal theory of assumption of
risk and involve a person who has fallen on ice or snow. The
advantage of this approach is that it narrows the search to a
legal theory but still leaves room for variations in the specific
facts. [Wes89]

To understand the query, it helps to know that ! is a "root expander"
(so assum! matches any term with the root assum), * is a "wild card"
matching any character, and /5 means that the term on the right must
occur with five words of the term on the left. As we see later on, many
people have difficulty with Boolean searches [Bor86b, Hil83, TK74] —
even when they know what the symbols mean.

Usually it takes several attempts to get a satisfactory search result.
In most commercial IR systems, including WESTLAW, the query-refining
process has a tedious trial-and-error quality attributable to the five interaction characteristics found in "standard" IR.

Because the system has no history, the user can't refine the *search*, but
must instead refine the *query* and tell the system to execute an entirely
new search. Because the command paradigm is used together with typed
input, users cannot indicate what was good or bad about the previous
result, nor can the system tell them what is wrong — except to say that
thousands of documents (i.e., too many) satisfy their query. The output
bandwidth is also so small (only 20 lines of a 100-page document or a
multipage listing of documents are visible at one time) that it is hard for
users to tell whether the cases being retrieved are satisfactory.

One suggestion West offers is to narrow the search to progressively
finer grained portions of the document [Wes89]. For example, rather
than searching the entire text of a case for a descriptive term, WESTLAW
supports restricting the search to the synopsis — a short summary that
is not officially part of the court decision. If this is insufficient, the user
can ask to search only the "topics" — a list of one-line issues or points of
law that a West editor uses to describe the case. Note that West's suggestions for refining the query involve a shift from user-selected indexing to
controlled-vocabulary expert indexing done by West's editors, similar to
the more familiar subject indexing done by the Library of Congress. The
user has shifted from finding any documents matching his or her word
choice, to essentially looking in a West-generated subject catalog.

2.3   Seeing Connections

One of the problems with the baseline interaction described earlier is
that the user cannot take advantage of relationships between documents.
This is especially unfortunate in law, where citations between cases are
extremely important.   In fact, an online legal citation service called
Shepard's[5], available through WESTLAW, allows a user to find all court
decisions citing the case being examined. By following these citation
pointers, the user can find new and possibly relevant cases. Even with
this extension to standard IR, the connections are somewhat limited. Although they join documents in a particularly meaningful way for the legal
domain, they may not be the associations a user would like to draw.

2.3.1   What's in a Trail?

In his 1945 *Atlantic Monthly* article "As We May Think," [Bus45] Vannevar Bush proposed a hypothetical information system of the future
called the *memex*. Bush's memex was to be a sort of microfilm reader by
which the user could access whole libraries of information. Bush realized
that it would be difficult to locate information, and — just as in standard
IR systems — once one search was completed, the query process had to
be started all over again:

> The human mind does not work that way. It operates by
> association. With one item in its grasp, it snaps instantly to
> the next that is suggested by the association of thoughts, in
> accordance with some intricate web of trails carried by cells
> of the brain. It has other characteristics, of course; trails that
> are not frequently followed are prone to fade . . . [Bus45]

The solution Bush proposed was simple: Allow any item to be connected
to any other item to form a "trail." Once joined, each could be instantly
recalled by pressing a button when the other was found. Furthermore,
the user could then follow the trails instead of the original order (if any)
of the items:

> It is exactly as though the physical items had been gathered
> together from widely separated sources and bound together
> to form a new book. It is more than this, for any item can be
> joined into numerous trails. [Bus45]

---

[5]Shepard's is a registered trademark of Shepard's/McGraw-Hill, which has also supported this research by allowing the use of their data.

Bush's idea is often cited as one of the original inspirations for the concept of hypertext [Con87]. Certainly hypertext systems allow their users to follow links between documents, and (at least in the case of authoring systems), to form these links.

Whatever Bush's intention, there is another interpretation of the *trail* concept that may be even more compelling. This is the notion of trails as paths which gradually form through repeated use of various sequences of documents.

When sidewalks follow unnecessarily long trajectories, pedestrians inevitably trample a more efficient path in the grass; hikers in the woods often form all sorts of trails, some intentionally, others gradually emerging as many people rediscover the same route to a scenic view. It is this type of trail one can imagine in Bush's memex.

The popularity of a trail will increase its width and ease of discovery; this in turn will encourage others to use it more. Some users may prefer to follow trails less traveled, or simply trample through the woods at random (i.e., moving from document to document in ways that others have not anticipated). A document that spawns a new paradigm may be the terminus of many converging trails.

Though Bush doesn't follow up on the idea of memory decay, he does refer to "side trails" and "general trails," as though the well-traveled ones are more noticeable or easier to follow. He also speaks of a "new profession of trail blazers."

In addition to simply forming connections, Bush's trails allow the memex to embody the research and learning of a whole community of users:

> The lawyer has at his touch the associated opinions and decisions of his whole experience and of the experience of friends and authorities. The patent attorney has on call the millions of issued patents, with familiar trails to every point of his client's interest. [Bus45]

These two ideas — connections emerging through use and the development of shared knowledge — are essential to interacting with SCALIR. Though they can be found in at least one interpretation of Bush's idea, they were passed more directly from Belew's Adaptive Information Retrieval (AIR) system [Bel86].

2.3.2 To AIR is Human

AIR is an interactive system for bibliographic information retrieval. AIR combines user browsing with feedback and learning. In particular, whenever a user indicates that certain retrieved items are worthy of further search, the system automatically creates links between them. Thus any future query or retrieval involving one of the items causes the others to be included as well. Although AIR's users have to indicate which items they liked, they do not have to explicitly instruct the system to connect them; indeed, they may not be aware that new links are being formed.

Through the creation of new links (and an additional adaptation mechanism described in chapter 4), the system gradually learns what the human users think various terms refer to. If a user has been responsible for some of AIR's inferences, he or she is more likely to rely on it. If others have contributed as well, each user gets additional benefit from it. Belew calls this approach "democratic knowledge engineering" [Bel86] to distinguish it from AI's traditional "knowledge engineering," which relies on a single expert.

2.4   Methods of Inquiry

A fundamental part of any interaction between a user and any retrieval system is how the user expresses a request for information. As we have seen, the traditional method in an IR system is to form a string of search terms joined by Boolean and positional connectives. This query paradigm may have originated in data retrieval systems, also known as database management systems (DBMSs). In fact, IR systems are often perceived as special cases of DBMSs in which the data being retrieved are documents.

As discussed in chapter 1, this perception is incorrect; there may not be a correct answer in an IR system. Accordingly, it is quite possible that the question-and-answer mode of interaction is inappropriate for the IR domain. In fact, two alternatives have already emerged: *query by example* and *retrieval by reformulation*. Interestingly, both were developed with data (as opposed to text) retrieval in mind, yet both seem especially well suited for IR.

2.4.1   Query by Example

In the theory of relational databases, queries can be expressed in an algebra of primitive operations known as *relational algebra* or in a set-theoretic descriptions resembling predicate calculus. Many database management systems use the algebraic approach as the foundation for their query language; these languages often add little more than syntactic sugar to make them seem easier to use.

For example, suppose that employees, their salaries, and their departments were kept in a relation R. The salaries of employees in the sales department can be expressed algebraically as

$$\pi_{\text{salary}}(\sigma_{\text{department}="\text{sales}"}(R))$$

where the π and σ indicate the use of the project and select operators, respectively [Ull82]. In SQL, a widely used commercial database query language, the same query would be written

```
select R.salary where R.dept = "sales"
```

Basically, the reserved word select is being used to express the database concept projection, and the word where to express selection. The SQL statement may use more English-like terminology, but there is a simple 1–1 mapping to the algebraic expression.[6]

A radically different approach to entering database queries was query by example (QBE), introduced by Zloof in 1975 [Zlo75]. QBE is based on the set description approach (more formally, on domain calculus). Instead of giving a command to execute certain operations, a user could now "show" the system an example of the type of data to be retrieved. Instead of responding to a command-line prompt, the user would be presented with a form-like depiction of the data. The QBE interaction is thus like showing a group of people how to fill out a form; you write "your name here" in the appropriate space and all the forms come back with each individual's name in that space. In particular, the QBE equivalent of the salary query above is shown in Figure 2.4. The P instructs the system to print that attribute or result.

Zloof believed that QBE could allow nonprogrammers to express complex requests to their database systems. In his original paper, he described seven unique attributes found in QBE:

1. The user has the perception of manual table manipulation.

2. The user has a pre-established *frame of reference*, i.e., the tables.

3. The user can easily pre-identify the relations to be used, resulting in an early reduction in the scope of the data base.

---

[6]In fact, SQL contains aspects of both the algebraic and predicate calculus approaches, in part because the SQL expression (unlike the parenthesized relational algebra expression) does not specify an ordering for the operations; a well-designed system will choose the optimal order of evaluation. Nevertheless, the example illustrates the form of a typical SQL query.

EMPLOYEE	SALARY	DEPARTMENT
	P.	sales

Figure 2.4: The salary query in QBE.

4. As opposed to linear-type languages where the user is constrained to one degree of freedom, here the user has multi-degrees of freedom in that the sequence of filling in the tables ... is immaterial. This implies that given a data base the system does not constrain the user's thinking process. ...

5. The sequence of ... steps is also immaterial.

6. It follows from 4 and 5 that [the query is] declarative and highly non-procedural.

7. Due to the decoupling features inherent in Query by Example, it can handle rather complicated queries without relinquishing simplicity. [Zlo75]

Aside from the relative ease of the form-filling approach from the user's point of view (Zloof's point 1), QBE allows users to see what their results were going to look like syntactically (point 2).

Though Zloof does not express the idea in this way, the critical feature is that *the representation used for query and response is nearly identical.* This insight seems to recur periodically in computer science; the Von Neumann architecture (in which programs and data could be stored in the same place) and the LISP programming language (in which programs and data could be constructed from the same syntactic elements) are two previous examples.

QBE seems especially well-suited for the task of document retrieval. Users often begin research wanting "articles like this one," and they must rely on their own knowledge (and often that of a librarian) to determine what "like this one" means and how to translate that set description into a sequence of IR commands. One of the most valuable insights of the vector representation approach in IR (see chapter 4 for details) is that documents and queries could use the same representation. This feature is also present in SCALIR.

2.4.2 Retrieval by Reformulation

QBE alleviates the need for users to know what attributes to specify in formulating a query. Despite this benefit, the QBE approach still operates essentially in command mode: The user writes a query, the system displays a response, and the process repeats. IR users, however, are likely to encounter some difficulties with this approach, because a user's information need is rarely completely satisfied by a single query. Finding all the relevant information may become a tedious trial-and-error process.

Williams' RABBIT system [Wil84] was intended to provide an alternative. RABBIT introduced the principle of *retrieval by reformulation*, in which the distinction between query and response was blurred. Queries became an incremental interactive process through which users gradually homed in on the most useful data — possibly data they didn't know existed in advance. The impetus for retrieval by reformulation is a particular psychological theory of long-term memory [NB79, WH81]. RABBIT contained a KL-ONE-encoded knowledge base about various specific domains, but the reformulation principle is a general one.

Suppose someone wanted to eat out at a restaurant in a strange city. In a traditional knowledge representation system (of the sort often programmed in introductory AI classes), the request "Suggest a restaurant" might generate the response

```
Are you willing to spend more than $25 per person?
```

or

```
      Please select type (enter first letter):
American Chinese French Italian Japanese Seafood
```

and so on until only one item matched. This would then be displayed for the user, by now perhaps passed out from hunger.

RABBIT, in contrast, would display information (location, price range, menu, etc.) about a *single* restaurant — say, Joe's Pizzeria on Market Street — and also list the names of others. The user could then respond,[7] "Oh, I meant a Chinese restaurant" or "Is there anything closer to my hotel?"

---

[7]The user's response takes the form of pointing at attributes to change and selecting restrictions or generalizations from menus. RABBIT does not use a natural-language interface.

There are two distinct benefits of this approach. One is that the user can take advantage of recognition; seeing an example provides a basis for critiquing the search. The user doesn't have to know what dimensions of variation are available or what the choices are for each dimension, nor does he or she have to (alternatively) wade through several levels of menus or prompts.

The second benefit is that *the system always responds with information*. It may not be the choice the user is looking for (hence the reformulation), but it is preferable to no choice at all. Too many computer systems in use today have been designed to give responses like

```
ERROR %%Q-UNSPEC, Underspecified Query.
```

RABBIT's solution is also preferable to an overwhelming set of choices and questions. The system is responding in a reasonable manner to the pragmatics of the question; Grice's maxims [Gri75] should hold here as in human conversation.

In a sense, RABBIT turns QBE on its head. Instead of the *user* entering *queries* of the form "find me something like this," the *system* gives *responses* of the form "how about something like this" — what we might call "retrieval by example." In an ideal information retrieval system, both types of interaction should be possible.

2.5 Browsing

In the previous section, I discussed alternatives to the traditional method of query formulation that may be necessary when there is no correct answer to the query. There is still another aspect of many information retrieval tasks not yet addressed: *The user may not know what he or she is looking for.* If the user's goal is to find out the answer to a factual question — such as "Who was the first human in space?" — then the problem is relatively easy. The answer may even appear in the title of a document displayed in a retrieval set (say, *Yuri Gagarin, the World's First Spaceman*).

Contrast this situation with the following task: An attorney's client is a songwriter who thinks a TV commercial is a slightly altered version of one of his songs. The attorney tells her paralegal to research the law and see whether the client has a case. The IR research task is difficult — and different from the fact retrieval problem — in several important ways:

- There is no way to query *all* of the relevant issues, because the user doesn't know what they are before researching the topic.

- There is no way to know which responses are even germane to the problem (much less on point) without examining the documents themselves.

- As a result of these two problems, there is no way to know when the search process should be terminated. There may always be more documents related *in some way* to the query topic.

As a result of these difficulties, the user is likely to adopt a rather different strategy: browsing. Cove and Walsh describe browsing as "information retrieval where the initial search criteria are quite vague" [CW88]; Thompson and Croft say it is "an informal or heuristic search through a well connected collection of records in order to find information relevant to one's need" [TC89]. These definitions and others include the idea of a fairly unplanned process in which the user moves from one item or set of items to another by means of one or more associations — spatial[8] (this book was next to that one on the reshelving cart), chronological (this issue of the journal came before the one I was looking for), conceptual (this book keeps referring to cybernetics — are there books on that?), and so on.

It is common to see browsing characterized as the "opposite" of searching. Browsing is viewed as a directionless process in which users hope something useful will magically pop up, whereas searching is a logical procedure in which users know exactly what they want and recognize it when they get it. In fact, real searches are neither so directed nor so random. Users may have only a vague idea in mind, but they generally recognize a useful item when they see it. Furthermore, the jumps to new search directions are often caused by "reminding," the process of retrieving something from memory without consciously searching for it. Both of these principles stem from the well-known result in cognitive psychology that people are much better at *recognition* than *recall* [Kla80].

This turns out to have enormous importance for the design of an IR system; it will be a recurring theme throughout this work.

Bates, who has studied people's information search habits extensively [Bat79a, Bat79b], characterizes this search process as "berry-picking," and contrasts it with traditional notions in IR of search as directed and browsing as random [Bat91]. The term *berry-picking* conveys much of its meaning with vivid imagery: I know berries of the right kind when I see them, I have some ideas about where to look for them, I probably won't plan a route, seeing a few can lead to a promising patch, more berries are better

---

[8]Of course, spatial relationships between books in a library are not accidental.

than fewer, but I'll probably know when I have "enough," and so on. Nevertheless, I will use the term *browsing* for the same phenomenon, not just in the sense of aimless meandering.

Several IR systems have been designed to support browsing. One of the most comprehensive is Croft and Thompson's I^3R System [CT87, TC89]. In addition to querying the system in a variety of ways (by example, with terms and Boolean connectives, in natural language), the user of I^3R can view a document and simultaneously examine its "nearest neighbors," where proximity can be the result of statistical similarity, citation, reference, synonymy, and so on. The basic idea of browsing through a network of associations is not new (in fact, it is a basic mode of operation in a hypertext system), but the range of associations available in I^3R is.

One of Croft and Thompson's most notable observations is that:

> The browsing process can be viewed as a semiautomatic version of a spreading activation search of the knowledge-base network.... [In standard spreading activation search] the spread of activation is controlled by a mechanism such as a threshold on the activation level. In the I^3R browser the spread of activation is controlled by the user. [CT87]

The SCALIR system uses both types of spreading activation, automatic and user-controlled.

2.6   Adaptation

An important part of any intelligent system is its ability to adapt to changing conditions, hopefully improving its performance. Though interest in adaptive systems has waxed and waned over the years, the idea has a long history in artificial intelligence research and an even longer one in control theory. In general, the idea of an improving system seems natural and desirable.

The same argument can be made for user/system interfaces. As Rissland comments, "Everyone expects the 'ideal' interface to change over time, specifically, to get 'better'" [Ris84]. However, the issue is not so clear. Although some interface changes may be perceived as helpful (such as allowing shortcuts for experienced users), others — even "improvements" — might interfere with most users' work. For example, most people who work with the UNIX[9] operating system would be unhappy

---

[9]UNIX is a registered trademark of AT&T Bell Laboratories.

if it suddenly replaced its commands with different names, even if they were more mnemonic.

There is no simple rule governing which aspects of a system should be allowed to change and which should be kept the same. Even a cautious rule of thumb, such as allowing changes to the system but not the user/system interface, is difficult to follow. Automatic improvements to a compiler, for example, may necessitate different error messages. In the information retrieval domain, nearly every aspect of the system comes in contact with the user. This may be why adaptive systems have not made much headway in IR.[10]

The idea of adaptive IR dates back at least as far as the late 1960s, when Brauen extended Salton's vector approach to allow changes to document representation in response to user feedback [Bra71]. This kind of adaptation might be considered *global*, since it affects all users of the system. Since then, there has been little support for further research on adaptive IR; Belew's AIR [Bel86, Bel89] system and Gordon's genetic algorithm approach [Gor88] are notable exceptions. (All three of these systems will be discussed further in chapter 4.)

Resistance to adaptive IR is understandable. Many people like the idea of important or frequently-used documents being made more easily accessible, but then are outraged when others are consequently less accessible. (This happens all the time at overcrowded libraries, where infrequently used books are relocated from the stacks to an off-site storage facility, much to the dismay of the rare person who needs them.)

Another type of adaptation in interacting with IR systems involves tracking individual user preferences or queries and selecting the most effective search strategy or presentation format accordingly. This is the approach advocated by Croft [Cro84]; no changes are made to his system's representation of documents or its retrieval rules. Although a system like this certainly adapts, the only permanent traces of adaptation are in the user profiles induced by the system. This is related to the idea of selective dissemination of information (SDI) systems, which often have "filters" tuned to different users' interests. These are examples of *local* adaptation, in that each individual's behavior affects the systems' responses to only his or her own (future) searches.

Despite its difficulties, I believe that global adaptation — actually changing the representation of documents — is beneficial and even necessary for future IR systems. Because no retrieval method is perfect, some items will always be incorrectly retrieved, and some of these will

---

[10] Another obstacle may be the difficulty of evaluating adaptive systems by traditional IR measures.

be completely off-base. (For example, a retrieval system might return a child's alphabet book *Apple to Zebra* in response to a query about fruit.) Systems supporting "relevance feedback" allow the user to report which items he or she did and didn't like. If an item reported to be irrelevant keeps being retrieved — perhaps even the next day when the user resumes the research — then the system will be judged "stupid" and users will be reluctant to rely on it.

Ultimately, the case for global adaptation must be adjudicated by the users. If users get more benefit from adaptation — by their own perception — than it costs them in occasional confusion or annoyance, then it is a useful feature. Neither AIR's user study nor SCALIR's was extensive enough to answer the question, and the partial results are mixed. Nevertheless, the collective expertise provided by an adaptive IR system — like that of an experienced librarian — seems too great a resource to ignore.

2.7   Implementation-Level Interface Issues

Throughout this chapter, I have discussed general aspects of interaction with information retrieval systems, but I have said little about the specific form that interaction can or should take. It is the latter issue that this section considers.

Much has been written about various paradigms for interacting with computer systems. Often these discussions attempt to dichotomize the interface world into such categories as "command-line interfaces" (CLIs) and "graphical user interfaces" (GUIs), with the implicit assumption that these are comprehensive, mutually exclusive classifications. Such classifications are often a prelude to a study (or, in unfortunate cases, a polemic) about "which is better" for some set of tasks or group of users.

Because there are many attributes that can be varied about the user/system interface, there are actually countless intertwined "paradigms." For example, the terms *command-line interface, conversational interface,* and *natural language interface* usually[11] share the idea of a user entering text by typing, but encompass a wide variety of ways for this to occur.

One of the most compelling interface ideas which seems to be steadily gaining adherents is the *direct-manipulation interface* (DMI) approach. As characterized by Shneiderman, who coined the term, there are three features which seem essential to the concept:

---

[11] But not always. See, for example, Brennan's characterization of direct manipulation interfaces as conversational [Bre90].

- continuous representation of the objects and actions of interest

- physical actions or labeled button presses instead of complex syntax

- rapid incremental reversible operations whose impact on the object of interest is immediately visible. [Shn87, p. 201]

Of course, these characterizations are subject to individual interpretation (How rapid is "rapid"? How does one define "the objects of interest"?), and it is not surprising that several authors introduce the concept by giving examples of it.

Yet somehow the idea of a DMI has come to mean a system in which the user manipulates graphical representations of *physical objects in the everyday world*. Shneiderman's own suggestion for a DMI interface to a bibliographic system has this property:

> A basic system could be built by first showing the user a wall of labeled catalog index drawers. A cursor in the shape of a human hand might be moved over to the section labeled "Author Index" and to the drawer labeled "F-L." Depressing the button on the joystick or mouse would cause the drawer to open, revealing an array of index cards with tabs offering a finer index.... Depressing the button while holding a card would cause a copy of the card to be made in the user's notebook, also represented on the screen. Entries in the notebook might be edited to create a printed bibliography or combined with other entries to perform set intersections or unions. [Shn87, p. 206]

At first glance, these ideas have some immediate appeal. The user is presented with visual representations of familiar objects — drawers and cards from a card catalog — which can be directly moved about on the screen in a manner analogous to using their real-world referents. He does not have to learn the syntax of a new system and translate this to the task at hand.

What is wrong with this approach? To paraphrase Shneiderman's own terminology, the card catalog model mistakenly focuses on the task *syntax* rather than its *semantics*. In other words, instead of using ideas about the concept of retrieving information stored in documents by finding relevant pointers to them (task semantics), we are using ideas about *the way the task has been traditionally performed* — its syntax. Just as the use of a typewriter as an analogy for word processing is as often harmful as helpful [CMN83], restricting our notion of IR browsing to those dimensions currently supported by the library's (physical) card catalog[12] limits our design of electronic systems unnecessarily. In short, the *task*, not features of our current tools for accomplishing it, should drive the design of the system.

This analysis should not be interpreted as a critique of representing physical objects in user/system interfaces. Indeed, Pejtersen has implemented a system in which the user moves through a "book house" where pictures of physical objects are used as cues for searching areas of interest [Pej89]. For example, the "room" with children's books is depicted easily by having children in it. Icons represent available search dimensions, such as a globe for searching by geographically organized subject.

The point is that the desiderata of direct manipulation are the attributes that give the user a model world to explore [HHN86] and provide a feeling of "first-personness" or direct engagement in that world [Lau86]. As Hutchins et al. point out in their assessment of direct manipulation interfaces:

> If we restrict ourselves to only building interfaces that allow us to do things we can already do and to think in ways we already think, we will miss the most exciting potential of new technology: to provide new ways to think of and to interact with a domain. [HHN86, p. 118]

This parallels my view of SCALIR's user/system interface; its realization will be discussed in detail in chapter 10.

2.8   Who's in Charge Here?

A recent trend in artificial intelligence is interest in the notion of *intelligent agents*. The idea is that rather than trying to build a system with general intelligence, it makes more sense to try to incorporate many small goal-directed subsystems — agents — each of which is adept at a well-constrained task. A typical example is "an agent that could sort your mail and remind you of your appointments, like a secretary," which underestimates the vast amount of world knowledge and common sense required to do those tasks in a useful manner.

In any case, agents are supposed to provide a happy medium between the passive system that requires the user to do everything and the

---

[12]Or, in the legal domain, the set of tools discussed in chapter 5: court reporters, digests, citation index volumes, and the West key numbering system.

overzealous hyperintelligence (think of HAL in the film *2001: A Space Odyssey*) that forbids the user to do anything. Agents are goal-directed, so they can take some initiative and ease the burden on the user. But they "report back" to the user and follow his or her instructions, allowing the user to remain in control of the task. Because each agent has only a small area of "expertise," the user is not threatened.

In some circles, one hears the argument that the direct-manipulation paradigm has reached its limit of usefulness, that a DMI requires user to be responsible for tasks that could easily be delegated to agents. The IR task is occasionally portrayed as such a task, easily delegated to the "research assistant" or "reference librarian" agent. I believe this view is mistaken for several reasons:

- The IR task is extremely difficult. Finding all documents about a certain subject is not comparable to reminding someone of tomorrow's appointments.

- The IR task is user-oriented. It is the user's information need that must be satisfied, not the agent's.[13]

- Human searchers change their task and their view of completion as they work (see Section 2.5).

- An a priori characterization of the information need may not exist; users don't know what it is they don't know.

These points do not imply that there is no role for agents in IR. Rather, it suggests that the idea of an omniscient, objective IR agent is misguided. However, this is not the only alternative, as the Guides system [OSKD90, LOD90] demonstrates. In Guides, different agents ("guides") represent different points of view; the system searches each user-suggested topic according to the interests of the different guides. Rather than attempting to replace the user, the guides allow him or her to view alternative notions of relevant documents and stories.

Bates has also written about the role of delegation and intelligence in IR systems. She emphasizes the preference of many users to control their searches and points out how that affects the task of IR research:

Therefore ... we do not ask the usual question "How can we automate everything in an information retrieval system?" Rather, we ask, "Which things shall we automate and which not?"

---

[13]This contrasts with tasks such as programming, where the attainment of the goal (roughly speaking, converting an algorithm into a program) may not affect the user at all. An optimizing compiler might be thought of as a useful agent assisting in this task.

> ...If we design an information retrieval system and inter-
> face intended to be controlled during the search process by
> the user, then we may want to design *whole new capabilities*
> that are not relevant when the entire process is taken out of
> the searcher's hands. So, let us reword that last question more
> precisely: "What capabilities should we design for the system
> to do, and what capabilities should we enable the searcher to
> exercise?" [Bat90]

If users are to maintain control of the search process, then they must be
kept "in the loop" at all times, even though "the loop" itself may change.
This can be achieved by giving users the ability to manipulate the task's
model world.

But what about the limitations of DMI? I believe that the apparent
limitations result from too narrow a notion of what objects can be manipulated. As discussed in Section 2.7, DMIs need not require the depiction
of physical objects, nor must the depiction of physical objects require
using them only as they are used in the real world.

Furthermore, there is no limit to the complexity of the objects users
can manipulate. Just as humans use *chunking* to remember as many complex entities (such as chess game configurations) as simple ones [Kla80],
so a system can use *representational chunking* to allow its users to directly
manipulate, with the same amount of effort, a word, document, or library.

2.9   A Framework for Interaction with an IR System

This chapter began with the observation that the physical representation
and organization of a document or collection of documents (such as a
library) affects the way one interacts with them, and this in turn affects
the context in which they are understood — their meaning. It then described the way in which most IR interaction works today, and presented
alternatives to this approach. It is now possible to postulate a framework
for interaction with an information retrieval system.

There is no single correct way of interacting with a system; appropriate interaction is task- and user-dependent. Therefore we cannot characterize how all IR systems should interact with their users; the tasks of
a student writing his or her first term paper and a lawyer researching a
case are simply incommensurate. Nevertheless, it is possible to outline a
general framework within which one can design a specific user/system
interface:

The information retrieval task consists of meeting the information need of the user. Accordingly, the user should be a participant in all aspects of the task, and the system's behavior should be responsive to the behavior of the user. In particular:

1. The expression of a user's information need (the query) and the system's attempts to fulfill it (the retrieval) should use the same representation. This gives the user a sense of perspective and supports both query-by-example and retrieval-by-example.

2. The query process and the retrieval process should be intertwined and incremental, so that the user can browse and change the search goal during the search process.

3. The user should participate directly in the model world, both by directly manipulating the objects and perceiving the processes (e.g., retrieval) in it, all at the appropriate level of abstraction.

4. Chains of association should emerge from the user's behavior, without requiring explicit commands. In particular, when two or more items are reported to be relevant to the same query, the system should permanently associate them. The more often this happens, the stronger the associations should be.

5. The system should exhibit adaptation to the user's behavior (i.e., it should alter its representation of documents as the users' knowledge becomes incorporated into the system).

6. Adaptation should be global, so that each user may benefit from the experience of other users.

These principles — instantiated for the particular task of legal research — underlie much of the design of SCALIR's user/system interface, which will presented in detail in chapter 10.

Chapter 3

Knowledge Representation, Meaning, and Text in AI

A main source of our failure to understand is that we do not com-mand a clear view of the use of our words. — Our grammar is lacking in this sort of perspicuity. A perspicuous representation produces just that understanding which consists in "seeing connex ions."

— Ludwig Wittgenstein,
Philosophical Investigations [Wit58, 122]

One of the most important problems in artificial intelligence (AI) is the attempt to support natural language communication with artificial sys-tems. This task is believed to require vast amounts of knowledge which the system must somehow learn or be given. This chapter is concerned with issues surrounding the representation of knowledge. I describe some desirable properties of representations, and examine the represen-tations used in SCALIR. In particular, I argue that knowledge represen-tation systems must have "unbounded depth," the ability to represent an unspecifiable amount of knowledge. Text, together with the representa-tional tools provided by a system like SCALIR, is one such system. This suggests a way in which adaptive IR systems may provide an "end-run" around some problems that have plagued AI in general, and natural lan-guage processing in particular. SCALIR's users provide the connection to the world that grounds the meaning of the system's representations. Before discussing these issues, however, I begin with a brief description of some of the terminology used throughout this work.

37

3.1   Characterizations of AI

One of the most troublesome aspects of AI seems to be that few people agree on just what the term means. Some claim that it would be easy to understand the meaning of artificial intelligence if we only could agree on the meaning of intelligence. Others treat "artificial intelligence" as a single lexical item, with various definitions (I have paraphrased them and listed some of the authors who seem to hold each view):

- Building computer models of human cognitive processes in order to understand those processes better [Bod77, CM85].

- Getting computers to do things that seem to require intelligence when done by humans [BF81, Min68, Nil80, Win77].

- Getting computers to do things that people currently do better [Ric83].

- Getting computers to think — to have or be minds [Hau85].

The first definition portrays AI as a tool for the scientific study of cognitive systems. The second and third definitions, in contrast, share the idea of imitating the behavior of cognitive systems, rather than trying to understand the mechanisms that cause that behavior. The final definition suggests the idea of actually creating cognitive systems.

My own view of AI encompasses all of these goals, viz., *AI is the use of computational mechanisms to understand and create cognitive systems.* The term *computational mechanisms* may include more than just the traditional von Neumann stored-program digital computer. I do not believe that any existing AI research program, completed or proposed, comes remotely close to creating a cognitive system. Nevertheless, I take this to be a goal of AI.

3.1.1   Connectionism as AI

The past 5 years or so have seen an enormous rebirth of an approach to AI called *connectionism*. Connectionist models — also variously called *neural networks, parallel distributed processing (PDP) systems, neurocomputers,* and so on — are based on the general idea that a massive interconnection of simple processing units, such as are found in the brain, may serve as a model for an intelligent machine. The idea of modeling neurons, or at least drawing inspiration from the architecture of the brain, has a history at least as long as the rest of AI [Heb49, MP43, Ros58, vN58]. However, it is only very recently that connectionism has developed into a full-blown subdiscipline, with its own conferences (several each year in the United States alone), journals, and so on.

Many connectionist researchers emerged from disciplines which previously made little use of computational models, such as physics and neurobiology. They were concerned more with modeling specific phenomena than with creating intelligent machines. People from other cognitive sciences often found that connectionist models offered a new and different approach that avoided some of the problems of traditional AI models.

As a result, many researchers began to treat connectionism and AI as two completely distinct (and competing) approaches. When interest in connectionism was rekindled in the mid-1980s, almost no connectionist papers could be found in the proceedings of the AI or Machine Learning conferences and journals. Meanwhile, the Cognitive Science Society meetings "began to resemble connectionist pep rallies," as Smolensky puts it [Smo88].

This view of "AI vs. connectionism" is mistaken. AI is a discipline of computer science and cognitive science, whereas connectionism is a paradigm or approach for doing research on cognition. The confusion arises from treating them as mutually exclusive alternatives; it depends on the assumption that AI comprises only "the type of research historically described in existing AI textbooks[1]" rather than including new approaches to the problems of understanding (simulating, etc.) cognition. Some connectionist research is clearly AI — by any of the definitions mentioned earlier — whereas other connectionist research may not be.

Alternatively, the "AI vs. connectionism" confusion may arise from simply using the term "AI" as a shorthand for "the symbolic approach to AI," or what Haugeland has called *GOFAI*, for "Good Old Fashioned AI" [Hau85]. He summarizes this view as being based on the belief that cognition is computation, and specifies "the claims essential to all GOFAI theories" as:

1. our ability to deal with things intelligently is due to our capacity to think about them reasonably (including subconscious thinking); and

2. our capacity to think about things reasonably amounts to a faculty for internal "automatic" symbol manipulation. [Hau85, p. 113]

Haugeland's criteria are similar to Newell's Physical Symbol System Hy-

---

[1]Now that at least one AI textbook discusses connectionism [RK91], this misunderstanding should become less common.

	Standard	**Alternative**
Techniques used	mainstream AI	connectionism
Assumptions made	symbolic AI	sub-symbolic AI

Table 3.1: Ways of slicing AI research.

pothesis [New80], which says essentially that manipulation of symbols is a necessary condition for an intelligent system. Advocates of GOFAI are committed to the explicit use of symbols; connectionists are not. Many believe that a simple symbol manipulator will never be capable of intelligent behavior because the symbols are meaningless or "hollow." This issue will be discussed further in Section 3.4.

Thus it appears that there are two ways in which one might try to pit "AI" against "connectionism." One is by saying "AI means 'standard AI techniques,' and connectionism isn't one of them." The other is by saying "AI means symbol manipulation (GOFAI, Physical Symbol System Hypothesis, etc.), whereas connectionism advocates sub-symbolic systems." Lots of confusion arises because, depending on what one means by "nonsymbolic," many traditional AI systems fall at least partly on the nonsymbolic side. Furthermore, connectionism is not the only nontraditional approach that opposes the premise of symbol-manipulation.

To clarify this issue, I use the term *mainstream AI* to refer to the standard AI techniques (from which connectionism was historically excluded), and *symbolic AI* to refer to AI research which accepts the GOFAI or Physical Symbol System view. These distinctions are shown in Table 3.1.

Are these distinctions valid? In other words, is there really anything that distinguishes mainstream AI from connectionism, or symbolic AI from sub-symbolic AI? The answer to the first question is obviously yes, because we define mainstream AI to exclude connectionism. The second question is nontrivial; in fact, it is the subject of much of chapter 6. Although I will defer discussion of the problem until then, the answer turns out to be yes as well.

3.2 Desiderata for Knowledge Representations

What is knowledge? This question has puzzled philosophers for millenia. Proposed answers, such as "knowledge is justified true belief" [Lew46], simply move the hard question elsewhere, to the concept of *belief*. Explaining what it means to believe something, or more generally, to "have a propositional attitude" (that is, to believe a proposition P, fear that P, hope that P, and so on) has proved no easier than explaining what it means to know something.

It might seem that without a good understanding of knowledge, it makes little sense to talk about knowledge representation — yet AI researchers have done just that for several decades. In part, this is due to a lack of awareness of work in philosophy on the part of people in AI. A more important reason is one of terminology; an AI researcher will say "I will define 'knowledge' to be 'facts about the world,' and thus my system will represent knowledge." For example, Brachman and Levesque believe that knowledge representation

> ...simply has to do with writing down, in some language or communicative medium, descriptions or pictures that correspond in some salient way to the world or a state of the world. [BL85, p. xiii].

It is this meaning of the term that I use as well.

The remainder of this section describes a set of desirable properties for knowledge representations. Unfortunately, some of them conflict; there are always tradeoffs. It is nevertheless instructive to identify the desiderata, and then assess our actual representations according to how well the desired attributes are achieved.

3.2.1 Avoiding the Acquisition Bottleneck

Many AI systems have been built to operate on "toy" domains. Rather complete knowledge bases are manually constructed for these tiny domains, the system works more or less as advertised, and the system's concept is said to be demonstrated "in theory." As Dreyfus pointed out [Dre79], few of these systems have ever been actually scaled up to real-world problems. The problem is that the actual domains are often *several* orders of magnitude larger than the toy domains, and the solutions often require computations that grow exponentially with the size of the knowledge base.

Attempts to use the same strategy for more general tasks leads to what Lenat called the *knowledge acquisition bottleneck* [Len83]; because the knowledge must be manually encoded, it can only be inserted into the system at a constant rate. A graduate student may be able to encode a few tens or even hundreds of rules (or other "knowledge atoms") about a small domain; the student's time is cheap and the domain is finite. But experts draw on vast amounts of knowledge. Chess masters, for example, are believed to recognize some 50,000 board configurations [Ber73]. Suppose we define *expertise* in terms of knowing 50,000 "chunks" of domain knowledge. Optimistically assuming that it takes a graduate student only one month to build a 100-item knowledge base (where an "item" depends on the domain, but corresponds to an expert's "chunk"), it would take 500 months — over 40 years — to scale up the system. (By way of comparison, Guha and Lenat describe the Cyc project — an attempt to encode common-sense knowledge — as a "decade-long, two person-century effort" [GL90]).

Of course, the problem is greater than just the length of time required to enter the knowledge. If one person does it, the resulting representation will reflect only his or her own view of the domain. This view is likely to become increasingly idiosyncratic as he or she spends an entire career doing the encoding. Furthermore, it is quite possible that some of the knowledge entered at the start of the effort will be obsolete by the end.

In practice, of course, the task would be divided among many individuals. However, this introduces a second problem: inconsistency. It is unlikely that a set of "knowledge encoding rules" can be constructed so rigorously that different people will encode the same item exactly the same way. Indeed, if such rules were known, we wouldn't need the knowledge engineers.

Nor does the scaling problem lie only in the sheer size of the domain. In many cases, the number of interactions increases exponentially. Anyone who has tried to write or modify a rule-based system can attest to the danger of unexpected interactions. When attempting to scale up the system, there may be too many interactions for any one individual to keep track of, and multiple encoders may unwittingly cause interactions with their colleagues' representations. Finally, some attributes cannot be not scaled indefinitely; techniques that worked for smaller cases may simply break down. Just because we can build 10- and 100- story buildings doesn't mean we can build 10,000-story ones with the same technology.

3.2.2   Learnability

Clearly, the manual encoding of knowledge is infeasible for many problems; it is simply too slow and difficult. As Guha and Lenat remarked, "manually entering assertion after assertion ... is akin to teachers [having to] instruct by surgically manipulating brains" [GL90, p. 57]. One obvious alternative is to use *learning* as a means of knowledge acquisition. If we can get the system to learn, then we can avoid the knowledge acquisition bottleneck . In particular, if the system can be designed so that the "power law of learning" [NR81] holds, a learning system might acquire knowledge at an progressively increasing rate.

Although some learning is clearly necessary, it is not a panacea. Many forms of learning require human preprogramming to specify the rules for the representations the system is to learn. But these rules, like the knowledge base itself, may not scale easily. Once the learning mechanism is set up, the system must be provided with "experiences" or "instruction." In the former case, the system may not encounter the situations needed to learn certain facts. In other words, it is not guaranteed to be exposed to enough data. In the latter case, human intervention is again required to construct a set of training examples that will illustrate all possible dimensions of variation. Even if the system is exploratory, human intervention is often required to assist in determining which of its discoveries are important [LB84].

3.2.3 Comprehensibility

An alternative to specifying the nature of the representations to be learned is to provide a very general mechanism for learning associations or classifications. This is the approach used in connectionist and other statistical learning models. One advantage is that these systems can often generalize; they do not need to "memorize" all the data they are expected handle correctly.

However, connectionist or other sub-symbolic learning often introduces a new problem: the representations constructed may not be comprehensible to the system's human users. As Belew and Forrest explained, comprehensibility is one of the crucial advantages of symbolic learning:

> A key feature of symbolic knowledge systems is their ability to retrace inferences so that the system's behavior can be debugged and explained. This capability depends on the comprehensibility of both the symbols making up the knowledge base and the inference procedures operating on this representation.... [BF88, p. 217]

If representations are not comprehensible, then users may not trust the system's inferences, however well it performs.

In many connectionist systems, the representations learned can be elucidated to some degree. There are various techniques, such as hierarchical cluster analysis, principal components analysis, or simply graphing certain hidden unit weights. The use of these techniques underscores the importance of being able to understand learned representations.

On the other hand, comprehensibility should not be an excuse for oversimplification. As McDermott pointed out, calling the main loop of the program UNDERSTAND does not give the system understanding [McD81]; this type of terminology is merely a misleading exercise in wishful thinking.

3.2.4 Informability

Despite the value of learning, there are many situations in which it is unnecessary, and therefore inappropriate. These are the cases in which not only is the desired knowledge available a priori, but it is also in a form isomorphic to (or at least analogous with) the way in which it will be represented. In these instances, learning is simply wasted effort.

Simon illustrated this point repeatedly in his skeptical paper, "Why Should Machines Learn?" [Sim83]. Discussing the parameter learning that occurred in Samuel's checker-playing program [Sam63], Simon pointed out that "if Samuel had known the right evaluation function at the outset, he would have put it in the program; he would not have gone through all the learning rigamarole" [Sim83, p. 31]. Summarizing, he said:,

> [W]hat is the place here for learning research in AI? ... If we understand the domain ourselves, if we understand physics, why don't we just choose an internal representation and provide the problems to the system in that internal representation? What's all this learning and natural language understanding about? [Sim83, pp. 33–34]

Of course, only some representations have the desirable ability to directly "implement" knowledge, or to have knowledge "implanted" in them; I call these *informable* representations.

3.2.5 Adaptivity

Whether a system's initial knowledge is acquired by "hardwiring" or by learning, it will often be necessary to alter the knowledge base later on. It may be that new knowledge needs to be added to the system; in this case, the existing knowledge should not be lost. Alternatively, some part of the existing knowledge may need to be modified. Again, this should be possible without reconstructing the entire representation.

Representations able to handle these two types of modification (which correspond roughly to *accretion* and *tuning* in Rumelhart and Norman's model of human learning [RN78]) are said to be *adaptive*. Adaptivity is extremely useful, since it means that representations can be kept current in a changing environment.

Occasionally, a modification may take the form of cancelling some previous information. An adaptive representation should be able to preserve the rest of its knowledge even when explicitly removing or cancelling one portion of it.

It is important to distinguish between the concepts of learnability and adaptivity. Learnable representations are those that acquire their knowledge through learning, whereas adaptive representations are those which can continually update their existing representations. It is possible to have nonlearnable systems that are adaptive, as well as learnable systems that aren't.

3.2.6 Unbounded Depth

Most traditional knowledge representation methods involve the a priori specification of what features of the domain are to be modeled. For example, a "clue" program to understand murder mysteries might use a frame-based representation in which the slots for **detective, victim, murderer, means, motive,** and **opportunity** (among others) would be filled in. The fillers may in turn be structured objects — subframes — with their own slots. Although this may continue for a few levels, there will still be a finite number of *predetermined* dimensions of variation. For many problems, the combinatorial number of possible representations is quite sufficient.

The problem with these prespecified knowledge bases is that the types of inferences one can draw — in other words, the types of knowledge one can access — is severely limited. Although there may be an infinite *number* of inferences (using such axioms as $A \rightarrow A \vee B$), they are all restricted to the language identified by the designer of the representation. With the murder mystery knowledge base, we probably could not ask the symbolism of the detective's clothing, or the allegorical nature of the plot. Even if all that information were somehow made available to the system, the representation simply provides no way to express it. In fact, *there is no way to know what features of the knowledge must be represented until the knowledge needs to be accessed* — and then it is usually too late. Even if part of the design task involves trying to identify what the system will be used for, there may be no way to foresee what will be important in the future. This is especially true of the legal IR task, as will become clear in chapter 5.

I will use the term *unbounded depth* to describe those representations which, in contrast, have (theoretically) infinite expressive capacity. This can only be achieved by having at least part of the representation *not* predetermine what features are relevant. It implies some infinitely dense continuous space (like the real line) in which there is always another point between any two items being observed. Such representations might well contain knowledge that was not known to the person providing it. They might also contain knowledge that is not immediately accessible.

Of course, all this expansiveness does not come for free; there are diminishing returns. Because there is no such thing as infinite precision, the fidelity of the inferences gradually degrades as one continues to isolate and magnify smaller and smaller portions of the representation. This is analogous to the way in which holograms became increasingly blurry when cut into smaller pieces.

3.3   Semantic and Connectionist Networks

Having seen what properties we would like our representations to have, it is useful to preview those actually used in SCALIR — semantic and connectionist networks. This section provides a general background and definition of each type of representation, and attempts to assess whether each possesses any or all of the desirable properties listed earlier.

3.3.1   Representing Knowledge in Semantic Networks

In the mid-1960s, Quillian proposed a model of semantic memory that was intended to account for the behavior of people given "compare and contrast" tasks. Quillian's model consisted primarily of a network of associations between nodes representing words. This became known as a *semantic network*. Quillian believed that the meaning of a word was simply the set of other nodes to which it was related:

> ... [A] word's full concept is defined in the model memory to be all the nodes that can be reached by an exhaustive tracing process, originating at its initial, patriarchical type node, together with the total sum of relationships among these nodes specified by within-plane, token-to-token links.   [Qui85, p. 101, italics removed]

(The "type nodes" were the words being defined, whereas the "token nodes" included all the words used in the definitions. A "plane" was a part of the network corresponding to a particular meaning of a word.)

In order to test the model, Quillian developed the idea of a *spreading activation* search, which could be visualized as "slowly expanding spheres of activated nodes around each patriarch" [Qui85, p. 110]. Because the goal of the model was to study the compare-and-contrast task, Quillian activated two "patriarch" nodes and then recorded the points at which the spheres of activation intersected. This was implemented by what would later be called a *marker-passing* scheme:

> The program simulates the gradual activation of each concept outward through the vast proliferation of associations originating from each patriarch, by moving out along these links, tagging each node encountered with a special two-part tag, the "activation tag." Part of this tag always names the patriarch from which the search began, that is, the name of the concept within which the current node has been reached. Now, the program detects any intersection of meaning between the two concepts simply by asking, every time a node is reached, whether or not it already contains an activation tag naming the other patriarch, that is, showing that this node has previously been reached in the tracing out of the other concept. [Qui85, p. 110]

Among the important concepts introduced by Quillian were first, the idea of a variety of link types representing different relationships, and second, the ability to pass multiple marker types, each maintaining their identity. As will become clear in chapter 6, these two properties were essential to the use of a semantic network in SCALIR.

In the years following Quillian's research, many other semantic network models were proposed.[2] A critical development was the use of explicit labels on different link types to determine how to spread markers selectively. In particular, links indicating predication, instantiation, or subclass/superclass relationships — often called IS-A links — took on special status.

IS-A links ushered in a concise representation of properties known as *inheritance hierarchies*. As shown in Figure 3.1, inheritance hierarchies were essentially taxonomic trees (more recently called *ontologies*) that associated properties with the most general class possible. Thus one could now assert that birds fly without having to separately mention that robins fly, canaries fly, and so on; these subclasses would *inherit* the properties of their superclass. Indeed, the idea of inheritance hierarchies built around

---

[2]A very clear explication of important network models is given in [Bra85].

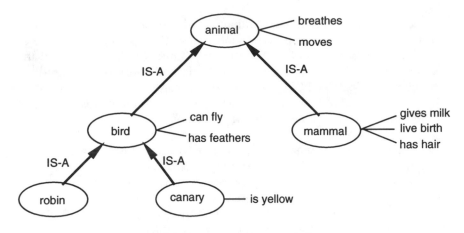

Figure 3.1: An inheritance hierarchy.

IS-A links is so widespread that the network shown in Figure 3.1 might well serve as a picture of a "canonical" semantic network.[3]

An obvious problem with the network in the figure is that it if, as Quillian intended, a node is defined by its relationships, then the network makes no allowance for the possibility of birds that don't fly. To avoid this problem, most semantic network models have treated properties as *defaults* which can be overridden if a more specific node contradicts them. This is shown in Figure 3.2. Thus the nodes are viewed as *assertions* rather than as *definitions* [BFL85]. "Definitional" nets can be characterized by simple first-order predicate logic, whereas defaults and exceptions require nonmonotonic formalisms [ER85].

The clustering of default properties (or events) around prototypical entities is a hallmark of frame [Min75], script [SA77], and schema [Rum75] models. Indeed, the distinction between semantic nets and frames has blurred to the point where formalisms for systematically relating entities in semantic networks (such as KL-ONE [BS85]) are often referred to as "frame representation languages."

For the purposes of this work, the following definition will be used:

Definition 3.1 *A semantic network is a labeled directed graph consisting of:*

- *Nodes, representing instances or classes of concepts, that have states consisting of sets of marker tokens.*

---

[3]Brachman, however, has argued [Bra83] that the concept of inheritance should play no role in discussions of the ability of semantic networks to represent knowledge.

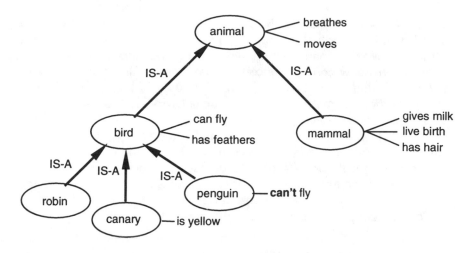

Figure 3.2: An inheritance hierarchy with exceptions.

- *Directed arcs (also called links), representing relationships between nodes, that have labels drawn from a small finite set.*

- *A finite set of marker types, which can be instantiated to mark nodes.*

- *Marker-passing functions, that for each node, link label, and optional external input compute which markers should be passed along the link.*

"Marker-passing" refers to adding a new marker token to the state of the node at the "receiving" end of the link, if that marker type is not already present .

Note that this definition says nothing about special hierarchy-forming links such as IS-A, although it certainly allows for them. This avoids some of the problems (such as distinguishing between instantiation and class membership) that have plagued many semantic network models [Woo75, Bra83].

Semantic networks have the virtue of being informable, in that they facilitate the encoding of a priori knowledge. They are also extremely comprehensible. This property is particularly useful when (as is the case with SCALIR), the links in the network correspond to relationships familiar to the system's users.

However, semantic networks do not score high on the knowledge acquisition scale. They must be constructed by hand, unless there already exist real-world artifacts (which may themselves have required previous knowledge engineering) whose structure is to be isomorphically mirrored. (This is fortunately the case with SCALIR's semantic network, which will be described in chapter 7.) Nor are they generally adaptive, although there are some well-known semantic network systems that are able to learn new concepts once they have originally been constructed [Win75]. Perhaps their biggest drawback is their lack of depth; the only inferences one can make from a semantic network are those based on the existence or nonexistence of links.

In SCALIR, the semantic network nodes represent specific instances (of documents) or concepts (topics of law), and the links correspond directly to explicit, pre-existing relationships between them (such as the overruling of one court case by another). There is no notion of inheritance per se, nor are there nodes representing sets or classes. Thus many of the conceptual problems with semantic networks do not arise.

3.3.2   Representing Knowledge in Connectionist Networks

Connectionist models are based on the idea of very simple processing units which compute a function of their weighted inputs. There are several formal descriptions of connectionist models that support extremely general types of computation, such as the ability of a unit to compute different functions on different inputs [FB82, RHM86].

For the purposes of this work, I use a somewhat more restricted notion of connectionist networks, which nevertheless adequately describes many if not most of the networks in current use:

Definition 3.2 *A connectionist network is a weighted directed graph such that:*

- *Each node (also called unit) i at time t has a real-valued state $a_i(t)$ known as its activation or output.*

- *Any node i can be connected to any other node j by arcs (also called links) with real-valued weights w_{ij}.*

- *The new state of a node $a_i(t+1)$ is a function of its previous state $a_i(t)$, the weighted sum of previous states of its neighbors $\sum w_{ij}a_j(t)$, and external input $x_i(t)$.*

For conciseness, we can represent the information about the network by a vector a of states of all the nodes and a square matrix **W** of weights.

There are a few differences between this model and some of the other well-known models. First, any node can receive external input. This means that the model does not need to be layered in the sense of a feed-forward PDP net, though it subsumes layered nets. Second, general recurrence occurs through asymmetric, directed links. Third, there is no distinction between the activation of a unit and its output. Finally, each unit can compute only a single function of its inputs; in other words, there is only one "site" per unit.

Note also that the model does not restrict how the link weights are to be determined. This is consistent with the variety of weighting schemes used in connectionist research; some networks require that the weights be determined a priori [Hop82, MR81, Sha88], whereas others allow or require the weights to adapt to (hopefully) satisfactory values. SCALIR uses both types of weight determination: initial weights are computed by a mechanism described in chapter 7 and then refined by a learning mechanism explained in chapter 9.

How is knowledge represented in a connectionist network? The simple answer is that, to paraphrase Rumelhart et al., *the knowledge is in the weights* [RHM86]. Further, knowledge is accessed by initiating and observing *patterns of activation* propagating through the network over time. As Rumelhart et al. explained,

> [I]t is the connections ... which primarily differentiate one model from another. This is a profound difference between our approach and other more conventional approaches, for it means that almost all knowledge is *implicit* in the structure of the device that carries out out the task rather than *explicit* in the states of units themselves. Knowledge is not directly accessible to interpretation by some separate processor, but is built into the processor itself and directly determines the course of processing. It is acquired through tuning of connections as these are used in processing, rather than formulated and stored as declarative facts. [RHM86, pp. 75–76]

It is this "knowledge-through-use" idea that has prompted some researchers to describe connectionist representations as "proclarative" [Cottrell, personal communication, 1988].

There are many general algorithms for adjusting the weights of connectionist networks to solve various tasks. This learnability is one of the model's greatest strengths. It is also nearly a necessity, since hand-coding the weights is difficult for all but the simplest tasks. In other words, these models are not very informable. Furthermore, they generally fail to develop comprehensible representations; some sort of analysis is needed to tell "what the net is doing."

Their ability to learn overcomes the acquisition bottleneck to some degree, although there are doubts about how well they can scale. Complex problems require larger networks, which in turn require a much longer

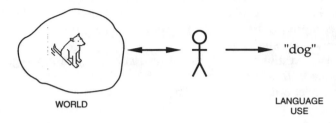

WORLD

LANGUAGE
USE

Figure 3.3: The grounded symbols of a human language user.

training period to learn the desired task. As we will see later on, scaling is less of a problem if the entire network does not need to be involved for every task.

Most significantly, many connectionist representations are deep. The set of salient features they can represent is unspecified and theoretically unbounded. The representations are the result of the network's training or "experience," the input-output data to which it has been exposed. Existing knowledge can be modified or incorporated into new knowledge, though it can sometimes also be destroyed.

Of course, most connectionist systems are simply extracting regularities from the environment, finding the dimensions of maximum variance. Furthermore, "the environment" is still whatever the trainer or programmer chooses. Thus a network trained to distinguish words from nonwords by receiving ASCII input and binary targets cannot say anything about the word's visual appearance, any more than we can tell what song is playing on the radio by standing next to the station's transmitter; that input is simply not available. But although connectionist nets are data-dependent, there are no a priori constraints on which regularities of this data the system can identify.

3.4 Representation and Meaning

For a system to truly represent knowledge, the symbols or other structures that are supposed to be the representations must stand in some meaningful relationship to the things in the world that they represent. Human language users participate in a variety of direct experiences with the world; their use of symbols refers to their representation of these experiences. This is shown in Figure 3.3. However, this has generally

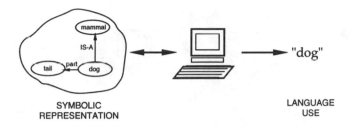

SYMBOLIC
REPRESENTATION

LANGUAGE
USE

Figure 3.4: Ungrounded symbols in a traditional AI system.

not been the case with AI systems. In a typical AI system, for instance, something representing the concept *dog* does not bear any relationship to dogs in the real world. Rather the *dog* concept is defined by its properties or class memberships (e.g., a *dog* is defined to be 4-legged domesticated canine carnivore). But those concepts (such as carnivore) refer to further concepts, and so on. Even if we can define all concepts in terms of some small atomic set (such as Schank's semantic primitives [SR74]), the atoms themselves have no meaningful semantics. Figure 3.4 shows this relationship; the system has a representation and produces (or takes in) natural language symbols, but the world is not present anywhere in the model. This is often called the *symbol grounding* problem in AI. As Harnad explained:

> ...[T]he meanings of elementary symbols must be grounded in perceptual categories. That is, symbols, which are manipulated only in virtue of their form (i.e. syntactically) rather than their "meaning" must be reducible to nonsymbolic, shape-preserving representations. Semantics can only arise when the interpretations of elementary symbols are "fixed" by these nonsymbolic, iconic representations. [Har87, p. 11]

Many critics have attacked AI research for its failure to recognize the inadequacy of ungrounded symbols. Perhaps the best-known critique is Searle's "Chinese Room" problem [Sea78]. Searle compared the understanding of a typical natural language processing program to an English-speaking person locked in a room, answering questions in Chinese by following a set of complex English instructions for writing one Chinese character when another appears. He argued that

> [T]he formal symbol manipulations by themselves don't have any intentionality: they are meaningless; they aren't even *sym-*

53

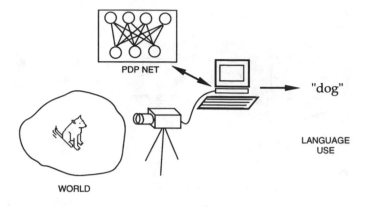

Figure 3.5: Artificial grounding by perceptual input.

bol manipulations, since the symbols don't symbolize anything. In linguistic jargon they have only a syntax but no
semantics. Such intentionality as computers appear to have
is solely in the minds of those who program them and those
who use them, those who send in the input and who interpret
the output. [Sea78, pp. 300–301]

Dreyfus, attacking much of the formalist tradition in Western philosophy
in addition to AI, arrived at a similar conclusion: "since intelligence must
be situated it cannot be separated from the rest of human life" [Dre79, p.
62]. Winograd and Flores, following Heidegger, offer a related critique
[WF86] that points out limitations of computers without physical bodies
and contexts.

3.4.1 Grounding by Observation

Ideally, we would like our knowledge representations to have real semantics; that is, to have meaning grounded in experience with the world.
Although this may never be fully attainable, it is not an all-or-nothing
proposition. We can work now on representations that are *more* grounded,
even if we cannot suddenly impart true knowledge of the world to a dis-
embodied system.

It seems that in order to have symbols grounded in the human language sense, the artificial system would need to actually participate in
the physical world. For example, a system with visual input could have a
more grounded representation of spatial relationships than one without.
This is shown conceptually in Figure 3.5. This is the approach taken by

Bartell and Cottrell in their "movie description network" (MDN) [BC91].
As Cottrell et al. describe the approach:

> We assert that the mapping of predicates to the world is the
> fundamental issue in semantics: We must know the meanings
> of the individual elements of the theory before we can form
> a theory of the whole. We propose that the mapping is one
> that is *acquired* through interaction of a learner with the world,
> during which the learner forms associations between linguis-
> tic entities and concrete objects. That is, meaning is grounded
> in perception. [CBH90, p. 307]

This network is shown a sequence of visual input patterns ("movies")
which, viewed in succession, shows a ball moving in a given direction.
The system's task is to "subtitle" the movies, describing the action occurring. The system's descriptions take the form of sequentially turning on
units corresponding to the current action — the four directions of motion (up, down, left, right) and two speeds (slowly and quickly). So its
subtitle for a typical movie corresponds to the statement "rolling down
and left quickly."

The MDN approach seems promising for a long-range effort to develop an artificial language user with grounded semantics. However,
there are two problems. First, there is no way to bootstrap the system; it
must be trained from an initial random configuration. As the complexity
of the task increases, the amount of training required does also. Even
if it were theoretically possible to build a system that used language as
we did (that is, with symbols grounded in perception), it might take as
long for the system to acquire language as it takes humans — though
this might be acceptable if the system could then be replicated.

A more serious problem is that although this type of system interacts
with the world, it does not have the opportunity to interact with other
language users. Given that the artificial system has different experiences
than we do, its symbols — however well grounded — will not have the
same meanings that ours do.

3.4.2 Grounding by Communication

What might a compromise between ungrounded symbols and full perceptual grounding look like? It would have to have some kind of semantics
related to the world, yet it should be a "plug and play" system that does
not require extensive training to be useful.

As we have argued previously [BR88], an adaptive information retrieval system (such as AIR or SCALIR) may possess the desired at-

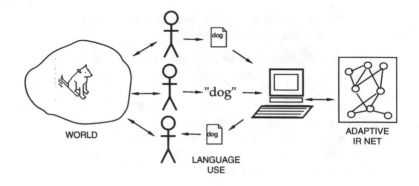

Figure 3.6: Language use in an adaptive IR system.

tributes. These systems manipulate examples of written language (text documents) and develop associations for words in accordance with the contexts in which they occur. This is reminiscent of Wittgenstein's view of meaning: "For a *large* class of cases — though not for all — in which we employ the word 'meaning' it can be defined thus: the meaning of a word is its use in the language" [Wit58, 43]. This view of meaning depends critically on the notion of language as communication. The people communicating, whether through speech or text, must use the same conventions; they must be participating in same language game, to use Wittgenstein's terminology.

A traditional IR system provides a (one-way) communication link between authors (of the documents in the system) and readers (users of the system). The system is a passive conduit for information. An adaptive IR system, however, allows users to cause changes to the representation, and thus to communicate their ideas about the meanings of words and documents to other users. The system plays an active role in the process, developing a consensual repository of knowledge that no individual could have provided. By repeated exposure to a large and diverse set of word uses in context, the system gradually learns what words and documents mean to its users.

Thus in addition to starting with a representation of word contexts, the adaptive IR system has the benefit of actually participating in an ongoing interaction with its human users. This is shown in Figure 3.6. Each of those users interacts daily with the world, so the system's knowledge is not frozen in the statistical properties of the text. Such a system may be locked away from direct participation with the world, but it has a window on human communication. Thus we might describe the situation as a "Chinese Room with a View," sidestepping Searle's problem without attempting to build an artificial person. Rather than rejecting Searle's view of meaning being in the minds of users, this approach embraces it as a virtue.

A critical attribute of adaptive IR is that the behavior from which the system learns is the result of users' interactions with text. The text itself contains knowledge carefully conveyed by its author. Indeed, text may be viewed as another type of knowledge representation. In fact, it has many of the desirable properties discussed in Section 3.2.

First, text is certainly comprehensible, as is evidenced by its role in human communication, even across large temporal and spatial distances. Even the extensive AI research aimed at developing artificial systems that can generate and understand natural language is motivated by the desire to facilitate communication with human users — why else go to all that trouble?

Second, text is a grounded representation, almost by definition, because it is the product of a human's natural language use. The authors themselves interact with and perceptually experience the world, and their language uses are grounded in that experience.

Third, text is a deep representation, because there are no a priori constraints on the inferences one can make from a document. Belew [personal communication, 1990] has illustrated this property with an enlightening exercise for an information retrieval class; he asks students to write down all the inferences they can make from the first paragraph of a newspaper story. A sentence beginning "Soviet President Mikhail Gorbachev flew to Geneva ..." conveys not only that a certain event (PTRANS, in Schank's terminology) took place, but also that when the sentence was written, the Soviet Union still existed under that name, that some some constitutional reforms had already taken place (since he wasn't described as "General-Secretary Gorbachev"), that Geneva is the name of a place that has an airport, and so on.

Furthermore, the meaning of a text may change over time and in different social contexts. This is not merely a tenet of current literary criticism; it is a fundamental property of common law. Judges continue to find new meaning in old decisions, and offhand remarks — even footnotes — often become cornerstones of later law. (This is discussed further in chapter 5.)

Meaningful text, of course, is not easy to generate. Thus one might say that a textual knowledge representation suffers severely from the acquisition bottleneck. Although it is undoubtedly difficult to convey knowledge in text, people have been doing it successfully for centuries, and much of that text is now available online. In SCALIR, the text forms the primordial soup from which the other representations — the connectionist and semantic networks — draw their strength.

Chapter 4

Approaches to Information Retrieval

Information retrieval[1] (IR) is a rich field with a long history dating back to the 1940s. These decades of research have produced some extremely powerful techniques that have revolutionized, among other things, bibliographic research. However, despite the progress, many — perhaps most — IR systems are far less powerful than we would wish. There are serious problems limiting IR system effectiveness, and competing suggestions about how to overcome them. In this chapter I follow a particular landscape of IR research, highlighting certain problems with traditional IR methods and describing various methods used to alleviate them. Before proceeding, though, it is worth being clear on exactly what an IR system is supposed to do.

4.1   The Information Retrieval Task

The task of an information retrieval system is simple: *to retrieve documents that satisfy a user's information need.* The simplicity of the task is deceptive, however, because each aspect of it raises many questions.

What is a "Document"? In IR, this may not be the typical book or journal article, but rather any contiguous collection of free text[2] — for

---

[1]Sometimes known as "automatic" or "computer-assisted" information retrieval, to distinguish it from manual methods.

[2]There is also interest in systems that retrieve images and other nontext objects, but I do not discuss them here, nor does most of the work in IR apply to them.

example, paragraphs, electronic mail messages, or (as in SCALIR) court decisions.

What Constitutes "Retrieval"? In some IR systems (such as Dow Jones News Service), the full text of the document itself is retrieved. In other systems, only a surrogate of the document is retrieved. This might simply be a library catalog number, or it might contain more information such as an abstract. In either case, a user must then physically retrieve the item by (for instance) going to the library.

Who is "a User"? In some cases, the typical user of the system will be the one who ultimately needs the information. In other cases, a skilled intermediary (such as a reference librarian) does the actual interacting with the IR system, and then relays the information to the end-user. Usually these intermediaries are far more skilled at using the IR system than the end-user, but they may be less knowledgeable about the domain of the document corpus.[3]

What is a User's "Information Need"? A simple view is that the information need is just what is described in the user's request for information or *query*. Typical queries are expressed in some artificial syntax, but some systems allow natural language requests. A more complex view of information need holds that because the user doesn't yet know the answer to the problem that motivated the search, he or she cannot directly express the need as a query. As Belkin et al. explained:

> ... [T]he user, faced with a problem, recognizes that her/his state of knowledge is inadequate for resolving that problem, and decides that obtaining information about the problem area and its circumstances is an appropriate means toward its resolution. There are certainly occasions when one might be able to specify precisely what information is required to bring the state of knowledge to a structure adequate for resolution of the problem, but it seems obvious that the more usual situation will be that in which what is appropriate for the purpose is not known in advance. [BOB82, p. 63]

In part, which view one adopts depends on whether "the task at hand" is believed to be using the IR system to search for documents, or "retrieving information" in the general sense.

What Does it Mean to "Satisfy" this Need? This is perhaps the most difficult and hotly debated question. If we view queries as roughly the expression of an information need, then satisfying the need is most commonly described by a notion of *relevance*. The task of an IR system is often

---

[3]This is often the case in a law firm, where more senior members of the firm (e.g., partners) give research instructions to more junior members (or paralegals).

stated as "retrieving relevant documents." Unfortunately, there is significant disagreement about what constitutes relevance and how to measure
it, and even whether it is an appropriate concept at all [Coo71, Sar76].
Problems with relevance are part of the central motivation for the SCALIR
approach, so it is worth elaborating this point.

Relevance is difficult to grasp because it is *subjective* and *relative*. *Subjectivity* simply means that two users may differ in their opinions about
whether a document is relevant, even if both issued the same query.
Therefore any general statements we make about the effectiveness of a
system may not hold for particular users. *Relativity* means that a document might be judged irrelevant if retrieved in context A, but relevant if
retrieved in context B. So although we may be able to rank all documents
in the corpus according to relevance and choose an arbitrary number of
"most" relevant ones, we cannot separate the collection into a "relevant
set" and a "nonrelevant set."

Relevance also depends on the user's ultimate information need. If
a document was relevant with respect to a query early on in one's research, it may be judged irrelevant later because it no longer fills part
of the information need (having done so already earlier). An even more
paradoxical situation arises when a user is searching for a particular document believed to contain an answer to a specific problem. When the
user finally locates the document, she or he discovers that it does not,
in fact, contain the desired answer. So was the document relevant with
respect to a query designed particularly to find it?

So far I have said little about the actual retrieval (i.e., *how* the information need is satisfied). In the simplest view, the system gets queries
as input, searches a database of documents, and outputs those that are
relevant. This is shown in Figure 4.1. However, it omits several features. First, it is generally not the documents and queries themselves
that the system manipulates, but representations of them. Second, the
user should appear as a participant in the system. This revised view is
shown in Figure 4.2.

Once the user sees the system's response, he or she can express opinions about how well it satisfied the information need. This is known as
relevance feedback (see Section 4.5.3), and is generally used to automatically
change the query. However, it can also be used to change the documents,
as discussed in Section 4.5.4. These feedback loops produce the picture
in Figure 4.3.

By now it should be clear that IR is a complex task in which it is hard
to even say what a "right answer" would be. This stands in marked contrast to the task of a database management system (DBMS), in which the
user is interested in an exact answer to an exact question, such as "How

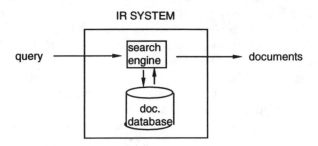

Figure 4.1: A simple view of retrieval.

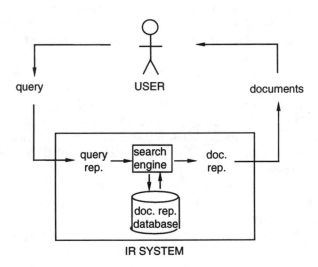

Figure 4.2: A better view of retrieval.

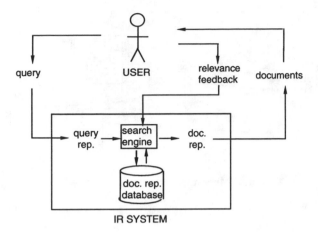

Figure 4.3: Retrieval with relevance feedback.

many employees earning over $50,000 work in the research division?"
We can argue about the effectiveness of an IR system and the relevance
of its responses, but this question does not even make sense for a DBMS;
it either gives the correct answer or has a bug in the program.[4] Many
authors have commented on the different nature of the IR and DBMS
tasks; see, for example, [vR79].

4.2   The Two "Classical" Approaches

Although there are many different ways to design an IR system, two
approaches have dominated the field for the past 30 years. Although
few people advocate using the simple versions that follow, it is worth
understanding them to appreciate the enhancements that can be made.
By "approach to IR," I mean specifically how documents are represented
and accessed in the system.

---

[4]Although there is ongoing research about DBMSs that can handle more complex and
possibly ambiguous questions, such as "who no longer works in the research lab" (the
system must infer that people who have left the company altogether — perhaps at some
later date — are not of interest). Nevertheless, the open-ended issues of database research
are still different from those in IR.

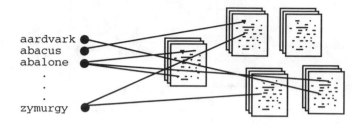

aardvark •
abacus •
abalone •
.
.
.
zymurgy •

Figure 4.4: Searching with an inverted file.

4.2.1 Inverted Files

Suppose that queries consisted of a single term, and finding relevant documents consisted of simply finding documents that contain that term. One strategy we might take is to simply search all the documents (in whatever order they appear in the collection) and list those in which the term appears. This may seem like an inefficient method, but it made more sense in the early days of information retrieval, when batch processing systems were fairly common. Many users would submit their requests (perhaps by handing punched cards to an operator), which would be collected together and then run on the system. Thus while scanning document 1, the system could check if it contained any of the hundreds of terms different users asked about. Because the system had to scan every document, the set of all documents was viewed as a so-called *direct file* to be searched.

With the advent of interactive terminals, the direct file method no longer made sense. Why search the corpus over and over when we could simply determine once and for all which documents contain which words? This is the motivation for the *inverted file*. In this approach, a table is made of every unique word[5] occurring in the corpus. Each word in the table has an associated list indicating the location of every occurrence of that word in the corpus. For simplicity, we can imagine the location as being a document number, but in fact many systems specify the exact position of the term in the document. Either way, the location serves as a pointer to the text itself. This is shown in Figure 4.4. Instead of searching the documents directly, we search the table, which is ordered by terms (hence the name "inverted file"). This is extremely efficient, particularly

---

[5]Actually, any words from a *stop list* or *negative dictionary* — articles, prepositions, and so on that have no content — are generally omitted.

because clever data structures such as tries or hashing schemes can be used to locate the inverted file entries in very short times. A disadvantage is that the index often takes up as much space as the text itself.

Inverted-file-based systems routinely use Boolean query languages, in which a user's query must be expressed as a list of terms joined by the connectives of Boolean algebra[6]. It is clear why the use of Boolean queries is so closely associated with the inverted file approach; Boolean queries are easy and efficient to implement with an inverted index. Recall that each entry in the inverted file contains a list of documents in which the term occurs. If the user wants documents containing the terms *artificial* or *intelligence*, we can simply take the union of the index entries for each of the two terms. If the user wants documents containing both terms, we can take the intersection of the entries. If the user wants documents about *artificial* but not *intelligence*, we can take the set difference. Thus there is a simple mapping between Boolean queries and the operations easily supported by an inverted file.

The simplicity, efficiency, and power of the inverted file approach has given it enormous popularity in commercial IR systems. Indeed, almost all commercial IR systems vended use this approach. Some significant enhancements have been added — such as additional connectives that allow "proximity searching" (e.g., to find all the documents in which the terms *artificial* and *intelligence* occur within five words of each other) and wild card expanders (that support searches on any term with the same root). Nevertheless, the basic nature of the systems has remained the same.

Unfortunately, there are many problems with the inverted file/Boolean query approach. For one thing, there is evidence that users have difficulty expressing their queries in Boolean algebra. Furthermore, this approach imposes an unrealistic view of relevance: A document is either relevant or it isn't. This can be alleviated somewhat by presenting the retrieved set of documents in order, from most to fewest occurrences of the term, but this is a partial solution at best.

4.2.2 The Vector Model

Both of the previous problems are avoided by an insightful approach known as the *vector model*. In this model, documents are represented as vectors of terms. In the simplest case, we can simply put a "1" in the appropriate component of a document vector if a term appears in it, and

---

[6]Well, almost. Boolean query languages generally replace the unary negation connective with the binary BUT NOT, where A BUT NOT B is equivalent to $A \land \neg B$.

	term$_1$	term$_2$	$\cdots$	term$_m$
doc$_1$	w_{11}	w_{12}	$\cdots$	w_{1m}
doc$_2$	w_{21}	w_{22}	$\cdots$	w_{2m}
$\vdots$	$\vdots$	$\vdots$		$\vdots$
doc$_n$	w_{n1}	w_{n2}	$\cdots$	w_{nm}

Table 4.1: A term $\times$ document matrix.

a "0" if the term does not appear. Or, we can store integers representing the number of times the term occurs. To eliminate artificial differences between counts in long and short documents, we may want to normal-ize the numbers. This generalizes to a notion of *term weighting*; each document is represented as a vector of term weights indicating essen-tially how well that term describes the contents of that document. Many methods for assigning the weights are possible (see [SB88b] for a com-parison of the best-known). We can summarize the entire representation of documents by a *term $\times$ document* matrix, as shown in Table 4.1.

In addition, the vector model represents queries themselves as term vectors. To retrieve documents, the system simply looks for those docu-ment vectors which are most similar to the query vector. Various simi-larity measures are possible, but a common one is the cosine of the angle between the query vector and the candidate document vector [Sal68]. Specifically, the similarity between a document vector D and a query vector Q can be expressed as:

$$similarity(D, Q) = cosine(D, Q) = \frac{\sum_{i=1}^{n}(D_i \cdot Q_i)}{\sqrt{\sum_{i=1}^{n} D_i^2 \cdot \sum_{i=1}^{n} Q_i^2}}. \qquad (4.1)$$

Note that this always computes a value in the range [0,1], regardless of the magnitude of the term weights or the length of the vectors.

To retrieve documents in the vector model, the system simply finds the document vectors that are most similar to the query vector. This is shown geometrically in Figure 4.5. This has several advantages over the inverted file approach. First, the matching is continuous rather than binary. Instead of one set of documents being retrieved and the rest not retrieved, all the documents are ordered in terms of their similarity to the query. This means that the system (possibly under user control) can be set up to use any threshold to determine how many documents to retrieve. It could, for example, retrieve only the top ten documents, or only those which had a similarity score above a certain value. Second, it supports the use of weighted query terms, by which the user can indicate that he

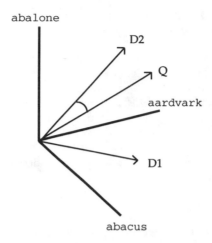

Figure 4.5: Retrieving documents with the vector model. Only three dimensions are shown, but there is actually a dimension for each index term.

or she is more interested in some aspects of the problem than others. This technique can be used as a generalization of Boolean queries [SFW83] if this is desired.

Another advantage of the vector model is that, because queries and documents use the same representation, a query can simply be a document vector. In other words, the user may ask to see all the documents "like this one." This is the query-by-example approach discussed in chapter 2. Similarly, the same techniques used to find similarities between queries and documents can be used to find similarities between documents and other documents. This allows the use of hierarchically clustered document files [SM83], in which queries are first matched to the document clusters[7] that are most similar, and only then to the documents within the chosen clusters. This can dramatically reduce the computational search effort.

4.3 Standard Evaluation Techniques

In order to understand some of the problems with the classical approaches, it is useful to examine how the performance IR systems are typically evaluated, and to give examples of the types of errors they make.

---

[7]More specifically, to a "centroid" vector that is the average of all the document vectors in that cluster.

```
...office of President, Art. II, s 1, cl. 5; in the
Extradition provisions, Art. IV, s 2, cl. 2, and the
superseded Fugitive Slave Clause 3; and in the Fifth,
Twelfth, and TWENTY-SECOND AMENDMENTS, as well as in ss 2
and 3 of the Fourteenth Amendment. But in nearly all these
instances, the use of the word is such that it has
application only postnatally. None indicates, with any
assurance, that it has any possible prenatal application.
```

Figure 4.6: One part of the *Roe v. Wade* Supreme Court decision. The phrase "second amendment" was found in "twenty-second amendments."

4.3.1 Retrieval Errors

There are two types of mistakes an IR system can make, which (in terminology borrowed from signal detection theory) are called "misses" and "false alarms."

A *false alarm* occurs when an irrelevant document is (incorrectly) retrieved. This is a frequent occurrence, though it is less common in a vector model with a good term-weighting scheme than in an inverted file system. As a simple example, consider the following legal research query:

```
"second amendment" AND "bear arms"
```

When run on one standard system[8], this search retrieved (among others) the case *Roe v. Wade*, which deals with the issue of abortion and not with the right to bear arms. Why was this case retrieved, when it is so obviously irrelevant? The text of the case offers the solution. Figure 4.6 shows how the string "second amendment" was found, in the string "twenty-second amendment." Figure 4.7 contains another part of the decision in which Justice Blackmun quoted another judge explaining the role of all the rights guaranteed by the United States Constitution — the right to free speech, the right to bear arms, and so on.

Another source of false alarms is *polysemy*, the fact that words have multiple meanings. A search about free speech in a park will undoubtably retrieve cases dealing with parking lots and garages, people named Park, and so on.

A *miss* occurs when a relevant document is not retrieved. This also happens often in standard systems, because the documents are indexed

---

[8]The search was performed using WESTLAW, with the SCT (Supreme Court) database. It is important to emphasize again that the problems illustrated are endemic to current CALR technology, and are *not* specific to WESTLAW.

As Mr. Justice Harlan once wrote: '(T)he full scope of the
liberty guaranteed by the Due Process Clause cannot be found
in or limited by the precise terms of the specific guarantees elsewhere provided in the Constitution. This 'liberty'
is not a series of isolated points priced out in terms of
the taking of property; the freedom of speech, press, and
religion; the right to keep and BEAR ARMS; the freedom from
unreasonable searches and seizures; and so on. It is a ra-
tional continuum which, broadly speaking, includes a freedom
from all substantial arbitrary impositions and purposeless
restraints...and which also recognizes, what a reasonable and
sensitive judgment must, that certain interests require particularly careful scrutiny of the state needs asserted to
justify their abridgment.'

Figure 4.7: More of the *Roe* case.

lexically rather than conceptually. This problem is equally common in
both classical approaches. As an example, suppose someone wanted to
retrieve court cases dealing with the question of whether using a VCR to
record movies shown on television constituted copyright infringement.
The query[9]

"copyright" AND "infringement" AND "VCR"

fails to retrieve a landmark Supreme Court case on the subject, *Sony v.
Universal*. A brief examination of the some of the text (shown in Figure 4.8) shows why: the Sony Betamax was described as a "videotape
recorder," "video tape recorder," and "VTR," but not as a videocassette
recorder or VCR.

4.3.2 The Recall and Precision Measures

In traditional IR, the entire document corpus is viewed as being divided
into two disjoint sets, relevant documents and nonrelevant documents,
with respect to a given query. Furthermore, the contents of the relevant
set is assumed to be known. There is a fixed-size retrieval set, and its
complement, the set of documents not retrieved for that query. These
four sets are shown in the Venn diagram in Figure 4.9. If the IR system
were perfect, the relevant set would be coextensive with the retrieved

---

[9]This search was also run on WESTLAW, this time with the FIP-CS (Federal intellectual
property cases) database.

Petitioner Sony manufactures millions of Betamax VIDEO TAPE
recorders and markets these devices through numerous retail
establishments, some of which are also petitioners in this
action. [FN2] Sony's Betamax VTR is a mechanism consisting
of three basic components: (1) a tuner, which receives
electromagnetic signals transmitted over the television band
of the public airwaves and separates them into audio and
visual signals; (2) a recorder, which records such signals
on a magnetic tape; and (3) an adapter, which converts the
audio and visual signals on the tape into a composite signal
that can be received by a television set.
...
DISSENT:
...
The introduction of the home VIDEOTAPE recorder (VTR) upon
the market has enabled millions of Americans to make
recordings of television programs in their homes, for future
and repeated viewing at their own convenience. While this
practice has proved highly popular with owners of television
...

Figure 4.8: Excerpts from *Sony v. Universal*, a case about VCRs.

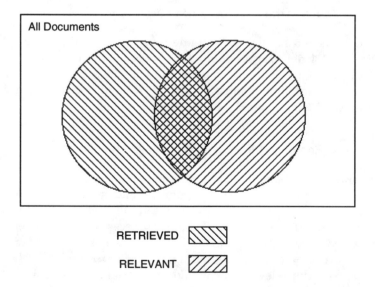

Figure 4.9: The relationship of retrieved and relevant sets, and their complements.

set. Although this is impossible, there are at least two measures we can use to see how closely the sets overlap.

The first measure, called *recall*, indicates how much of the desired material was actually found. It is defined as

$$\text{recall} = \frac{|\text{REL} \cap \text{RET}|}{|\text{REL}|} \quad (4.2)$$

where RET and REL are the retrieved and relevant sets, respectively. Low recall corresponds to many misses, in the terminology used above.

The second measure, *precision*, indicates how much of the retrieved material was actually useful. It is defined as

$$\text{precision} = \frac{|\text{REL} \cap \text{RET}|}{|\text{RET}|} \quad (4.3)$$

Low precision corresponds to a high rate of false alarms.

An alternate measure of false alarms, less common than precision, is *fallout*, which indicates what proportion of all unwanted material has been retrieved:

$$\text{fallout} = \frac{|\text{NONREL} \cap \text{RET}|}{|\text{NONREL}|} \quad (4.4)$$

Unlike either recall or precision, fallout is sensitive to the size of the collection, and thus may be viewed as a better measure of selectivity than precision.

There are many problems with these measures. First, they do not evaluate variable-length retrievals such as those produced by typical vector systems, which generally give the n best-matching documents, and then allow users to see more if they desire. Second, they do not give an evaluator a single number by which to compare effectiveness of IR systems. In fact, improvements in recall can often be made at the expense of losses in precision, and vice versa. For these reasons, many other measurements have been proposed, such as *normalized recall* [SM83] and *expected search length* [Coo68]. Each of these other measures has its adherents, but recall and precision continue to be the most common tools for evaluation in IR. A typical way to get around the problems without abandoning the traditional measures is to report precision at several fixed levels of recall.

4.4 Rethinking the Classics

The classical approaches to IR have many benefits. They are very efficient, widely used, and well understood. The vector approach, in particular, has continued to improve over the years as better term weighting schemes are discovered. Despite these successes, there are three major problems with "standard IR."

1. *Trial-and-Error Interaction.* In a classical IR system, each query is viewed as a single retrieval *event*, rather than viewing the entire search session as a *process*. As a result, the session becomes a trial-and-error interaction in which the user keeps attempting entirely new queries until she or he finds a reasonable set of documents. This issue has already been discussed in chapter 2.

2. *Brittle Retrievals.* Because classical IR systems search for documents containing the text string matching the query, rather than using a representation of the documents' meanings, it is very difficult to get all and only the desired documents. This was illustrated by both of the sample searches presented in the previous section.

3. *Inability to Learn.* In classical IR systems, the structure of the system is static. Each user is given the same responses, each time, even if they have indicated that these responses are incorrect. For example, one would like to be able to indicate to the system that the *Roe v. Wade* abortion case is an erroneous response to the query about the right to bear arms, and have the system correct the problem. This issue was also discussed in chapter 2.

Because the examples used to illustrate these problems are merely anecdotal, it may be tempting to view them as anomalous. Isn't it possible that the performance of classical IR systems is quite high, despite occasional mistakes? Unfortunately, at least one major study of IR effectiveness indicates that this is not the case.

In 1985, Blair and Maron published the results of a study they did of legal research using a commercial IR system [BM85]. The database consisted of some 40,000 corporate documents (not court decisions). The IR system used, IBM's STAIRS/TLS, was considered "state of the art" for commercial systems; it was basically an inverted file system with Boolean queries, augmented by proximity searches and a "thesaurus linguistic system" (the TLS in its name) that allowed the construction of additional term-term associations.

The study examined the results of actual users doing actual searches needed for a case. The information requesters were lawyers on the case. They would give research questions to assistants familiar with the IR system, who would formulate STAIRS queries, check them with the lawyers, and run them on the system. The assistants would then bring the results to the lawyers, who would make suggestions for refining the search, and the process would repeat. This continued until the lawyers believed that they had found 75% of the relevant documents (in other words, until

	Minimum	Maximum	Average
Precision	19.6%	100.0%	79.0%
Recall	2.8%	78.7%	20.0%

Table 4.2: Results of the Blair & Maron study.

they believed recall had reached 75%), including 100% of those "vital" to the case.

To measure recall, the experimenters used systematic generalizations of the queries to search promising subsets of the unretrieved documents [Bla90]. Two primary techniques were used. First, the Boolean connectives of existing queries were modified to produce alternative but similar retrieval sets. For example, if an initial query had been $A \wedge B \wedge C$, they would use the three modified queries $A \wedge B \wedge \neg C$, $A \wedge C \wedge \neg B$, and $B \wedge C \wedge \neg A$. Second, synonyms were substituted for the search terms to form related queries. In addition, other parts of the collection were randomly selected. The experiment was conducted in such a way that the lawyers were unaware whether the retrievals they were evaluating were the result of their paralegals' queries or of the experimenters modified samples.

The results are summarized in Table 4.2. *The average recall rate over 51 retrieval requests* (each of which contained many query iterations) *was only 20%.* Furthermore, for those documents considered "vital" — 100% of which were required — recall was only 48.2%.

The Blair and Maron study contained two separate but related results [Bla90, BM85, BM90]. The first was the extremely low overall recall rate. This was largely due to the fact that so many different words were used to refer to the same thing. For example, a query concerning an industrial accident failed to retrieve documents that referred to it as "the incident," "the event," or "the subject of our last meeting." The second finding was the mistaken belief by users that they had found most or all of the relevant material. Blair and Maron believe that this is the result of the crucial observation, discussed in chapter 2, that people are better at recognition than recall [Kla80]. Without having read all 40,000 documents, the lawyers simply had no idea how many relevant documents they had not yet found.

It is also important to note that the recall figures for the Blair and Maron study are *upper bound* estimates of the true recall. This is due to the fact that their sampling techniques probably did not find all the missed relevant documents, thus the denominator of the recall computation was artificially small. Furthermore, the researchers in the study were unusually well-equipped to use the system effectively:

> The lawyers who used the system had been working on this particular litigation for over a year and were not only intimately familiar with the issues in the complaint, but had been instrumental in supervising the selection of the documents on the database. Each of these documents was germane to at least one of the 13 issues in the complaint. The paralegals who did the searching for the lawyers had been the ones who actually selected (under the lawyers' guidance) the documents to be included in the database. In addition, they had a great deal of training in the use of STAIRS by IBM personnel and had the continuing support of their technical staff. [BM90, p. 440]

Thus one might expect that typical users of a typical system would actually have even less success finding the relevant documents.

The STAIRS study argued against simple full-text indexing for large document sets. It could be argued that some of the problems Blair and Maron cite (such as "output overload") could be overcome by a vector-based system that used a good term weighting scheme and ordered its output by relevance. Certainly this would be a major improvement. However, there is further evidence that even with this more sophisticated approach, low recall (or, in the case of a system which retrieves all the documents in order, low normalized recall) will still be a problem.

The difficulty that plagues even the best "classical" IR models is known as the *vocabulary problem*, and has been studied in several domains [FLGD87]. As described by Furnas et al.,

> The fundamental observation is that people use a surprisingly great variety of words to refer to the same thing. In fact, the data show that no single access word, however well chosen, can be expected to cover more than a small proportion of users' attempts. [FLGD87, p. 964]

What the vocabulary studies found was that over a variety of tasks, when two people were asked to give a name for something (e.g., a keyword for a recipe), there was less than a 20% chance that they chose the same name. In other words, if something is indexed by one person's term, another person has an 80 to 90% chance of failing to find it using the term he or she thinks of. Even the "best" name — the one chosen most often — results in a 65 to 85% failure rate.

The results of the study are summarized as follows:

> Simply stated, the data tell us *there is no one good access term
> for most objects*. The idea of an "obvious," "self-evident," or
> "natural" term is a myth! Since even the best possible name is
> not very useful, it follows that *there can exist no rules, guidelines
> or procedures for choosing a good name, in the sense of "accessible
> to the unfamiliar user."* [FLGD87, p. 967].

Consider the consequences of this conclusion for information retrieval.
One person writes a document, using terms *she* considers important to
the topic being discussed. Another person formulates a query, using the
terms *he* considers important. The chance of the two overlapping is very
small.

One solution might be to abandon automatic indexing methods and
rely on manual experts to determine the content of documents. This
certainly has some advantages. For instance, the indexer may choose
terms from a closed vocabulary (such as Library of Congress subject
headings) that the researcher has access to. So although I might not
have chosen the term *cybernetics* to describe AI literature, I can see from
the list of subjects that that term must have been used by the indexer.
But manual indexing is extremely time-consuming and expensive (since
it requires experts familiar with indexing techniques and the domain
area). Furthermore, the vocabulary problem immediately resurfaces if
any index terms may be assigned, except now the end-user's query term
must match the indexer's instead of the author's.

One additional problem with classical IR is the way in which performance is measured. Traditional evaluation methods assume that the
set of relevant documents is somehow known omnisciently. As we have
seen, relevance is not something that can be determined once for all users
in all situations. Even if relevance were absolute, relevance judgements
are not available for most corpora in practice. This has led many IR researchers to evaluate the performance of their systems on test collections
for which documents relevant to a set of standard queries have been
identified. These relevance judgements were made by expert but fallible
humans who had to examine every document to determine the relevant
set. Thus too few IR systems are tested in naturalistic settings with real
users.

Furthermore, it is often assumed that recall and precision are the
only criteria worth evaluating. For example, van Rijsbergen cites the six
measurable quantities suggested by Cleverdon:

   (1) the *coverage* of the collection, that is, the extent to which
       the system includes relevant matter;

(2) the *time lag*, that is, the average interval between the time
    the search request is made and the time and answer is
    given;

(3) the form of *presentation* of the output;

(4) the *effort* involved on the part of the user in obtaining
    answers to his search requests;

(5) the *recall* of the system ... ;

(6) the *precision* of the system .... [vR79, p. 145]

He then goes on to say that the first four are "readily assessed," and
that users will be satisfied as long as recall and precision are high. In
fact, user effort is complex and difficult to measure. With few exceptions
(such as work by Belkin [BOB82] and Borgman [Bor86a]) IR researchers
generally ignore this problem.

4.5 Variations and Alternatives

Research in information retrieval has not stood still since the development
of inverted files and the vector model. Many of the problems already
described have been recognized for years, though there is ongoing debate
about their severity. This section describes some of the enhancements
and alternatives to the classical models that have been tested. Those that
provide the foundations for some of the concepts in SCALIR are covered
in more detail than those that represent orthogonal approaches.

4.5.1 Thesaurus Construction

The vocabulary problem suggests that a document could be relevant to
a query and yet not be retrieved, because different terms were used in
each. Suppose, though, that an IR system converted the user's search
terms to semantic categories and searched for documents matching those
concepts. (Of course, the documents would need similar conversion.) For
example, whether one asked for "car" or "automobile," the system might
search for **personal-passenger-vehicle**. In theory, this would improve
recall, because the synonymy problem would go away. Precision would
also improve, because we'd be using some "Platonic form" of the term
rather than the string itself, which might be polysemous.

Alternatively, we could simply search for documents that matched not
only the query term, but also documents indexed by words considered
similar to the query terms. This would probably not improve precision

(indeed, it might make it worse), because the system has broadened its notion of matching. However, it should improve recall considerably.

Both of these structures — the semantic categories and the set of associations between terms — may be considered different types of *thesauri*, as the term is used in the information retrieval literature. The well-known Roget's thesaurus is similar in spirit to the first approach; Roget's divides the world into general types of things, and each type into subtypes. If Roget's were used as an IR thesaurus, queries to any of the lists of related words would be replaced by a search for their concept. Kim [Kim73] suggests that thesauri of this type are the conceptual inverses of dictionaries; they map from concepts to words rather than from words to concepts. Unfortunately, these thesauri are too general to be helpful in IR. Furthermore, they are based on individual attempts to carve up the world in a meaningful way, which (as philosophers, naturalists, and AI researchers can attest to) is an extremely difficult task.

Librarians use another type of thesaurus for indexing. According to the ANSI committee on Library and Information Sciences:

> [A] thesaurus is defined as a compilation of words and phrases showing synonymous, hierarchical, and other relationships and dependencies, the function of which is to provide a standardized vocabulary for information storage and retrieval. [ANS80, p. 9]

This type of thesaurus simply contains entries and cross-references, where the latter must be (according to the ANSI standard) one of **USE**, **UF** (used-for), **BT** (broader term), **NT** (narrower term), or **RT** (related term). When documents using one term are actually indexed by another, a **USE** entry is created. For example, there might be an entry that says "Planet X — **USE** Pluto." **BT** entries alert the user to a broader term that may help expand a search, e.g. "magazines — **BT** periodicals." Related terms suggest "lateral" variants to search (e.g., "Democratic Party — **RT** Republican Party"). Each entry has an inverse, such as "Pluto – **UF** Planet X." These thesauri are constructed manually and are meant to help improve manual search; they contain many different kinds of associations and make no claims to being semantic maps.

In IR research, many people have considered the idea of automating the thesaurus creation process. Whether the goal is identification of semantic primitives or simply graphing the relationships between words, one will need a way to group them. Thus research on thesaurus creation often goes by the name "automatic keyword classification."

Salton and Lesk experimented with a variant of the first type of thesaurus as part of the SMART project [SL71]. However, the words were mapped not to semantic primitives, but to a numbered "concept." The terms grouped under a concept were not synonyms, but simply related. The relationships were determined by a term-term similarity measure analogous to the document-document similarity metric given in Equation 4.1. Instead of comparing the similarity of rows of the term × document matrix, its columns were used. The result is that terms often found in the same documents would be lumped under the same concept. For example, the term *cryogenic* belonged to the same concept as *superconduct*.

Although the Salton and Lesk experiments were successful (in the sense that the thesaurus modestly improved precision and recall), Salton found that greater improvements arose from document clustering, rather than term clustering, and by investigating better term weighting schemes.

Sparck Jones adopted the second approach in her landmark study of keyword classification [Spa71]. Like Salton and Lesk, Sparck Jones initially based her thesaurus on term co-occurrence statistics, rather than syntactic or semantic information. After thoroughly exploring many alternatives, she concluded that many assumptions fundamental to automatic thesaurus creation were not always correct. In particular, she found that it was impossible to focus on improving recall alone.

Although both research efforts demonstrated the value of thesauri in certain situations, it is fair to say that the idea of automatically associating terms has not lived up to its promise.

4.5.2   Natural Language Processing

IR systems attempt to retrieve documents about (relevant to) the items queried by its users. As we have seen, this is an elusive task; not every document containing a query term is about that topic, nor will every document about the topic contain that term. If the system could actually *understand* the document, in some sense, then it could make better decisions regarding its relevance. This understanding is the goal of an entire area of AI research, known as natural language processing (NLP). Although a general discussion of NLP is beyond the scope of this work, it is useful to examine a couple of NLP approaches that have been used to try to improve IR systems.

One approach might generally be characterized as *syntactic*. It is motivated by the idea that retrieval could be improved simply by parsing the text and refining the indexing and search processes according to grammatical constraints. As a simple (if unrealistic) example, suppose one were interested in finding documents about cans. In a simple Boolean system, every document containing the term *can* — for example, one containing the sentence "In this system, the user can exit at any time by pressing X" — will be retrieved. A system using term weights might perform better, but the overall frequency of the term *can* might prevent the retrieval of many relevant documents.

In a syntactic system, however, it is generally assumed that the user is searching for noun phrases, and that a system should be indexed accordingly. Thus documents containing the noun "can" would be retrieved, but those containing the auxiliary "can" would not. A syntactic parse can identify parts of speech, thus allowing separate weighting for homographs (different words with the same spelling). This technique can be extended in various ways. For example, a document might be indexed only by noun phrases that occur as subjects of sentences. Salton and Smith [SS89] review a few such techniques.

Parsing noun phrases is itself an extremely difficult problem. To use a well-known example from Sparck Jones and Tait [SJT84], it is difficult for a program to know that a "high frequency transistor oscillator" does not refer to a type of "high oscillator" or "frequency transistor" (neither of which exist, of course). The high error rate, and the common technique of suggesting alternate possible parses, have discouraged many IR researchers from using syntactic techniques. However, improvements in parsers and the increased availability of machine-readable dictionaries may improve the prospects for syntactic processing in IR.

A rather different approach to applying NLP to IR is based on attempting to achieve some *semantic* representation of the document. This approach is perhaps more prevalent in question-answering or story-understanding systems, such as DeJong's FRUMP text-skimming system [DeJ79], which provided one-sentence summaries of UPI news stories. These systems generally use a less complete parser, concentrating instead on identifying particular phrases used to instantiate what DeJong calls "sketchy scripts." Mauldin [Mau86, MCT87] has proposed using the FRUMP parser as part of an IR system.

Rau and Jacobs' SCISOR [JR88, Rau87] is another example of a question-answering system which can be viewed as a natural language processing approach to IR carried to its logical extreme. The assumption made in SCISOR is that an IR user really is after information in the documents, not the documents themselves; thus the system supports natural language queries about its domain (corporate takeovers) and responds with natural language answers or summaries of events. SCISOR is not an IR system in the traditional sense, but it suggests an alternative that may be increasingly desirable for many applications.

4.5.3 Relevance Feedback

One of the most important ideas to emerge from the SMART project was the concept of *relevance feedback* [Ide71, Roc71]. After presenting its response to each query, the SMART system gives users the opportunity to indicate whether they found each document relevant or not relevant to the query. This information is used to form a new query:

> The query reformulation process is then based on the following complementary operations:
>
> 1. Terms that occur in documents previously identified as relevant by the user population are added to the original query vectors, or alternatively the weight of such terms is increased by an appropriate factor in constructing the new query statements.
>
> 2. At the same time, terms occurring in documents previously identified as nonrelevant by the users are deleted from the original query statements, or the weight of such terms is appropriately reduced. [SM83, p. 123]

As a result, the reformulated query is closer in document space to the relevant items. Figure 4.10 (based on Salton's figures [SM83]) shows this conceptually. Although the technique is shown for a vector model, it can be used in many IR system — even when no weighting is used — by simply adding and subtracting query terms.

Rocchio points out that if the set D_R of R relevant documents in a collection of size N were known in advance, then it would be possible to construct an optimal[10] query, Q_{opt}, in which each term k has weight:

$$(Q_{opt})_k = C(\frac{1}{R} \sum_{i \in D_R} t_{ik} - \frac{1}{N-R} \sum_{i \in D_{N-R}} t_{ik}) \qquad (4.5)$$

where C is a constant and the t_{ik}'s are the weights of the term k in document i [Roc71]. Of course, we don't know the entire set D_R, but we do know the set $D_{R'}$ reported relevant by the user, and the set $D_{N'}$ reported not relevant. This suggests a way to approximate the optimal query based on the available information.

Rather than simply replace the user's initial query Q with this pseudo-optimal one, which might be radically different, we can combine them to form a new query that retains some of the original while moving in

---

[10]That is, one that maximizes the overlap between the retrieved and relevant sets.

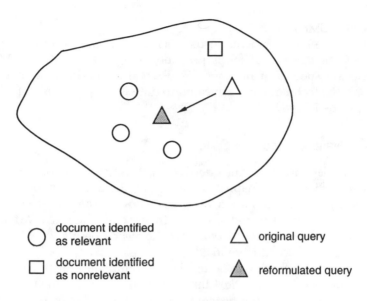

 document identified as relevant

□ document identified as nonrelevant

△ original query

▲ reformulated query

Figure 4.10: A conceptual view of relevance feedback.

the desired direction:

$$Q' = \alpha Q + \beta(\frac{1}{R'} \sum_{i \in D_{R'}} d_i) - \gamma(\frac{1}{N'} \sum_{i \in D_{N'}} d_i) \qquad (4.6)$$

where d_i is the vector representing document i. The parameters α, β, and γ are chosen to balance the desired importance of the initial query, the documents marked relevant, and those marked irrelevant. This is just the algebraic description of the operation shown geometrically in the figure.

Salton reports that the SMART experiments suggest making β higher than γ, because

> [T]he set of relevant documents with respect to a given query may be expected to be located in a reasonably homogeneous area of the the document space .... The set of nonrelevant items, on the other hand, is normally much more heterogeneous. The average nonrelevant item may therefore be located almost anywhere in the document space, and subtraction of the corresponding terms removes the query from that area of the space without specifying a definite alternative direction. [SM83, p. 145]

Although there are many variants of this process, it generally improves the response — measured in precision for specific levels of recall — by

10 to 20% [SM83].

Of all the enhancements to the classical IR models, the evidence in favor of relevance feedback is probably the most incontrovertible. Yet despite the success of relevance feedback in experimental IR research systems, the technique has appeared to date in only a couple of commercial systems [Wey89].

4.5.4   Dynamic Document Space

Initial queries rarely produce perfect retrievals, for a variety of reasons outlined earlier in the chapter. In particular, the terms that users employ to describe their information need may not be the terms used in the documents, or used to index them. In general, this means that every query will retrieve some documents the user doesn't want, and miss some he or she would have liked.

Relevance feedback can be used to reformulate a query, and the retrieval improves. But the next time that user — or anyone else — gives the same initial query, the system responds with the same irrelevant documents, and misses the same relevant ones. This problem suggests a natural modification of the relevance feedback concept: Rather than having the system modify the query to be more like the desired documents, it can modify the *document* representations to be more like the query. This is known as a "dynamic document space," and was implemented by Brauen as another part of the SMART project [Bra71].

Brauen's technique is shown geometrically in Figure 4.11. It uses the following algorithm:

1. For documents designated as relevant, which must be rendered more similar to query Q:

    a. A query term *not* present in the document is added to the document with a weighting factor of α.

    b. A query term also present in the document receives increased importance by incrementing its weight by a factor β.

    c. A document term not present in the query is decreased in weight by a factor $-\gamma$.

2. For documents designated as nonrelevant which must be rendered less similar to the query:

    a. Document terms also present in the query are rendered less important by decreasing their weight by a factor of $-\delta$.

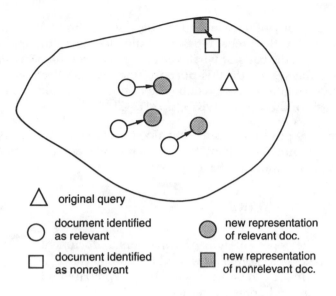

△ original query

○ document identified
  as relevant

● new representation
  of relevant doc.

☐ document identified
  as nonrelevant

▨ new representation
  of nonrelevant doc.

Figure 4.11: Document space modification.

b. Document terms absent from the query are increased
   in weight by a factor ϵ. [Bra71]

Brauen's experiments resulted in recall and precision improvements of
5 to 10%. Despite this success, the dynamic document space approach has
rarely been in later IR systems; two exceptions are discussed as follows.
This might be due to a perception that users would be uncomfortable
knowing that their IR system may give different answers to the same
query at different times. This issue is discussed further in chapter 10.

4.5.5 Probabilistic Retrieval

In recent years, many IR researchers have experimented with probabilistic
approaches. Although some of these ideas date back at least as far as
the early 1960s [MK60], they have become more widespread since the
introduction of the model by Robertson and Sparck Jones in 1976 [RS76].
This model relies on what Robertson [Rob77] called the *probability ranking
principle*:

If a reference retrieval system's response to each request is a
ranking of the documents in the collection in order of decreas-

ing probability of relevance to the user who submitted the request, where the probabilities are estimated as accurately as possible on the basis of whatever data have been made available to the system for this purpose, the overall effectiveness of the system to its user will be the best that is obtainable on the basis of those data. [vR79, pp. 113–114]

In practice, this principle means that documents should be ranked according the conditional probability that each is relevant, given that it has a certain representation. By Bayes' theorem,

$$P(\text{Rel}|X) = \frac{P(X|\text{Rel})P(\text{Rel})}{P(X)} \tag{4.7}$$

where X is the representation of a particular document (a vector of terms); an analogous expression is used for nonrelevance. Thus the problem reduces primarily to figuring out what the probability that each term indexes relevant and nonrelevant documents.

Unfortunately, there are many difficulties in assigning these probabilities. Often unrealistic independence assumptions must be made, or an impractical number of joint probabilities must be computed. In either case, the estimates are based a single individual's relevance judgements.

4.5.6   Genetic Adaptation

Gordon has proposed the use of an adaptive model that uses Holland's Genetic Algorithm (GA) [Gol89, Hol75] to evolve document representations [Gor88]. In Gordon's model, each user's term relevance judgements are used to form a competing description of the document. The fitness of each description is then evaluated, and a new generation of descriptions replaces the old. The fitness (called μ in the GA literature) of a description g at a given time is its "matching score":

$$\mu(g) = \frac{1}{M} \sum_i J(g, q_i) \tag{4.8}$$

where each q_i is one of the M queries for which this document is relevant. (Gordon's experiment was unusual in that subjects identified queries for which specific documents were relevant, rather than documents relevant to specific queries.) J is a measure of overlap between the document description and the query, known as *Jaccard's coefficient* [vR79]. It is defined as

$$J(X,Y) = \frac{|X \cap Y|}{|X \cup Y|}. \tag{4.9}$$

Each new individual contains portions of its "parents"; more fit individuals will participate in the production of more offspring. Holland's algorithm guarantees that the most useful subdescriptions (called *schemata* or "building blocks") will gradually dominate the population [Hol75].

Gordon's model was developed under very constrained experimental conditions, and may not be practical for real-world IR problems. In particular, it requires a separate evolution of document descriptions for *every* document in the corpus. This entails keeping around all the competing document representations, of which there must be tens or even hundreds for the Genetic Algorithm to function optimally.

Despite these restrictions, Gordon's approach is notable in that it provides yet another data point demonstrating the feasibility and power of the dynamic document space model described earlier. Gordon's experiments demonstrated that what he called "document redescription" could in fact improve both recall and fallout.

4.5.7 Parallel Implementations

Recent developments in parallel processing have suggested new approaches to the IR problem. In particular, Stanfill and Kahle [SK86] have developed a IR system designed specifically for the Connection Machine[11] (CM), a massively parallel SIMD[12] hypercube architecture containing up to 65,536 processors [Hil85]. A version of the system, called DowQuest, is now used commercially by the Dow Jones News Service [Wey89].

The Stanfill and Kahle system uses the concept of *signature files* to represent individual documents[13]. A signature file is essentially a kind of hash table in which each unique word gets a multivalued hash index, and the bits corresponding to each index in the table are set. To execute a retrieval, the system broadcasts a query signature to all processors simultaneously, each of which then performs a logical AND of the bits in its own tables corresponding to the bits set in the query. If the result is true, the processor reports a match. Unfortunately, there is some chance that the match will be spurious, because it is possible that the union of

---

[11]Connection Machine is a registered trademark of Thinking Machines Corporation.

[12]Single-Instruction stream, Multiple Data; in other words, each processor is doing the same operation at the same time, but on different data.

[13]As Salton pointed out [SB88a], this idea dates back to at least the 1950s, when notched cards were used for document storage and needles were used for retrieval.

bits set for two or more terms will include all of the bits representing a third, queried term.

In the implementation reported by Stanfill and Kahle, each processor stored two tables of 512 bits, each of which held up to 35 words. If a document contained more than 35 unique words, multiple tables were chained together. The test database contained about 32,000 documents.

The technique can be enhanced further if simple weighted queries are used. Instead of simply reporting a match, the processors can add up the scores of the query terms found and report a total. The CM supports a global maximum operator that allows the highest-scoring processor to be found in one time-step, and then disabled. By repeating this process, the documents can be retrieved in rank order.

In addition to its unique parallel implementation, the DowQuest system includes the capability for relevance feedback. Users can mark responses as good or bad; a new query uses a weighted sum of all the terms in the marked documents, with terms in good and bad documents getting positive and negative weights, respectively. As mentioned in Section 4.5.3, the DowQuest system is nearly unique in its use of relevance feedback for a commercial application. Given the proven success of relevance feedback in experimental IR systems, the DowQuest designers are to be commended for making this available to actual end users. Unfortunately, the interface ultimately employed was so poor that, according to at least one informal study, users never actually took advantage of relevance feedback[14].

From an IR perspective, the Stanfill and Kahle results were mixed. There has been some controversy about the speedup figures claimed for the system. Both Salton [SB88a] and Stone [Sto87] have criticized the signature file approach, comparing its performance unfavorably with the vector method and with inverted files, respectively. Despite some attempts to refute these criticisms [Sta88], Stanfill has since advocated a new approach using a variant of the inverted file, partitioned to take advantage of the CM architecture [Sta90, STW89].

4.5.8   Latent Semantic Indexing

One of the most interesting new techniques in information retrieval, and one that shares many of the ideas motivating SCALIR, is the *Latent Semantic Indexing* (LSI) technique developed by Dumais et al. [DFL+88, DDF+90]. As described by Deerwester et al., the LSI approach provides

---

[14]It should be noted that the designers of the system had no association with the interface of the commercially vended system.

a new way to attack the vocabulary problem in IR:

> We assume there is some underlying latent semantic struc-
> ture in the data that is partially obscured by the randomness
> of word choice with respect to retrieval.... We take a large
> matrix of term-document association data and construct a "se-
> mantic" space wherein terms and documents that are closely
> associated are placed near one another.... As a result, terms
> that did not actually appear in a document may still end up
> close to the document, if that is consistent with the major
> patterns of association in the data. [DDF+90, p. 391]

LSI can be viewed as a significant generalization of the standard vector
approach. The vector model normally supports first-order associations
between terms and documents. As Salton pointed out [Sal68], if the term
$\times$ document matrix is X, term-term and document-document similarities
can be computed by the products XX^T and X^TX. Eigenvector decomposition or principal components analysis can be used to identify clusters
of terms or documents.

These early analytic approaches lacked two things. First, they only
operated on the square term-term or document-document matrices. Thus
they could be used for clustering, but not directly for retrieval; terms and
documents were represented in two different spaces. Second, they were
never explicitly used to reduce noise.

LSI overcomes both these problems. Using a technique known as
singular value decomposition (SVD) [Str88], the initial term $\times$ document
matrix X can be expressed as the product of three matrices: a diagonal
matrix S_0 consisting of the "singular values" of X, and two matrices
T_0 and D_0 that represent terms and documents, respectively, *in the same
space*. This is shown in Figure 4.12 [DDF+90]. This is similar to the
eigenvector decomposition of a symmetric matrix. In fact, the columns
of T_0 are the eigenvectors of XX^T, the columns of D_0 are the eigenvectors
of X^TX, and the singular values on the diagonal are the square roots of
the nonzero eigenvalues of both XX^T and X^TX.

The primary insight of the LSI technique comes not in using the SVD,
but in using a *reduced description* of the space to eliminate noise. Because
certain permutations of rows and columns in the SVD leave the result
unchanged, it is possible to sort S_0 so that the singular values appear
in decreasing order of magnitude. By choosing only the k largest values
and setting the rest to zero, a reduced model $\widehat{X}$ is obtained, as shown
in Figure 4.13. This reduced matrix can be used to perform the typical
similarity matches (e.g., cosine) used in vector retrievals. As a result, two
documents (or a document and a query) that might not have been similar

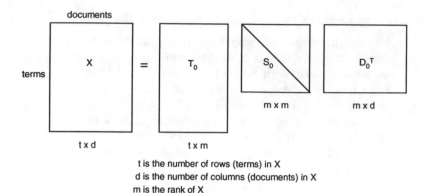

t is the number of rows (terms) in X
d is the number of columns (documents) in X
m is the rank of X

Figure 4.12: Decomposing a term × document matrix using the SVD.

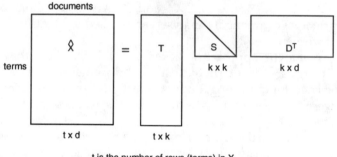

t is the number of rows (terms) in X
d is the number of columns (documents) in X
k is the chosen number of dimensions in reduced model

Figure 4.13: The reduced model used in LSI.

in the original space end up close together in the "semantic" space of the reduced model.

Deerwester et al. [DDF+90] report several experiments in which the LSI technique outperformed or equaled standard vector methods. A typical experiment involved a 100-factor SVD of a roughly 6,000 term by 1,000 document matrix, where a document consisted of a title and abstract.

There are a few problems with the LSI approach which have not been satisfactorily resolved. The decomposition itself is an extremely computationally intensive operation. Once the reduced model is in place, there is no reliable way to add new documents to the corpus without recomputing the SVD. Finally, deciding the number of singular values to

88

use is currently determined in an ad hoc fashion according to empirically measured retrieval performance. Despite these difficulties, LSI shows great promise for overcoming the vocabulary problem.

4.5.9 Spreading Activation and Connectionism

Much of IR research might be characterized as an attempt to identify associations between items of interest (usually terms and documents), and to exploit those associations for retrieval. The classical inverted file and vector methods identify certain types of first-order term-document associations. Document space modification attempts to refine and improve some of these associations. Latent Semantic Indexing attempts to extract higher order associations. Thesaurus construction identifies chains or clusters of term-term associations. It is thus not surprising that several researchers have independently arrived at the idea of representing those associations explicitly in some kind of network, and using spreading activation search (defined in chapter 3) to locate relevant items. Although the singular value decomposition can be used to calculate all higher order associations in advance, spreading activation computes these associations locally and at run time as part of the retrieval process.

Cohen and Kjeldsen's GRANT system [CK87] is one such attempt. GRANT represents information about the research interests of various funding agencies; users enter proposals and the system reponds with potential funding sources[15]. But GRANT relies on a manually constructed semantic network, with markers propagating across labeled links in response to logical constraints. As we shall see in chapter 6, such systems are only one way to implement the idea of spreading activation.

An alternative is the connectionist approach (also defined in chapter 3), in which activation is represented as a real-valued quantity which spreads through a network of unlabeled, weighted links. The first connectionist IR system was developed in a small experiment by Mozer [Moz84]. It used an interactive activation model [MR81, RM82] in which nodes for terms excited nodes for documents, while each document node inhibited all other documents. Nodes to be queried were given initial activation, which then spread through the network, with the most active nodes eventually considered to represent the retrieved items. Chapter 8 describes the system in more detail.

A much larger-scale connectionist IR system was Belew's AIR (for Adaptive Information Retrieval) system [Bel86, Bel89]. AIR, though developed without knowledge of Mozer's system, shared several of the lat-

---

[15]GRANT is thus not a traditional IR system, in the sense of retrieving documents.

ter's attributes: AIR used a connectionist network in which documents and terms were represented as nodes and associations between them were represented as weighted links. Activation, initially placed only on query nodes, then spread to the neighbors of these nodes, their neighbors' neighbors, and so on. Nodes retained residual activity in order to allow a gradual accumulation across longer link paths. Eventually, a new set of active nodes was displayed as the response to the query. Thus documents could be retrieved even if the query terms did not explicitly occur in them.

However, AIR differed from Mozer's system in many respects. It used a unique network architecture in which directed links could occur between any two nodes. Activity calculations were done differently, with inhibition between nodes playing a much smaller role. Most importantly, AIR's network was designed to *learn* based on interaction with the system's users. AIR's interface allowed users to indicate which retrieved items they liked and didn't like, suggesting where to expand and prune the search. The system would use this feedback as a new query, allowing the user to in effect *browse* through the space of documents. At the same time, the feedback was used to slightly alter the representation of the documents, so that the system would learn from experience. This combination of dynamic document space modification, relevance feedback, and browsing was one of AIR's most significant features. Much of the work described in this book can be viewed as descended from the concepts developed in AIR; thus that system will often be referred to in some detail. In particular, AIR's retrieval process is discussed in chapter 8.

Other connectionist systems have addressed different aspects of the IR problem. Brachman and McGuiness' CRUCS system [BM88] used a connectionist implementation of a frame-based taxonomy of concepts. This allowed the system to utilize a combination-of-evidence approach to a traditional knowledge representation structure. Kwok [Kwo89] used a layered network to implement a probabilistic indexing scheme; the system could be trained to produce the optimal ranking of relevant documents. Though both of these systems included a "training" phase, neither was an adaptive system in the sense of learning from actual experience. A summary of these and many other connectionist IR systems can be found in [DRL90].

Salton and Buckley have criticized the use of spreading activation techniques in IR, demonstrating that at least one such system cannot compete with standard vector methods. However, the system they examined, Jones' "Memory Extender" (ME) [JF87, Jon86], was designed as a small experiment with a personal filing system, not as a general purpose

IR system. All initial weights in the ME network were constant, though the system gradually decayed the weights of less-frequently used files. (This adaptive weighting was not discussed by Salton and Buckley.) Activity in ME was allowed to spread through equidistant paths from a query to terms to documents. Neither Mozer's system nor Belew's has these restrictions; both of their systems allow for a gradual combination of evidence, higher order associations, and nonlinear associations. Thus it is at least premature to conclude that spreading activation systems are relatively ineffective in IR.

4.6 Taking Stock

This chapter has attempted to convey the richness of the IR task, its extreme difficulty, and the limitations of traditional approaches to the problem. These conclusions have motivated the design of SCALIR, which is outlined in detail in chapters 7 through 10. As we have seen throughout the previous section, they have also prompted a wide range of other research efforts over the past 25 years. Some of the techniques described have conclusively proven their worth and have slowly found their way to the marketplace. Others have barely been implemented experimentally, much less reduced to practice. Evaluation of all the systems — in particular, those that involve adaptation and/or user intervention — has been sparse and difficult. In many cases the results have been mixed or inconclusive. Yet each has provided the IR community with another tool for constructing better solutions to the problem of finding information in large bodies of text.

Chapter 5

Some Perspectives on the Law and Legal Research

The law always has been, is now, and will ever continue to be, largely vague and variable. And how could this well be otherwise? The law deals with human relations in their most complicated aspects. The whole confused, shifting helter-skelter of life parades before it — more confused than ever, in our kaleidoscopic age.

— Jerome Frank, *Law and the Modern Mind* [Fra63, p. 6].

This chapter is about law. Specifically, it is about the Anglo-American legal system — how law is made, how it is found, how it is perceived, and how these perceptions relate to the design of a computer system for legal research.

It should be emphasized that the opinions in this chapter are those of a legal layperson. I make no claims about the legal significance of my discussion. However, I hope that my outsider's perspective may provide different insights from those ordinarily found in law journals.

5.1 Their Word is Law

There are two primary legal traditions in Western civilizations. The first of these, *civil law* , is rooted in the *Corpus Juris Civilis*, a codification of Roman Law compiled under the direction of the emperor Justinian (527–565) [vMG77]. It comes to us more directly from the French *Code Civil*, begun in 1792 (shortly after the French revolution) and completed in 1804 under Napoleon. The legal systems of France and Germany are based on civil law, as is that of Louisiana. The basic idea of civil law is that the written set of rules is the ultimate arbiter of disputes.

The second legal tradition is the *common law*. Gradually emerging from the accepted practices of merchants in 12th-century England [vMG77], the common law is essentially the set of decisions made by judges over time. In a common law system, disputes are resolved by finding judicial precedent, not by looking up the appropriate rule. During litigation, each lawyer will try to find precedents that favor his or her side of the case; the judge decides which (if any) of these truly bear on the issue at hand.

The terms *law* and *legal system*, as used throughout this discussion, refer primarily to the legal system of the United States, and, to a lesser extent, the systems of other countries and individual states that have also descended from the British common law tradition.

In the United States, one may encounter three kinds of law. *Statutory law* is what most people think of as "law" — these are the laws written and passed by the U.S. Senate and House of Representatives. *Administrative law* is the set of regulations instituted by agencies of the Executive branch of government such as the Federal Aviation Administration. *Common law*, as described above, consists of judicial decisions. Although these three types of law each play a role in the U.S. legal system, we nevertheless basically follow the common law tradition. When a judge writes a decision, particularly one that interprets precedents in a new way, he or she is said to be "making" law. This doctrine of following precedents is known as *stare decisis*, which simply means "to stand by what has been decided."

The system of Federal Appellate courts is central to the legal system. There are three levels to the Federal hierarchy: District Courts (at least one per state), thirteen Courts of Appeals, and the Supreme Court. Each court is bound by its own precedents and those of higher courts, but not necessarily by the decisions of "sister" courts. (States have a similar distinction between trial and appellate courts, but the number of levels differs from state to state.)

A judge, in committing his or her opinion[1] to writing, serves as a kind of knowledge engineer, trying to extract the legal principles from a

---

[1]In legal terminology, *opinion* is a technical term meaning "the statement by a judge or court of the decision reached in regard to a cause tried or argued before them, expounding the law as applied to the case, and detailing the reasons upon which the judgement is based" [NC83]. The term *decision* is often synonymous, though it can also refer to the judgement on which the opinion is based.

set of facts. Yet at the same time, the process of creating new law from old is done in a parallel, distributed fashion — by many judges at many points in time. Any one judge can only interpret the statutes and the precedents; one decision alone rarely makes new law. But taken together, the words collectively written by the judges *are* the law. Somehow the knowledge has been embedded in the text of common law, and it is extracted, refined, and enhanced each time a judge (in a new piece of text) invokes a precedent. Thus the legal system itself can be viewed as a "text-based intelligent system," a new concept in AI.

This characteristic of common law — the extent to which it exists in the very text that describes it — is unique[2] among our social and scientific institutions. It stands in sharp contrast to a domain like medicine: Medical principles are described in medical texts, but the texts do not constitute medicine.

Belew questioned this analysis, arguing that the role of text in law is just one example of the way in which the artifacts of any institution serve to define it:

> Science also critically depends on the written record of journals, treatises, texts, etc. as a shared artifactual structure integrating the activities of individual scientists.
>
> The artifacts need not be textual, of course. It is hard to imagine financial institutions ... functioning without their ledger sheets.... In fact, every profession has its defining artifacts. [Belew, personal communication, 1991]

Although debate continues about whether the law stands alone in its use of text, there is agreement over the critical role of text in the law. It is this that makes the law both challenging and amenable to intelligent IR solutions.

5.2 Legal Philosophy: Formalism vs. Realism

Is there any logic to common law? Are there fundamental rules or principles that underlie judges' decisions? Or do these decisions depend, as one justice reportedly said, on what the judge had for breakfast? These

---

[2]Though there are similar examples: in religion, the Talmud (a series of commentaries about Jewish law, commentaries on the commentaries, and so on); and in pragmatics, Austin's "performative" sentences, such as "I hereby declare these games open" (in which the uttering of the sentence is the act it describes).

two positions represent two ends of a spectrum of philosophies of jurisprudence. I call the former position *formalism* and the latter *realism*.[3] In practice, most legal scholars concede a role for both positions; few have staked out the extremes. Nevertheless, there are very real differences between adherents of the two views, and as we shall see, each has different consequences for how one might approach the legal research problem.

For more than a century, legal scholars have been debating whether the process of law can be formalized by some calculus, list of rules, or set of concepts. Langdell [Lan87] was an early proponent of what became known as "mechanical jurisprudence." He argued that there were indeed a very concrete set of rules underlying the law.

Though Langdell's views are an extreme example of the formalist view, the general idea of legal principles is still quite popular. Perhaps its best expression came in the work of H. L. A. Hart, who viewed law as the superposition of what he called "primary" rules (which impose duties) and "secondary" rules (which confer powers):

> [M]ost features of the law which have proved most perplexing and have both provoked and eluded the search for definition can best be rendered clear, if these two types of rule and the interplay between them are understood. We accord this union of elements a central place because of their explanatory power in elucidating the concepts that constitute the framework of legal thought. [Har61, p. 79]

Despite the formalism of Hart's rules, he was well aware of their "fuzziness" in practice:

> Legal rules may have a central core of undisputed meaning, and in some cases it may be difficult to imagine a dispute as to the meaning of a rule breaking out.... Yet all rules have a penumbra of uncertainty where the judge must choose between alternatives. [Har61, p. 12]

Although this idea helped account for the inexactness of the actual process of law, it did not change the fundamentally rule-oriented nature of Hart's theory.

At the other end of the spectrum lie those who have always argued that (to oversimplify somewhat) law is just "what judges do." This view

---

[3] The reader is reminded of the disclaimer at the start of this chapter; this characterization of the law may not be shared by legal scholars.

was espoused by Oliver Wendell Holmes and later elaborated by scholars such as Jerome Frank and Karl Llewellyn. Frank and Llewellyn were
often viewed as leaders of a movement that became known as "legal realism," though they in fact represented a broad range of legal philosophies.
Llewellyn characterized the realists as being united by their opposition
to traditional assumptions about the static and isolated nature of law and
the role of rules or principles. Among the realists' concerns were:

> distrust of traditional legal rules and concepts insofar as they
> purport to *describe* what either courts or people are actually
> doing.... Hand in hand with this distrust of traditional rules
> ... goes a distrust of the theory that traditional prescriptive
> rule-formulations are *the* heavily operative factor in producing
> court decisions. [Lle62, p. 56]

Llewellyn acknowledged the use of rules for predicting judges' behavior
("That is their importance. That is all their importance, except as pretty
playthings" [Lle30, p. 14]). Frank relegates rules to an even smaller role:

> Viewed from any angle, the rules and principles do not
> constitute law. They may be aids to the judge in tentatively
> testing or formulating conclusions; they may be positive fac-
> tors in bending his mind towards wise or unwise solutions of
> the problem before him. They may be the formal clothes in
> which he dresses up his thoughts. But they do not and can-
> not completely control his mental operations and it is there-
> fore unfortunate that either he or the lawyers interested in
> his decision should accept them as the full equivalent of that
> decision. If the judge so believes, his thinking will be less ef-
> fective. If the lawyers so believe, their opinions on questions
> of law (their guesses as to future decisions) will be necessarily
> inaccurate. [Fra63, p. 141]

In addition to their opposition to the view of rules as law, the realists
emphasized the fundamentally social nature of the law, and its resul-
tant variety and change. Frank in particular talked about how judges'
preconceptions and prejudices, however unconscious, played a role in
the law[4]. This idea has recently been expanded by the Critical Legal
Studies movement [Ung83], which essentially views law as a product of
socioeconomic forces with no objective component.

---

[4]"[The judge's] own past may have created plus or minus reactions to women, or blonde
women, or men with beards, or Southerners, or Italians, or Englishmen, or plumbers, or
ministers, or college graduates, or Democrats" [Fra63, p. 115].

It is clear that a characterization of the legal *reasoning* process — and an attempt to model or assist it — depends on one's characterization of the law. As a simplistic example, a formalist might model legal reasoning with a rule-based expert system, whereas a legal realist might prefer a case-based reasoning approach. It is for this reason that AI and Law researchers such as Gardner [Gar87] attempt to situate their models in the appropriate jurisprudential context. This is equally true (if less obvious) for characterizing, modeling, or assisting legal *research*. In determining whether a case is relevant to a query, do we appeal to underlying rules, as a formalist analysis of law would suggest? The SCALIR project follows the realists, in that no set of rules is believed adequate for capturing the richness of what a judge or a lawyer might consider relevant.

5.3   The Dual Nature of the Legal System

From the previous conclusion, it might seem that the task of legal research is impossible. After all, if the holding of a case depended on what the judge had for breakfast, what would it mean to find other cases like it?

In fact, I believe that the key to designing an effective legal research system is to identify different aspects of the law and use appropriate tools to model them. This analysis[5], an extension of the arguments developed in [RB89] and [RB91a], is based on the observation that our legal system has a dual nature; it is both "connectionist" and "symbolic."

5.3.1   Symbolic Characteristics of Law

What does it mean to say the law has "symbolic" structure? Part of the answer will have to wait until chapter 6, which discusses what it means for a system to be symbolic. For now, though, it refers to ways in which the law can be thought of as composed of (or capable of being modeled by) the kind of symbolic representations used in traditional AI systems.

Symbolic Structure in Statutory Law. The most obvious example occurs in statutory law, where "laws" really are intended to be rules of behavior. Although their wording and their purpose is not always clear (as we shall see later), statutes can be viewed as if-then rules that could be expressed in a variety of symbolic formalisms such as a production system or first-order predicate logic.

---

[5]Robert French [Fre87] made a similar argument. However, he drew the analogy between common law systems and connectionism, and between civil law systems and symbolic AI. In contrast, the account presented in this chapter regards both connectionist and symbolic characteristics as extant in our essentially common-law system.

Consider, for example, §106 of the Copyright Act of 1976:

> Subject to sections 107 through 118, the owner of copyright under this title has the exclusive rights to do and to authorize any of the following:
> (1) to reproduce the copyrighted work in copies or phonorecords;
> (2) to prepare derivative works based on the copyrighted work;
> (3) to distribute copies or phonorecords of the copyrighted work to the public by sale or other transfer of ownership ...

Clearly, the basic thrust of this section is that IF certain conditions are met AND x is the owner of a copyrighted work THEN x has exclusive rights to reproduce the work, sell the work, etc. This is *not* a claim that every aspect of the statute is expressible in logic (indeed, few would believe this). It simply illustrates a rough correspondence between statutes and symbolic rules.

Structural Hierarchies. A second and more interesting way in which the law has symbolic aspects is the way it can be viewed hierarchically. There are many structural hierarchies in the law, such as the appellate court system already discussed, which constrains when precedents must be followed.

Perhaps the richest hierarchical structure in law is the West key number system, a taxonomy of law developed by West Publishing Company during the past hundred years or so. It is used to organize the topically compiled case digests. At the highest level, West organizes its "outline of the law" into seven "main divisions": Persons, Property, Contracts, Torts, Crimes, Remedies, and Government. Each of these areas is divided into a few subareas, and each subarea into perhaps 20 topics, for a total of around 400 topics. Each of these topics is then divided further into a couple hundred key numbers. Figure 5.1 shows a single path through the hierarchy from the root (all of law) to a specific key number ("Acts constituting [copyright] infringement.")

To an AI researcher, the West taxonomy (like other such classification schemes) bears a striking resemblance to a simple semantic network, inheritance hierarchy, or ontology. There is clearly an IS-A relationship between each node and its parent, with implicit inheritance. In a very real sense, the key number hierarchy is a symbolic representation of the law.

One might argue that the mere existence of a taxonomy of law is not especially significant for understanding how law works; taxonomies are often merely descriptive. There are two responses to this. First, I believe that taxonomies *do* tell us a lot about how to understand a

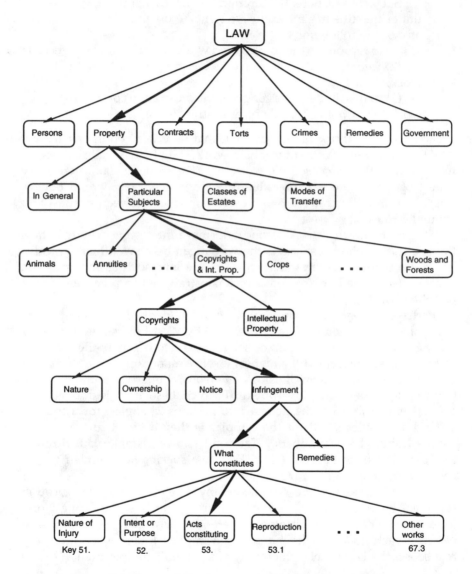

Figure 5.1: One path from root to leaf in the West taxonomy.

discipline. Eighteenth-century naturalists believed that fossils and rocks were basically the same because they belonged to the class "things found underground" [Gou88]. More importantly, the value of the key number taxonomy is evident in the way it is used in the law. Court decisions are the texts that constitute law, and every court decision published by West (which is often the only publisher, and often the official publisher) has headnotes labeled by key numbers in the taxonomy.

At a more superficial level, statutory law is also organized hierarchically, presumably representing its authors' conceptual framework for the topic at hand. For example, the Copyright Act of 1976 is divided into eight chapters, each dealing with a major issue — subject matter of copyright in Ch. 1, ownership in Ch. 2, duration in Ch. 3, and so on. Each of these is divided up into several sections concerned with more specific issues (e.g., §202, "Ownership of copyright as distinct from ownership of material object"), which may in turn be divided further.

Symbolic Nature of Citations. The third symbolic aspect of the law lies in the existence of explicit symbolic relationships between legal texts. The most important of these are the labeled citations indexed by *Shepard's*[6], a reverse bibliography that is described in Section 5.4. Each citing case is linked to each cited case by the existence of an explicit relationship such as "criticized," "harmonized," or "limited." (Although not all citations are labeled with a so-called *treatment phrase*, the mere existence and identification of a citation forms an explicit symbolic relationship.) A complete listing of Shepard's citation labels is given in Table 5.1; some of these are discussed further in chapter 7.

Again, the importance of citation relationships might be discounted on the grounds that other disciplines — most notably, science — use them as well. As with taxonomies, I have two responses. First, citators are increasingly important in these fields; the *Science Citation Index* is said to be used in academic tenure decisions. Second, legal citators are especially critical both because of the additional information about the type of relationships, and more so because of the role of precedent in common law. Citations tell a legal researcher which precedents the judge believed were relevant and which were not.

There are similar relationships within statutory law, though they are not catalogued and labeled. These are the cross-references, such as "except where noted in section x" and "as defined in section y."

Taken together, the taxonomy of law and the interrelationships of legal texts form a web which might be viewed as a semantic network, as shown in Figure 5.2. It is this very network that forms the symbolic side

---

[6]Shepard's is a registered trademark of Shepard's/McGraw-Hill, Inc.

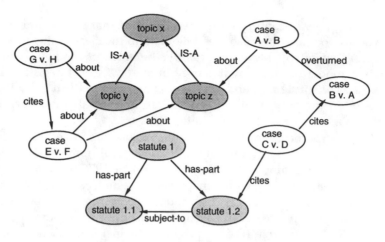

Figure 5.2: A semantic network for law.

of SCALIR.

5.3.2 Connectionist Characteristics of Law

The previous section suggested that symbolic structure exists and plays an important role in the law. However, this view of law does not tell the whole story. Law relies as much on ambiguity as on precision, on statistically emergent representations as on formal structures, and on analogy as much as deduction. In short, there are many aspects of the law that are similar to those found in a connectionist AI system (defined in chapter 3).

The most elegant analogy between our legal system and connectionism is that common law in particular is a *parallel distributed precedence* system: Law is made by the superposition of all the decisions of thousands of judges over hundreds of years at many levels and in many jurisdictions. Although there are occasional landmark decisions that obviously "make law," these are the exception. Generally, global concepts emerge from the interaction of a large number of local decisions, as in a connectionist network. Because the decisions that come to be incorporated in the law are distributed in time as well as space, this view is consistent with the realists' notion of law as a system constantly in flux, shaped by social forces around it. SCALIR was designed in part to mirror that social component.

The other way in which the law is analogous to a connectionist system is in its use of "noisy" representations and its ability to make sense of them. In the law, the noise — and the richness — stems from the use of natural language for legal texts. Although the "legalese" dialect in which statutes and court decisions are often written is commonly viewed (at least by laypersons) as conveying precision, this is generally not the case. As a leading scholar of legal writing puts it, "The language of the law is peculiar, not precise. Don't confuse peculiarity with precision" [Mel82]. This point is elaborated in the next section.

Section 5.1 discussed how legal texts (court decisions and statutes) actually *constitute* law, rather than merely *describing* it. But these texts are written in natural language, which has properties (such as polysemy and synonymy) that, as discussed in chapter 4 render them difficult to classify. Accordingly, SCALIR uses a connectionist network to represent the texts, handling their noise and — at least to some extent — maintaining their richness.

5.4 Legal Research

In this section I describe the basic tools and processes of traditional (that is, manual) legal research. The goal of legal research, whether manual or computer-assisted, is generally to find relevant court decisions that may serve as precedent for the issue at hand.

5.4.1 Research Resources

As discussed earlier, there are three kinds of law: statutory, administrative, and common law. Statutory law for the United States is published chronologically in a series of books called *Statutes at Large*. The statutes are then organized according to numbered topics called "titles" in the *United States Code*. For example, Title 17 constitutes the Federal copyright statute. Portions of the statute are cited by giving the title number, the abbreviation of the code, and the section number (e.g., 17 U.S.C. 101). Administrative law is similarly organized both chronologically (in the *Federal Register*) and topically (in the *Code of Federal Regulations*).

Federal common law is similarly arranged both chronologically and topically, but in each case there are several different and sometimes overlapping sources, depending on the court. The chronological compilations are called *reporters*, whereas the topical ones are called *digests*. However, unlike the codes for statutory and administrative law, digests contain only short descriptions of the cases, rather than the entire text of the decision. The entry for a given case in a reporter may contain not only the (majority) "opinion of the court" (usually written by a single judge), but also any separate opinions — dissenting or concurring — written by other judges.

Although there are often several competing reporters and digests, the ones compiled by West Publishing Company are the most widely used. In fact, in many cases the West reporters are the officially recognized record of the court.[7]

In addition to the text of the judge's decision, the West reporters include a series of *headnotes* listing the legal issues of the case.   Each headnote is tagged by a number, known as a *key number*, indexing that legal issue in a taxonomy of law developed by West over many years. This is the same taxonomy described earlier that is used to organize the topics in the digest. Headnotes are written by highly skilled editors — lawyers trained by West to perform the digesting task, summarizing the main points in a few short sentences.

Because the concept of precedent is so important in common law, it is not surprising that a special resource exists to identify each instance of one judge's decision citing another. This resource is *Shepard's Citations*, a series of published volumes that list every citation to a specific case. The citator serves as a kind of "reverse bibliography" for cases. But *Shepard's* includes additional information about the nature of the citation, in the form of a one-letter code indicating the relationship between the citing case and the cited case. There are two kinds of codes, one for "history" relationships (e.g., one decision overturned another decision), the other for "treatment" (e.g., one decision criticized another decision). These are listed in Table 5.1; comments are from Shepard's own descriptions.

5.4.2   Manual Research

During the process of legal research, any or all of these tools may come into play, although the chronological listings of statutes and regulations are less commonly used. A research session will very likely include digests, reporters, and citators, plus general references such as legal encyclopedias, *treatises* ("scholarly analyses of particular areas of law" [WW83] such as the four-volume *Nimmer on Copyright* [NN86]), and *restatements* (descriptions of well-established principles of common law).

For example, suppose a researcher was interested in the "fair use" exemption in copyright law. He or she might start with Nimmer's treatise to get a sense of some of the important issues and cases, and then look under the appropriate key number (say, 53.2 — Fair use and other

---

[7]One notable exception is at the Supreme Court level; the *United States Reports* is the official reporter, rather than West's *Supreme Court Reporter*.

HISTORY OF CASE		
Code	Description	Comments
A	affirmed	Same case affirmed on appeal.
CC	connected case	Different case from cited case but arising out of same subject matter or intimately connected therewith.
CF	certiorari filed	
DE	denied	
DM	dismissed	Appeal from same case dismissed.
GR	granted	
IN	US cert denied	Certiorari denied by U.S. Supreme Court.
	US cert dismissed	Certiorari dismissed by U.S. Supreme Court.
	US reh denied	Rehearing denied by U.S. Supreme Court.
	US reh dismissed	Rehearing dismissed by U.S. Supreme Court.
M	modified	Same case modified on appeal.
MI	mandate issed	
NP	not published	
PD	petition denied	
PG	petition granted	
R	reversed	Same case reversed on appeal.
S	superseded	Substitution for former opinion.
SC	same case	
V	vacated	Same case vacated.
TREATMENT OF CASE		
C	criticized	Soundness of decision or reasoning in cited case criticized for reasons given.
D	distinguished	Case at bar different either in law or fact from case cited for reasons given.
E	explained	Statement of import of decision in cited case. Not merely a restatement of the facts.
EX	examiner's decision	
F	followed	Cited as controlling.
H	harmonized	Apparent inconsistency explained and shown not to exist.
J	dissenting	Citation in dissenting opinion.
L	limited	Refusal to extend decision of cited case beyond precise issues involved.
O	overruled	Ruling in cited case expressly overruled.
P	parallel	Citing case substantially alike or on all fours with cited case in its law or facts.
Q	questioned	Soundness of decision or reasoning in cited case questioned.

Table 5.1: Shepard's citation labels.

permitted uses in general) in West's digest. This would give short descriptions of several cases. The researcher could then look up a few of the cases in the reporter. One case might seem promising, so he or she would "shepardize" it (that is, look it up in the citator) to see how other more recent decisions have treated it, and possibly look up some of the citing decisions in the reporter. These cases might have headnotes suggesting new digest topics, and so on.

Despite its critical role in a common law system, legal research is still not an exact science. Many tools have been developed to facilitate the process, but they are not fail-safe. As one guide to legal research wrote:

> Don't rely on summaries (e.g., case headnotes ...) as necessarily being accurate or authoritative statements of the law. Although such summaries are helpful guides, they can never substitute for the primary authorities [statutes, regulations, and court decisions] themselves....
>
> Remember that titles of sub-topics listed under various topics in case digests ... do not classify legal subject matter with scientific precision. [WW83, p. 75]

These caveats are important to keep in mind when we discuss ways to "computerize" the process.

5.5   Legal Information Retrieval

So far, I have discussed some general issues about information retrieval (in chapter 4), law, and legal research. In this section, I consider a problem involving all of these issues: legal information retrieval.

5.5.1   A Brief History of Computer-Assisted Legal Research

The idea of using computers to help find legal documents is not new. The general concept was suggested as early as the 1940s, and several research projects conducted in the early 1960s developed promising prototypes [Bin84]. John Horty's group at the University of Pittsburgh School of Public Health developed a system for locating health-related statutes; by 1965 they had experimented with court decisions. Horty advocated the use of what was then called "text" or "unindexed" retrieval — what we would today call full-text indexing (as opposed to manual indexing of the sort done by library cataloguers).

Horty's work inspired many others around the world and indirectly led to the creation of several extant legal IR systems. In particular, some members of the Ohio Bar Association who had been investigating the idea of legal IR heard Horty speak at their annual meeting and decided to pursue the concept [Har85]. Led by William Harrington, the Ohio group continued its contacts with Horty and eventually formulated a definition of the system they envisioned. As Harrington described it,

> The definition was the most important achievement of the Ohio project's first year — perhaps of the project's entire five years. The definition written by the Ohio group more than eighteen years ago is the basic definition of LEXIS and WEST-LAW to this day.
>
> In a few words, the Ohio group defined what it wanted as a nonindexed, full-text, on-line, interactive, computer-assisted legal research service. [Har85, p. 545]

By 1967, they created a nonprofit corporation called OBAR (for Ohio Bar Automated Research), which contracted with a firm called Data Corporation to develop the legal research system. When Mead acquired Data Corporation in 1969, they decided to expand the project into the nationwide commercial system that became known as LEXIS.

LEXIS, the first successful[8] computer-assisted legal research (CALR) system, came on line in 1973. LEXIS uses full-text inverted file indexing, with Boolean and positional keyword queries. Its databases now include most court decisions. By 1975, West Publishing Co. started their own CALR service, WESTLAW, which initially contained only case headnotes rather than the full text of the decisions. This proved to be an unpopular decision, and by 1978 WESTLAW offered both headnotes and full text. In addition, WESTLAW gives page numbers for the bound volumes in West's own reporter series. Due to the importance of West's reporters and digests in legal research, the presence of headnotes and page numbers often makes WESTLAW preferable to LEXIS.[9]

---

[8]An less successful effort was the system developed by Law Research Services (LRS), which used manual indexing. Founded in 1964, the noninteractive LRS service was eventually used by the majority of law firms in New York state [Tap73]. LRS was plagued by various hardware and financial problems, and by a lawsuit from West Publishing Company. During eventual bankruptcy proceedings, LRS agreed to destroy its database to settle the West suit [Bin84].

[9]Indeed, Mead's use of West page numbers in LEXIS spawned a major lawsuit [*West Pub. Co. v. Mead Data Cent., Inc.*, 616 F.Supp. 1571, affirmed 799 F.2d. 1219, certiorari denied 107 S.Ct. 962, 93 L.Ed.2d. 1010] eventually settled in West's favor.

5.5.2   What's Different About Legal IR?

Despite the enormous popularity of LEXIS and WESTLAW, there is evidence that these systems are less successful at finding relevant law than one might wish. This is illustrated in chapter 4 both by examples of CALR searches and by the evidence of limitations of any traditional IR technique. In fact, the problem of legal IR has special characteristics that make it somewhat different than that of general IR.

First, the notion of relevance in law is especially complex; a case might deal with the issues of interest but be judged less relevant by a lawyer because it was decided by a "sister" jurisdiction. Two documents which might seem closely related in a general IR system may thus be technically unrelated in law. In other words, the space of associations is more structured and, in some cases, discontinuous.

Second, legal researchers are often interested in higher recall than, say, a student writing a term paper. The student probably needs only a few good references; time is wasted poring over hundreds of possibilities. For a lawyer, however, the cost of missing a potentially relevant document is much higher; this may be the case that an opponent raises in court. Furthermore, the administrative structure of a law firm (in which legal research is often done by assistants, and billed accordingly to clients) encourages thorough research. (However, this may be more true for litigation than other aspects of law.)

Third, ambiguity (including what is known in the literature as vagueness, circularity, etc. [Ber89, Lam85, Lin88]) plays an unusually large role. Because this may run counter to our intuitions about law, it is worth elaborating further.

The most obvious form of ambiguity in law results from the fact that legal documents are written (more or less) in natural language. This makes ambiguities of both syntactic and lexical intent almost inevitable. Allen and Saxon [AS87] give many examples of syntactic ambiguity. For instance, a sentence that says "A and B unless C" might be interpreted as either "(A and B) unless C" or "A and (B unless C)." Note that the relevance of a case or statute could hinge on the associativity of a single clause. This type of problem has led Allen to propose programs to "normalize" law, identifying and eliminating this particular type of ambiguity.

Lexical ambiguity takes many forms. Often, a statutory term becomes ambiguous over time. To use an example from [Lin88], should the term *radio*, when written in older statutes, now refer also to television? Cable television? Videotex? Law is generally robust in the face of change; the meaning of legal texts changes to suit the times. This adaptive nature makes it difficult to formalize, however.

Another important type of lexical ambiguity is the use of what are known in the law as *open-textured* terms — those which require a subjective judgment to be correctly applied. Both statutory law and case law are filled with these sorts of concepts, such as *beyond a reasonable doubt, clear and present danger,* and *fair use.* These terms may be partly defined extensionally, by giving examples, but such definitions will never capture all future uses (nor are they intended to). Open-texture gives law much of its richness and flexibility, but it adds greatly to its ambiguity.

Perhaps the most blatant example of ambiguity occurs when legislators leave statutes "open ended." For example, unfair trade law [GKP86] contains this definition:

> The following unfair methods of competition and unfair or deceptive acts and practices ... are hereby declared to be unlawful:
>
> 1. passing off goods or services as those of another;
>
> 2. causing likelihood of confusion ... as to the source ... of goods and services;
>
> ⋮
>
> 13. engaging in any act or practice which is unfair or deceptive to the consumer.

Given the final clause, we might summarize this section (only slightly facetiously) as "an unfair practice is a practice which is unfair." Berman and Hafner noted many similar examples [BH88].

Given the ambiguity of the law, it is not surprising that commercial IR systems, which are based on surface properties of the text, have so much trouble. Existing CALR systems in particular also suffer from what Bing calls "the curse of Boole" [Bin87b]: a mistaken reliance on Boolean operators in queries and the use of binary rather than ranked relevance judgments. Given the subtlety of legal language, such an all-or-nothing mechanism cannot be sufficient.

5.5.3 Progress Toward Conceptual Legal IR

It is clear that there are severe limitations on the abilities of conventional IR techniques — particularly those used in commercial systems — to retrieve relevant legal documents. Although IR research has produced many enhancements to the basic techniques, legal IR remains a particularly difficult problem. One answer may be to shift from syntactic word-token-based approaches to *conceptual* representations and searches. In addition to improving recall, it seems plausible that a conceptual legal IR system would be more robust, less brittle, than a traditional system. Many research projects have attempted to do just that.

The WESTLAW system (in contrast to LEXIS) may itself be viewed as a first step toward a conceptual retrieval system. Because West's published documents are indexed by manually assigned key numbers, a user can query for cases that involve certain legal issues, rather than simply those that include certain words. In fact, SCALIR incorporates this same knowledge — West's taxonomy of the law — to improve retrievals. West's editors are in effect serving as knowledge engineers, trying to capture the judges' opinions in the terse representation of headnotes. However, West's dependence on manual indexing also makes it subject to the vagaries of any manual process, and it (like LEXIS) still suffers from the brittleness and ambiguity problems.

To achieve a more sophisticated method for conceptual retrieval, it might seem that the techniques of traditional AI would be effective. After all, if we could somehow represent knowledge of the law in some formal language, we could then search by meanings rather than by mere lexical items.

This was the approach taken by Hafner in her LIRS system [Haf81]. LIRS was among the first CALR systems to explicitly use AI techniques. It was able to do conceptual retrieval for documents dealing with the law of negotiable instruments; the database included 186 cases and 110 statute sections. Although this is a small number by traditional IR standards, it is an order of magnitude larger than many AI and law systems; this renders LIRS less subject to the common critique that AI works only on "toy" problems [Dre79].

Hafner manually encoded the cases using a frame-like "Document Description Language" to represent the legal basis of the lawsuit, the legal situation exemplified by the case, and so on. An example of a case described in this form is shown in Figure 5.3. The descriptors used correspond to parts of a semantic network representing a conceptual model of negotiable instruments law. For example, COA represents the legal concept "cause of action." The hierarchical structure of the statute — a portion of the Uniform Commercial Code (UCC) was also represented as a network.

LIRS used a simple command language which allowed for logical combinations of certain controlled vocabulary terms. For example, to find cases that describe dishonored instruments, and do not have a holder as the plaintiff, the user would enter

```
PL
    HOLDER
    INDORSEE
DEF
    INDORSER
COA
    C3414
EX
    SURRENDERED
    (DISHONORED CHECK)
HEX
    CONVERSION
LEFF
    (UNEX-DELAYED-IN-PRES (BASIS UCC3-501-1-B))
    (SURRENDERED (BASIS UCC3-605-1-B))
DEC
    ((NOT C-INST) (PREF (NOT OWNER)) (PREF (NOT HOLDER))
      (PREF (NOT LOST-STOLEN-OR-DEST)) (PREF (UNEX-DELAYED-IN-PRES))
      (BASIS UCC3-501-1-B) (BASIS UCC3-804) (BASIS UCC3-605-1-B))
    (UNEX-DELAYED-IN-PRES (BASIS UCC3-503-1-E) (BASIS UCC3-503-2-B)
      (BASIS UCC3-504-1))
    ((NOT OWNER))
    ((NOT LOST-STOLEN-OR-DEST))
    ((NOT HOLDER) (BASIS UCC1-201-20))
```

Figure 5.3: The document descriptors for *Dluge v. Robinson*, a sample case in the LIRS system [Haf81, pp. 159–160].

```
FIND CASES (DESC DISHONORED) AND NOT (PL HOLDER).
```

The system could then identify the cases and describe them using similar terminology. In addition, the user could ask for the retrieval of negatively and positively citing cases.

Although Hafner's approach used a very rich representation, it was limited by the need to manually encode each case. Furthermore, the representations — using the paradigm of symbolic AI — were able to capture only one view of the knowledge in the case, Hafner's own.

Another approach to conceptual retrieval is to use a knowledge representation formalism for the legal concepts, but not for the cases themselves. The conceptual structure would be used as a kind of "semantic thesaurus" to extend the query to all the terms that might actually be used in the relevant documents. Jon Bing has advocated essentially this approach.

Bing's *norm-based thesaurus* is a hierarchical formalism for representing legal norms (basic principles). Bing views the norms as being expressed as IF-THEN rules, which may be derived from normalized (in the sense of Layman Allen's work [AS85]) versions of statutory text [Bin87a]. For example, Bing suggests that one such rule for expressing part of the Norwegian social security statute would be represented like this:

```
IF
    entitled to basic pension
    AND
        spouse receiving old age pension
        OR
        spouse receiving invalid pension
        OR
        spouse receiving rehabilitation support
            while waiting for invalid pension
THEN
    basic pension
    EQUALS
    0.75 basic amount
```

[Bin87a, p. 47]

The chunks of normalized text would then be merged together to form a network. The network would be presented to the user as an "arrow diagram" with blocks indicating concepts like "entitled to basic pension," which contain more detailed subblocks. The disjunctions in the rule are displayed as multiple paths out of a node, while the conjunctions are

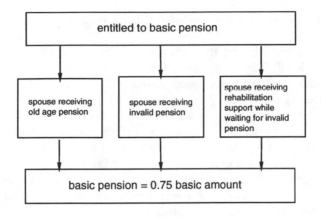

Figure 5.4: Bing's arrow diagram.

shown as successive nodes along a path. So, for example, the rule above might be presented to the user as shown in Figure 5.4.

Bing's idea is that the norm-based thesaurus would be used to improve basic text retrieval.[10] Queries use the *conceptor-based* strategy [Bin84, Bin88], which Bing has advocated as an alternative to Boolean queries. In this strategy, users are encouraged to think in terms of *classes* consisting of many interchangeable search terms; responses can then be ranked by class frequency as well as word frequency. In Boolean terms, a class C of search terms s_i is defined as

$$C = s_1 \vee s_2 \vee \ldots \vee s_n.$$

A query takes the form of a list of classes of interest. If there are three classes in the query, then the set of highest ranked documents corresponds to those containing terms in all three classes, the second set to those with terms in exactly two of the classes, and the third with terms in just one class. Thus the conceptor strategy combines some of the advantages of Boolean and frequency-ranking searches.

In Bing's legal IR system, a user might enter a query such as WIFE & DECEASE*, where the ampersand represents the class-combining operator described above and the asterisk is a wild-card expander. This would match a node containing both concepts (e.g., *spouse dead*). This in turn would cause the retrieval of all cases that contained the terms in the

---

[10]The norm-based thesaurus idea plays a role in many projects being investigated by the Norwegian Research Center for Computers and Law. Some of these involve modeling legal reasoning or providing legal expert systems; information retrieval is only one application of the concept.

spouse dead concept, such as *husband, wife, married, die, death, deceased,* and so on.

Thus the norm-based thesaurus carries the IR idea of thesauri to a conceptual level. Terms are related not on the basis of co-occurrence or semantic categories, but are based instead on their respective roles in the intertwined legal norms.

A third approach to conceptual retrieval is based on the assumption that a legal researcher is interested in finding a relevant *argument,* rather than a relevant case. There have been various efforts to construct formal models of legal arguments. For example, Marshall [Mar89] has experimented with a system for modeling Supreme Court oral arguments. She uses Toulmin's analysis of argument [Tou58] as a formalism for representing the court transcripts. So far, this type of model is of limited use for the IR problem; legal researchers are not generally searching databases of oral argument. However, Dick [Dic87] has proposed using a similar approach to representing case law. In Dick's system, a casebook on contract law would be used as the initial source. The arguments of each case — specifically, the *ratio decidendi* (reasons for the decision) [11] — would be represented using Toulmin structures. The final representation of the case would be a frame whose slots corresponded to Toulmin categories (claim, warrant, rebuttal, etc.), filled with a semantic case [Fil68] description of the language. Retrievals in the system would require questions to be "expressed in a logical form suitable for pattern-matching" [Dic87, p. 113].

A rather different approach to modeling legal arguments was taken by Ashley in his Hypo system [Ash90, RA87]. Although the purpose of Hypo was to help lawyers prepare a series of legal arguments, part of this task required the indexing and retrieval of relevant cases.

Hypo's "case knowledge base" (CKB) consisted of 30 cases in trade secrets law, manually encoded by Ashley in a hierarchical set of legal case frames. A critical part of Hypo's indexing and retrieval strategy was the concept of *Dimensions.* As explained by Ashley, Hypo's Dimensions

> encode knowledge of the features of a case that have relevance
> for arguing the legal merits of a claim. They represent factors
> that make a claim in a given fact situation stronger or weaker.
> If a Dimension applies to a fact situation, it means that the
> fact situation shares some factor in common with at least one
> case where a court decided the case because, or in spite, of
> the presence of that factor. [Ash90, p. 107]

---

[11] Dick argues that the casebook editor's notes will facilitate the process of distinguishing the *ratio* from the *obiter dicta* (other incidental comments by the judge).

Secrets-Voluntarily-Disclosed

Short Name: Secrets-Disclosed-Outsiders

Claim: Trade Secrets Misappropriation

Generalization: Plaintiff is strengthened the fewer disclosures to outsiders it has made of confidential information.

Focal Slot Prerequisites: "Plaintiff made some disclosures to outsiders."

Comparison Type: Greater-than versus Less-than

Range: 0–10,000,000

Pro-Plaintiff Direction: 0 disclosures

Figure 5.5: One of Hypo's 13 Dimensions.

Each case frame includes a top-level slot for the Dimensions that apply to that case.

The basic operation of Hypo involves getting information about a fact situation[12], retrieving cases sharing some Dimensions, and then generating arguments and counterarguments for ruling a certain way.

Hypo uses 13 Dimensions dealing primarily with issues of trade secrets, such as *Competitive-Advantage-Gained* and *Secrets-Voluntarily-Disclosed*, which is shown in Figure 5.5 [Ash90, p. 274]. Each Dimension has one or more "focal slots" such as (in the example from the figure), the number of disclosures of plaintiff's product. The focal slots have prerequisites, which are predicates that must be satisfied for this Dimension to be relevant ("plaintiff made some disclosures to outsiders"), and ranges indicating what kind of values, or magnitudes, can fill the slot (0–10,000,000 in the case of disclosures).

When a case is entered into the CKB, Hypo determines what Dimensions apply and the magnitudes of their focal slots. When a new fact situation is encountered, Hypo constructs a *claim lattice* of cases which share one or more dimensions with the current situation. The system can then recommend cases to cite[13] as well as "3-ply arguments." These are examples and counterexamples of points which favor each side, often distinguishing a potential precedent by contrasting the different magnitudes of focal slots. For example, Hypo may argue that case A is stronger for the plaintiff than case B, because only 7 disclosures were made in A as opposed to 100 in B.

---

[12]The "current fact situation" is the set of facts relating to the case at hand.

[13]Actually, the system distinguishes between the most on point cases (those most legally relevant to the current fact situation) and the best cases to cite.

Despite the importance of comparing focal slot magnitudes in assessing the strength of a precedent, Hypo did not use these to rank the retrieved cases. Rather, one case is considered more on point than another if the set of Dimensions it shares with the current fact situation is a proper superset of those the other case shares. Ashley argues that since there might be several most analogous cases, some of which may conflict with each other, it is inappropriate to try to rank them further. Rather, he suggests comparing them symbolically so as to elucidate the different ways in which the situation could be resolved.

Similarly, Ashley opposes the concept of weighting the factors, arguing (among other things) that factor weights might conflict with factor magnitudes, that there is no justification for assigning particular weights, and that numerical weights might obscure information used for symbolic comparisons.

5.5.4   Problems With the Traditional AI Approach

Each of the three approaches described previously is deeply rooted in the traditional AI approach. In each case a symbolic formalism was used to represent the knowledge of some aspect of law: cases and statutes (Hafner), legal norms (Bing), or legal arguments (both Dick and Ashley). Despite the promise of these three approaches, there are three problems which ultimately make each unable to handle the demands of a practical, full-scale legal information retrieval system.

The first problem is that each method requires a great deal of manual encoding of the legal knowledge. This is an extremely time-consuming task which requires a great deal of expertise. There are hundreds of thousands of cases, yet few AI systems can handle even 100. Bing is acutely aware of this problem, hence his system does not require any knowledge engineering for case law. Nevertheless, his formal representation of legal norms is itself a nontrivial task.

Ideally, the knowledge-encoding could be done automatically, using some kind of natural language understanding system which would translate cases or statutes into some formal representation. Yet this would require dramatic improvements in natural language processing (NLP). Furthermore, the most successful NLP programs have used stored chunks of knowledge about the world — knowledge which itself must be manually encoded for every topic that might possibly be encountered. As the magnitude of Lenat's Cyc project [GL90] indicates, this may be as large a problem as the one we started with — if it is possible at all.

The second problem is the fact that the formal representations correspond to one person's subjective opinion about what the case or statute or portion of law is really about. Yet there are many instances where there is disagreement about the implications of a certain decision. (If this were not the case, much of the legal machinery would not be necessary.) The situation grows worse when one expert cannot handle the entire job, as would certainly be the case with any sizable database of court decisions. In that situation, the different encoders might have different ideas about various points of law. In particular, they might use the same formalism to mean different things, or different formalisms to mean the same thing. This is essentially the age-old library indexing problem discussed in chapter 4.

Even if the previous two problems were overcome, there is a third and more serious problem. This is that judicial decisions simply do not contain a fixed set of facts and rules which can be enumerated a priori. An offhand remark, even a footnote, can become the basis for a new thread of the continually emerging law.[14]

In fact, any attempt to explicitly encode the "meaning" of a text in some knowledge representation formalism is doomed to fail. No derivative representation of the text can preserve the richness of the text itself. Once completed, the more concise representation will not contain the shades of meaning present in the original, and will by definition have omitted information judged irrelevant. But as we have seen, it is impossible to know in advance what is relevant unless one knows the specific reason the information is needed. Law is fundamentally variable; its ability to use static text in a dynamic world is one of its greatest strengths.

5.5.5 What Are the Alternatives?

At this point, the entire task may again appear futile. On the one hand, I have argued that traditional IR techniques will not suffice, due to the problems like synonymy and polysemy inherent in natural language. "Smarter," more conceptually oriented approaches are needed. On the other hand, I have claimed that traditional AI techniques do not provide a viable alternative.

What is needed is an approach that has the scalability and automation of IR, with the conceptual inference capabilities of AI but with dynamic, extensible representations. It is this combination of attributes I have tried to incorporate into SCALIR. Specifically, SCALIR uses a connectionist

---

[14]An example of this is Justice Stone's footnote to the 1938 case *U.S. v. Carolene Products Co.* (304 U.S. 144, 58 S.Ct. 778, 82 L.Ed. 1234), which became better known than the decision itself.

network to represent the contents of documents and their relationships. The initial network configuration is generated automatically by using statistical analysis techniques common in IR research. From this starting point, the network learns from its users, and can thus adapt to changing terminology or new interpretations of old cases. Furthermore, SCALIR incorporates a semantic network to incorporate any a priori knowledge already encoded, such as West's taxonomy of law or Shepard's citations.

Many of the ideas implemented independently in SCALIR were actually proposed years earlier by Ejan Mackaay. Mackaay, who had developed a standard CALR system called DATUM in the 1970s, proposed a new system (DATUM II) [Mac77]:

> The performance of a retrieval system in terms of recall and precision may be expected to improve by several features which should be considered in new designs:
>
> - the possibility of making corrections in existing files at reasonable cost ...
> - consolidating search experience in the system itself ("learning")
> - ranked presentation of search results
>
> Comfort may be affected by the following factors
>
> - uniformity of cost ...
> - reduction of the variety of commands the user has to master ...
> - reliance on "recognition" rather than "recall" memory in making options available to users ...
> - interactive operation, in particular for consultation of the dictionary of possible search terms, query formulation and searching, screening of search results.

Mackaay also intended DATUM II to use term weighting with inverse document frequency, relevance feedback to adjust the representation of the documents, and simultaneous access to the full text of the cases, sections of statute, and citation patterns. Though never completed, DATUM II would have realized many of the same goals which motivated the design of SCALIR.

5.6   Copyright Law: Briefest Course

The database used by SCALIR consists of Federal cases and statutes on copyright law. This area of law was chosen for several reasons (in addition to the interest of the author). First, it is a relatively small subject, so including all Federal cases was feasible. Second, it deals with issues likely to be familiar to potential readers of this work. Third, it is a rapidly changing area of law, so it is well suited for testing SCALIR's adaptive mechanisms.

To understand the examples used in later chapters, it is useful to know a little about what copyright law is and where it fits in with the rest of intellectual property law.

Intellectual property is generally divided into four areas: Patents, Copyrights, Trademarks, and Trade Secrets. Trademarks are indications of a firm's reputation, and trademark law cases often involve attempts to "palm off" one product as another. The law of trade secrets is connected with various unfair business practices.

Confusion often arises over the similarities and differences between copyrights and patents. Both are mandated in Article I, §8 of the United States Constitution:

> The Congress shall have power ... [t]o promote the Progress of Science and useful Arts, by securing for limited Times to Authors and Inventors the exclusive Right to their respective Writings and Discoveries ...

Both are intended to encourage public disclosure of intellectual achievements that might otherwise be kept private. The inducement for this disclosure is, in both cases, a type of limited monopoly granted to the author or inventor. However, both the subject matter and the nature of the monopoly differ between copyrights and patents.

Patents are basically intended to encourage innovation. A patent gives a 17-year monopoly to the inventor. The thing being patented can be either an object or a process; it cannot be an idea. Formulas, in particular, are off-limits; Einstein could not patent $E = mc^2$. (In recent years some patents on algorithms have been allowed, as processes, but this is still controversial.) The patented work must be *novel*; in particular, this means that an inventor has only 1 year to apply for a patent.

In contrast, copyrights were intended to encourage writing. A copyright gives an author a 50-year monopoly on the right to reproduce (hence "copy-right") the work, to license that right, and so on. In particular, the Copyright Act specifies [17 U.S.C. 106]:

> Subject to sections 107 through 118, the owner of copyright under this title has the exclusive rights to do and to authorize any of the following:

(1) to reproduce the copyrighted work in copies or phono-records;

(2) to prepare derivative works based upon the copyrighted work;

(3) to distribute copies or phonorecords of the copyrighted work to the public by sale or other transfer of ownership, or by rental, lease, or lending;

(4) in the case of literary, musical, dramatic, and choreo-graphic works, pantomimes, and motion pictures and other audiovisual works, to perform the copyrighted work publicly; and

(5) in the case of literary, musical, dramatic, and choreo-graphic works, pantomimes, and pictorial, graphic, or sculptural works, including the individual images of a motion picture or other audiovisual work, to display the copyrighted work publicly.

There are certain exceptions to the monopoly, such as the "fair use" exemption (17 U.S.C. 107) which permits others to copy an author's work for purposes of criticism, etc. In addition to literary works, copyrights cover paintings and other artistic works, musical compositions, films, choreography, and more. Computer programs were originally considered literary works (and sometimes also audiovisual works) for the purposes of copyright, but have since been explicitly listed as copyrightable subject matter by a 1980 amendment to the copyright law.

Unlike the situation for patents, there is no novelty requirement for copyrights, only an originality requirement. As Judge Learned Hand put it:

> Borrowed the work must indeed not be, for a plagiarist is not himself pro tanto an 'author'; but if by some magic a man who had not known it were to compose anew Keats's Ode on a Grecian Urn, he would be an 'author,' and, if he copyrighted it, others might not copy that poem, though they might of course copy Keats's. [*Sheldon v. Metro-Goldwyn Pictures Corp.,* 81 F.2d 29 (2d Cir. 1936)]

Just as ideas cannot be patented, they cannot be copyrighted either. Copyrights are granted for *the expression of an idea*, not for the idea itself. However, the boundary between expression and idea is not sharp; fictional characters, for example, have been found to be ideas in some courts, and expressions of ideas in others.

The current statute governing copyrights is the Copyright Act of 1976, which superseded the previous (1907) law. The 1976 Act instituted several important changes. Most importantly, it eliminated the requirement that a copyright must be registered with the copyright office. Under the current law, a work is copyrighted as soon as it is "fixed in a tangible medium of expression." In other words, copyrights are automatically granted to any original writing, musical composition, and so on. However, the copyright must be registered before an author can sue for infringement.

Many copyright disputes have centered around exactly what is meant by the terms *fixed* and *tangible medium of expression.* For example, the decision that read-only memory (ROM) chips could be copyrighted depended on convincing a judge that the semiconductor memory was indeed a tangible medium of expression.

Copyright law seems generally to be expanding to cover more and more items that were not previously considered subject to copyright. The "look and feel" computer interface cases, such as the recent *Lotus v. Paperback Software* (740 F. Supp. 37, D. Mass. 1990) decision and the ongoing *Apple v. Microsoft* case, are currently testing further expansion.

Chapter 6

Hybrid Vigor

> *The mating of individuals of totally unrelated strains, termed* out-breeding, *frequently leads to offspring that are much better adapted for survival than either parent, a phenomenon termed* hybrid vigor.

> — From an introductory biology textbook [Vil77, p. 675]

In this chapter I argue that for certain tasks, the optimal system is one that combines the best features of two AI paradigms. The two paradigms are not mainstream AI and connectionism (though these categories often coincide with the two paradigms), but *symbolic* and *sub-symbolic* systems. As promised in chapter 3, I describe exactly what makes these two paradigms different, and then consider ways in which they can be combined into *hybrid* systems such as SCALIR.

6.1 The Transduction Model

The debate over the proper role of symbolic processing in AI can take place at many levels. From a philosophical standpoint, one may argue about whether the symbols in an AI system actually stand for anything; this is often expressed as the *symbol grounding* problem [Har87], as discussed in chapter 3. From a psychological standpoint, one may argue about whether symbolic processing is needed for cognition [FP88, New80]. In characterizing hybrid AI systems, this discussion of the symbolic/sub-symbolic dispute will be restricted to a more modest domain: computational systems. In particular, the definitions of "symbolic" and "sub-symbolic" processing to be given are simply intended to provide a basis for answering the question, "What makes this AI system symbolic (or sub-symbolic)?"

It may be argued that answering this question serves little purpose; we should just build useful systems and not worry about testing their membership in artificial categories. But in fact, the question is of interest because we would like to understand what gives an AI system various properties. Just as an architect's design may be informed by a knowledge of structural mechanics, so the AI system designer may benefit from an understanding of the attributes that make a system symbolic or sub-symbolic.

The model used for the analysis of different types of processing is based on the following observation: *All computational systems can be characterized (at some level) as transducers.* They receive input from their environment, they undergo some internal state transition over time, and they produce output. The input may be a waveform or a mouse click, discrete or continuous, but there will be something in the environment that affects the behavior of the system. Similarly, *some* behavior of the system — perhaps a portion of its internal state — will be regarded as output by its users or its environment.

6.2 Symbolic Processing

Many mainstream AI tools and techniques, such as expert systems, frames, and heuristic search are commonly characterized as "symbolic" [New80]. Given the vast differences between these systems, what is it that they have in common? In other words, what does it mean to be a symbolic system?

Most people would agree that a symbol is an arbitrary entity that stands for something else, but among philosophers, agreement would probably end there. For example, Peirce [WB45] distinguished at least 66 different kinds of signs, many of which fall under the general concept of symbols. For the purposes of characterizing symbolic AI systems, we will not need to worry about reference (the "standing for") relation. To emphasize this, the term *label* will be used to describe the tokens often called "symbols" in AI systems:

Definition 6.1 *A label is a unique identifier belonging to a previously enumerated, fixed finite set.*

Note that the "previously enumerated set" can be quite large. For example, the set of all words in a given natural language at a given time

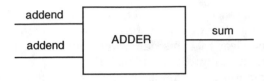

Figure 6.1: A simple adder is not symbolic.

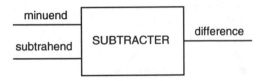

Figure 6.2: A simple subtracter *is* symbolic.

is satisfactory; the set of all arbitrary strings of 1's and 0's is not. From this definition, it is possible to characterize symbolic systems as follows:

Definition 6.2 *Symbolic systems are transducers whose next state is selectively determined by labels associated with the objects of computation.*

The "objects of computation" are the inputs and outputs and states of the system. "Selective" implies that when several state transitions are possible, the labels are used to determine what choice to make.

A small example is useful in illustrating the principle. Consider a simple abstract adding machine, shown in Figure 6.1. It works by taking the two values marked "addend" and writing their sum to the output. It is certainly a transducer; it takes two inputs and produces an output. It appears to have labels; the string "addend" is associated with each of its inputs. However, it is not symbolic in the sense defined above. The next state of the machine doesn't depend on the labels.

Now consider the abstract subtracter in Figure 6.2. It works by taking the value marked "subtrahend," subtracting it from the value marked "minuend," and writing the result to the output. This is also a transducer and also has labels. The subtracter, though, is also symbolic because the labels determine its state or action. It makes a big difference which value has which label.

Note that labels do not have to bear any meaning to a human observer; they could be "argument1" and "argument2" or "x" and "y." Furthermore, it isn't just that the input or output *channels* have labels; it is the data itself that is tagged. If subtraction required several time

125

steps to perform, each value would carry the appropriate label in the computation long after the input stimulus was removed.

It should be clear that this definition applies to typical AI systems, not just to certain arithmetic machines. For example, any system based on logic programming is symbolic because the state depends selectively on labels (variables) previously assigned to various inputs. Similarly, a production system is inherently symbolic.

This definition also makes clear what is symbolic about a semantic network. Links as well as nodes in the network are labeled, and the "activation" that spreads is itself typically a discrete marker whose label affects its treatment. The decision to pass or not pass a marker depends solely on the links' labels.[1] For example, many semantic networks allow marker propagation through IS-A links in only one direction, but bi-directional propagation through links with other labels.

The restriction that labels must be drawn from a finite set does not prevent learning; it affects the ways in which data are processed, not the data themselves. For example, it is permissible to add nodes to a semantic network, but not to add new types of links whose operation was not previously specified.

6.3   Sub-Symbolic Processing

The resurgence of interest in neurally inspired models of intelligence has raised the possibility of systems that are *not* symbolic. Furthermore, there is a notion that there is a level of processing *below* the symbolic level. Beyond this there is little agreement. Some authors, such as Hofstadter [Hof79, Hof82], stress the interaction of the two levels. Others — often opponents of connectionism such as Fodor [FP88] and Simon [Sim81] — consider any processing below the level of symbols to be a mere implementation detail, of no interest in understanding cognition.

Despite their differences on the significance of nonsymbolic systems, many researchers would agree that in practice these systems employ unstructured statistical inference on graded, continuous representations. Note that these attributes do not necessarily preclude the existence of symbolic processing; the concepts of *symbolic* and *sub-symbolic* presented are not mutually exclusive. This indicates a problem with the terminology, rather than a conceptual paradox; it is the reason I have referred to these systems elsewhere as "associative" [Ros90]. However, I have

---

[1] Hendler characterizes semantic networks that do not do this as "dumb" marker-passers in which "the links being traversed have little or no effect on the algorithm [Hen89a]. I believe there are very few in which the links really have *no* effect.

chosen here to stay with the sub-symbolic terminology suggested by Smolensky [Smo88], despite its problems, because it is familiar to most AI researchers.

As with symbolic systems, many researchers seem to know a sub-symbolic system when they see one, yet most definitions of sub-symbolic processing that have been offered are untestable. These definitions appeal to further notions like *subsymbols*, *microfeatures*, and *subcognition*, which, though conceptually useful, do not identify the *computational* properties that make a system sub-symbolic. For example, Smolensky gives the following "sub-symbolic hypothesis":

> The intuitive processor is a subconceptual connectionist dynamical system that does not admit a complete, formal, and precise conceptual-level description. [Smo88]

Another difficulty is that many of the descriptions, like this one, treat connectionism and sub-symbolic processing as interchangeable concepts. Although most connectionist models are paradigmatic examples of sub-symbolic systems, there are others as well, such as Holland's Genetic Algorithm [Gol89, Hol75]. These problems have motivated the characterization of sub-symbolic systems that follow.

In order to characterize the computational properties of sub-symbolic systems, two preliminary definitions are needed:

Definition 6.3 *A class C in a system S is **interchangeable** if and only if all functions allowed by S which operate on elements of C (whose domains are C^n for any integer n)*

- *map only to range C (i.e., $C^n \mapsto C$), and*

- *are infinitely many-to-one (i.e., the inverse image of any point in the range is an infinite set).*

The first condition insures that the functions can be composed indefinitely. The second condition allows this to be done in an unlimited number of ways.

An example serves to clarify the definition. The numbers in an idealized three-function calculator (one with infinite precision) are interchangeable. The only functions allowed by the system $(+,-,\times)$ each map $\mathcal{R}^n \mapsto \mathcal{R}$ — that is, the sum, difference, or product of any number of real numbers is always a real number — so the first condition is satisfied. Further, there are an infinite number of possible arguments to each function that produce any given result (e.g., if f is subtraction, and we want $f(x,y) = 2.5$, we can have $x = 5.0$ and $y = 2.5$, or $x = 1.25$ and

$y = -1.25$, and so on ad infinitum). Thus the second condition is met, and the numbers are interchangeable.

Interchangeability implies information loss. Any computation using a member x of such a class will proceed identically to its next state regardless of which of the infinitely many possibilities which map to x were used to get to the current state, hence the name "interchangeable."

Note that interchangeability is a characteristic of entities with respect to a system supporting a set of functions. It is the set of functions together with the type of the entities that makes the entities interchangeable. Real numbers are not inherently interchangeable, but they are in the hypothetical three-function calculator.[2]

Definition 6.4 *A class of parameterized functions is* **data-modulated** *if the values of the parameters are determined by characteristics of the specific examples of data to which the functions will be applied (as opposed to general properties of the computational mechanism or of the space from which the data are drawn).*

The setting of parameters is assumed to be a relatively infrequent operation that occurs only prior to or between evaluation of the functions.

Again, an example is illustrative of the concept. Consider a procedure which is given a sorted list and an item, and returns the position of the item. The algorithm used is: choose an item in the current list, and check to see if that is the item sought. If not, then repeat the procedure on the part of the list to the "left" or "right," depending on whether the sought item is smaller or larger than the chosen item.

The item can be chosen by any of a class of functions whose input is the list and whose parameter indicates how far down the list to choose the item. If we know nothing about the data, then we should set the parameter to $1/2$ (i.e., we'll look at the item halfway down the current list). If we know that the data are always four-digit integers, we can be smarter and look $n/10$ of the way down the list, where n is the first digit of the item being sought. In neither of these cases are the functions data-modulated, however. We have not set the parameter based on observing any actual data; we have used only general properties of the system and the data space to make this decision.

Now suppose we get to observe some actual lists, or better yet, some lists and some items sought. We might observe that, for instance, there are generally twice as many numbers beginning with higher digits than lower digits, yet this pattern does not hold for items sought. In this case,

---

[2]If this distinction isn't clear, try adding the quotient function to the calculator; the numbers are no longer interchangeable, because division by zero does not map to a real number.

the smart thing to do is to set the parameter to 1/3. This, finally, is an example of a data-modulated function.

These two definitions form the core of what it means to be subsymbolic:

Definition 6.5 *Sub-symbolic systems are those in which the function(s) for mapping from input(s) to output(s)*

- *operates on interchangeable, continuous quantities, and*

- *is data-modulated by continuous parameters.*

Connectionist networks are fundamentally sub-symbolic; the interchangeable quantities are generally called "activations" and the modulating parameters are called "weights." However, this definition encompasses other models such as the Classifier system [HHNT86], where message "intensity" is the quantity and classifier "strength" the modulating parameter.

There are two important attributes commonly associated with connectionist systems which are not present in Definition 6.5: *learning* and *distributed representation*.

6.3.1 Learning as Data-Modulation

Many sub-symbolic systems are adaptive; they learn to perform their task, or to improve their performance, through experience. This experience may occur in an actual use setting or it may be a special "training" phase. One virtue of sub-symbolic systems, and a common argument for their use, is their ability to learn. However, learning is not a condition for being a sub-symbolic system.

This should be evident from the fact that two of the best known connectionist (and sub-symbolic) models, Hopfield networks and interactive activation networks, do not have learning mechanisms. In a typical application of a Hopfield net [TH87], the weights are determined algorithmically. In McClelland and Rumelhart's model [MR81, RM82], the weights are set "by hand" in order to model certain empirical phenomena.

How is it that these systems can be sub-symbolic connectionist systems — have their knowledge "in the weights" — if they must be (knowledge-)engineered by hand, like rules in an expert system? The answer is that their weights are data-modulated; the Hopfield approach to the traveling salesperson problem, for example, sets the weights in accordance with the distances between specific cities in a specific problem. In other words, data-modulation subsumes learning.

In Section 6.2 we saw why semantic networks are symbolic systems. Now we can see why they are not sub-symbolic: they have no data-modulated functions. Even semantic nets with "weights" on the links (used to attenuate activation spread) and real-valued activations are not sub-symbolic, because the weights do not depend on the data.

6.3.2 The Localist/Distributed Controversy

One important feature of many connectionist systems is their use of *distributed* representations. Hinton et al. describe distributed representations as those in which "each entity is represented by a pattern of activity distributed over many computing elements, and each computing element is involved in representing many different entities" [HMR86, p. 77]. Distributed representations are contrasted with *localist* representations, in which there is a one-to-one correspondence between the elements doing the representing and those being represented.

In a typical localist system, specific features of the domain items are represented by specific components of the system. For example, a handwriting-recognition system network might have a single unit for each letter of the alphabet. In a distributed system, the units represent "microfeatures" which may play a role in several features or symbols simultaneously.

Although distributed representations play a significant role in the robustness of many connectionist systems, they are not a condition for sub-symbolic processing. This is due to the fact that *distribution is a relative concept*. Just as the handwriting net's feature (a letter) may be a story-understander's microfeature, one system's localist representation is another's distributed representation.

Suppose we wish to use alphabetic characters as input to a connectionist net. One approach is to use a localist representation — one unit per letter — as shown in Figure 6.3. Alternatively, we could use the more concise distributed representation in Figure 6.4. Because there are more than seven letters in the alphabet, each unit will have to play a part in representing more than one letter. In other words, the value at each unit is a microfeature of a letter. Unit 5, for example, is active both for the letters **D** and **N**, among others.

Finally, consider the coding scheme shown in Table 6.1. This is the familiar ASCII table, used to encode characters on most computers. Different bits in the code have different meanings, representing features of the characters such as case and printability. (Although ASCII does not use localist features for encoding case-insensitive alphabetic characters, one can imagine many schemes that would. For example, there might

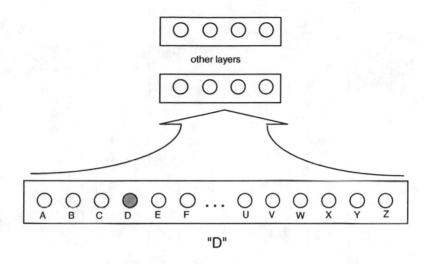

Figure 6.3: A localist representation for alphabetic characters, here indicating the letter **D**.

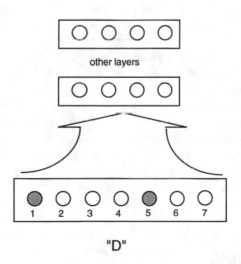

Figure 6.4: A distributed representation of the letter **D**.

		Bit 6→	0	0	0	0	1	1	1	1
		Bit 5→	0	0	1	1	0	0	1	1
		Bit 4→	0	1	0	1	0	1	0	1
Bit 3	Bit 2	Bit 1	Bit 0								
0	0	0	0	NUL	DLE	SP	0	@	P	'	p
0	0	0	1	SOH	DC1	!	1	A	Q	a	q
0	0	1	0	STX	DC2	"	2	B	R	b	r
0	0	1	1	ETX	DC3	#	3	C	S	c	s
0	1	0	0	EOT	DC4	$	4	D	T	d	t
0	1	0	1	ENQ	NAK	%	5	E	U	e	u
0	1	1	0	ACK	SYN	&	6	F	V	f	v
0	1	1	1	BEL	ETB	'	7	G	W	g	w
1	0	0	0	BS	CAN	(	8	H	X	h	x
1	0	0	1	HT	EM	)	9	I	Y	i	y
1	0	1	0	LF	SUB	*	:	J	Z	j	z
1	0	1	1	VT	ESC	+	;	K	[	k	{
1	1	0	0	FF	FS	,	<	L	\	l	|
1	1	0	1	CR	GS	-	=	M	]	m	}
1	1	1	0	SO	RS	.	>	N	^	n	~
1	1	1	1	SI	US	/	?	O	_	o	DEL

Table 6.1: ASCII: Distributed or Localist?

be a vowel/consonant unit.) Yet this is precisely the "distributed" representation used in Figure 6.4. Thus depending on one's perspective, the same encoding scheme is both distributed and localist.

Van Gelder [vG89] argued that the essential property of distribution is superposition[3], and that this notion (formally defined) is not subjective. One way he explains this is with the concept of a *distributing transformation*, which is a mapping from a content description function Γ to a representation description function Φ. Roughly speaking, a *strong* distributing transformation is one in which *any* part of the representation depends on *every* part of the contents being represented; a Fourier transform is one example. A *weak* distributing transformation is one in which any part of the representation depends on at least *some* part of the contents being represented; a linear associator is such a transformation.

But Van Gelder's concept of a *distributing transformation*, rigorously applied, would classify as distributing a transformation (e.g., a weight matrix) in which all entries are zero except one for each pattern. (Van Gelder [personal communication, 1989] referred to this as a "not very in-

---

[3]Indeed, he argued that the "Connectionist's Credo" (the Hinton definition given earlier) fails to define distribution.

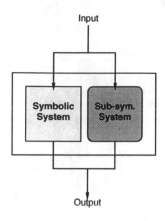

Input

Symbolic
System

Sub-sym.
System

Output

Figure 6.5: A degenerate case of a hybrid system.

teresting" weak distributing transformation.) This is technically correct; the resulting representation of any pattern would after all be different if any of the zeroes were changed. But this means that an identity matrix (1's on the diagonal, 0's everywhere else) is also a distributing transformation, and that the one-bit-per-letter encoding of the alphabet in Figure 6.3 could be a distributed representation if it were simply run through this matrix first.

6.4 Types of Hybrid Systems

Given these definitions of symbolic and sub-symbolic processing, the concept of a hybrid system results naturally:

Definition 6.6 *A* **hybrid system** *is a system in which the mapping from inputs to outputs results from both symbolic and sub-symbolic processing.*

Thus a hybrid system will rely on selective response to labels, use of interchangeable quantities, and data-modulated functions. Clearly there are many ways to achieve this. A degenerate case of a hybrid system would be a connectionist network and an expert system put "side-by-side" in the same box, each doing something different with its portion of the same input and producing its respective part of the box's output. This is illustrated in Figure 6.5.

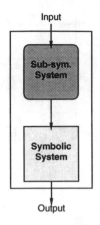

Figure 6.6: A loosely coupled hybrid system.

To distinguish between this rather uninteresting case and more powerful notions of hybrid systems, we introduce the notion of *coupling*. The coupling of a hybrid system is the degree to which the symbolic and the sub-symbolic mechanisms interact. In a *loosely coupled* system, each component (the symbolic and the sub-symbolic processors) can operate independently, though the result requires both parts. Loose coupling does not imply weakness, though the degenerate example given is certainly loosely coupled. A common useful form of loose coupling occurs when a problem requires a cascaded solution in which, for example, the outputs of a connectionist network are used as input for a semantic network, or vice versa. This is shown in Figure 6.6. Hendler's "marker passing over microfeatures" [Hen89c] is an example of such a system, as is Lange's ROBIN [LD89].

More complex is the *tightly coupled* hybrid system, in which the components interact and "pool their information" before the final output is produced. Figure 6.7 shows a conceptual view of tight coupling. In a tightly coupled system, each component will not produce the desired result unless the other component is active. A simple example is a system in which the outputs of a connectionist network activate a semantic network, which in turn activates the connectionist network, and so on. The subsystems may communicate in this iterated fashion, or via a blackboard or other medium, but in each case the end result could not have been obtained by "precomputing" the actions of either component.

134

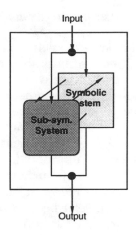

Figure 6.7: A tightly coupled hybrid system.

In the extreme case of a tightly coupled hybrid system, the components operate on the same objects of computation. This is the case in SCALIR; the semantic network and the connectionist network share the same nodes and represent activity using the same data structures. This is also the case in Shastri's variable-binding system [SA90], which uses a wave metaphor in which phase encodes "symbolic" information and amplitude encodes "sub-symbolic" activity.

6.5 The Symbolic/Sub-Symbolic Continuum

It is clear that computational systems may have characteristics of symbolic or sub-symbolic processing, or both. Each approach has its advantages, as will be discussed in Section 6.9. Before examining these, however, it is useful to examine the boundaries of the two paradigms, which form a continuum. We can gradually relax constraints on either side to get a system that lies somewhere in the middle.

A good place to examine the landscape of this continuum is the space between semantic and connectionist networks. It is clear from the definitions that semantic networks fall squarely into the realm of symbolic systems. They respond selectively to labels, and generally do not use continuous objects of computation. But what happens when we begin to add more "connectionist" attributes to a semantic network? Hendler discussed many of these techniques [Hen87, Hen89a], designed to im-

135

prove the performance of marker-passing systems. Does the system take on "sub-symbolic" properties?

A common problem with semantic networks is the exponential fan-out of marked nodes, which may result in markers being passed to the entire network. Suppose a semantic network designer wishes to avoid this problem, preventing too much of the network from being marked each time. We can imagine passing a number along with the marker. This number could be a counter for measuring path length. It could be incremented each time a link was traversed, and then used to terminate the search when it reached a certain threshold.

Now, for computational simplicity, imagine that each node decrements this counter, rather than incrementing it, and stops if the value reaches zero. This way the parameter becomes easily tunable; the programmer can change the desired path length of searches by starting the initially marked nodes with various quantities in the counters.

Suppose that too many nodes are still being marked. The programmer might want to introduce a penalty for fan-out as well as path length. Each time markers leave a node, their counters can be set to the incoming marker's counter divided by the out-degree of the node. (This technique was proposed by Hendler [Hen87].)

One last modification: Subtraction is too crude a control for path length; its effect is not proportional to the current magnitude of the counter. Instead of subtraction, we will multiply each counter by a value slightly less than one as it traverses a link. As an implementation detail to prevent roundoff errors, we will replace the integer counter with a real-valued one, and use real arithmetic for all our multiplications and divisions.

Clearly, this new system is closer to the center of the continuum than its predecessors. Yet even calling the counters "activations" and the product of the divisors and the multipliers "weights," this system does not meet the requirements for sub-symbolic processing. The "weights" bear no relationship to the data; there is no knowledge in them. The currency of the system, markers, are not interchangeable, because the system responds selectively to them depending on the link labels. Symbolic inference remains the fundamental processing operation.

Now suppose we started at the other extreme, with a feedforward connectionist net, a prime example of a sub-symbolic system. Again moving toward the center of the continuum, we could modify the system so that each node in the input gets different kinds of activation — colored blue or yellow, perhaps. All computation is done in some standard connectionist fashion, except that active nodes become tagged with the color of their activation: blue, yellow, or green (where the colors have mixed). We read off the output in the normal way, except for the following proviso: only green-tagged output nodes are considered active; all other output nodes are treated as having zero activity.

This system appears to have moved sufficiently far toward the center that it may be considered a tightly coupled hybrid system. It still meets the conditions for sub-symbolic systems; its weights are either learned or constructed to produce a certain mapping on the data, using interchangeable activation. But it also meets the conditions for symbolic processing; the mapping from input to output depends on a selective response to labels.

A third case is a system which lies at the boundary of the two approaches, but has the benefits of neither one. The system can be characterized in two ways. It is a semantic network in which there is only one kind of link (IS-A), and only one kind of marker. Alternatively, it is a connectionist network in which all nodes are localist and labeled, and all weights have the value one. Because there is only one type of link and marker, there can be no selective response on the basis of labels and the system therefore can do no useful symbolic processing. Because all weights are equal and independent of the data, the network cannot do meaningful sub-symbolic processing.

To summarize, it is clear that symbolic and sub-symbolic processing are not absolutes but rather two sides of a continuous space, as shown in Figure 6.8. Yet there are many paths connecting the two extremes. The ones which result from weakening the constraints of each approach until the two sources are indistinguishable turn out to be uninteresting. In contrast, the ones which result from combining properties of the other approach produce hybrid systems.

6.6 Motivation for Hybrid Approaches

In addition to the different computational properties outlined earlier in the chapter, the symbolic/sub-symbolic dichotomy is often described in terms of two views of cognition; Table 6.2 shows an informal characterization of the two views. Recently, many have suggested that both views are helpful in understanding cognition. As Norman explains:

> People interpret the world rapidly, effortlessly. But the development of new ideas, or evaluation of current thoughts proceeds slowly, serially, deliberately. People do seem to have at least two modes of operation, one rapid, efficient, subconscious, the other slow, serial, and conscious. [Nor86, p. 542]

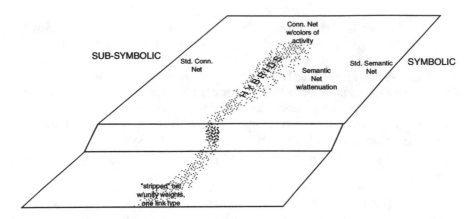

Figure 6.8: The space of symbolic and sub-symbolic systems. The "upper level" corresponds to useful systems, the lower level to nonuseful systems.

	SYMBOLIC	SUB-SYMBOLIC
AI Approach	Traditional	Connectionist
Inference	Rule-based	Statistical
Processing	Sequential	Parallel
Speed in brain	Slow (> 100ms)	Fast (< 100ms)
Robustness	Brittle	Graceful degradation
Precision	High	Low
Representation	Features	Microfeatures

Table 6.2: Comparison of two paradigms.

Because these two levels both have important roles to play, it is useful (at least for the present) to design hybrid systems which take advantage of techniques designed for both levels. (Similar arguments have been made by other proponents of hybrid systems [DP86, Dye91, Hen89b, Hen89c].)

Smolensky [Smo88] also mentions the possibility of systems which "involve both intuition and conscious rule interpretation" using hybrid mechanisms. However, he raises several doubts about the feasibility of such a project:

> How would the two formalisms communicate? How would the hybrid system evolve with experience, reflecting the development of intuition and the subsequent remission of conscious rule application? How would the hybrid system elucidate the fallibility of actual human rule application (e.g., logic)? How

Advantages for Sub-Symbolic Processing
Combining evidence
Graceful degradation
Adaptation
Magnitude information
Advantages for Symbolic Processing
Symbolic characteristics of problem
Task involving artifacts
A priori knowledge
Efficiency

Table 6.3: Situations favoring the use of sub-symbolic and symbolic systems.

> would the hybrid system get us closer to understanding how conscious rule application is achieved neurally?

Similar questions can be raised about a symbolic/sub-symbolic hybrid. Furthermore, SCALIR provides at least one possible answer to each of the first two questions.

These high-level cognitive analyses suggest why one might consider hybrid systems useful in general. For a specific task, one might believe that hybrid approaches offer "the best of both worlds." However, this ignores the added costs that the complexity of a hybrid system incurs. It is important to consider specific aspects of the problem domain and of the system goals; together these factors may determine whether a hybrid is appropriate. Table 6.3 suggests situations in which one approach or the other has an advantage. First, reasons to include sub-symbolic processing:

Combining Evidence. When decisions in a system should be made by a gradual accumulation of evidence from many sources, a sub-symbolic component is especially useful. In SCALIR, the relevance of a case to a query is such a judgment; it is not an all-or-nothing decision as could be expressed in a rule.

Graceful Degradation. Many symbolic systems are brittle; they break quickly when they reach the edges of their capabilities. Sub-symbolic processing, by virtue of its continuous representations, exhibits graceful degradation. The user can even be notified of the increased unreliability of the data; SCALIR does this by presenting less relevant cases farther from the center of its display.[4]

---

[4]This is described further in chapter 10.

139

Adaptation. There are many tasks that fall in the realm of symbolic processing, but also require adaptation, whether to different users, environments, or whatever. However, learning in many symbolic systems generally involves developing or modifying a concept expressed as a Boolean combination of predetermined features. Mitchell's version space algorithm [Mit77] and Winston's ARCH program [Win75] are two of the more elegant (and classic) examples of this approach. This is unsatisfactory when one doesn't know what the relevant features are. A subsymbolic component provides a mechanism for gradual, experimental adaptation during use. In SCALIR, for example, associations between documents and terms can be created, strengthened, or weakened, based on the browsing behavior of its users.

Magnitude Information. Symbolic approaches often rely on concepts of set membership and partial ordering, but do not explicitly use magnitudes (consider, e.g., Mitchell's algorithm [Mit77] or Valiant's learning model [Val84]). However, in many instances, magnitudes convey additional useful information. For example, in information retrieval, it is important to know not just that a document had the highest retrieval score, but what that value was and how it compares to others [vR79]. Was this merely the best of a bad lot? Is it nearly indistinguishable from the second-ranked document? Sub-symbolic systems preserve magnitude information, and thus can address these questions.

Second, reasons to include symbolic processing:

Symbolic Characteristics of the Problem. Some problem domains, such as symbolic integration, inherently involve the use of discrete representations. In the law, there are many such representations, such as the hierarchical taxonomy of the law formed by West Publishing's key numbers used to index cases. A symbolic component in a legal research system allows us to take advantage of the constraints provided by the existing representation.

Task Involving Artifacts. Humans solve many problems through the use of cognitive artifacts, artificial devices (such as an airline pilot's checklist) that enhance cognitive abilities [Nor91]. If we want a computer system to interact with humans and assist them at existing tasks, that system should be able to use our artifacts. For example, we use a certain notation for writing music which normally supports the representation of 12 distinct tones. Even though the frequency of sound waves is not inherently quantized or "symbolic," a computer-based music composition system would do well to accept and present the conventional notation. Many artifacts are used by lawyers to solve the legal research problem. For example, *Shepard's Citations* (described in chapter 5) lists not only what cases cited a case in question, but in what way — such as criticized, questioned, etc. Furthermore, the labels drawn from Shepard's standardized set have taken on the status of "reserved words," conveying meanings beyond (and often different from) their natural-language counterparts.

A Priori Knowledge. One of the primary virtues of sub-symbolic systems is their ability to learn by experience. However, if the system designer has a priori knowledge of the domain, this type of inductive learning may be inappropriate. First, the task may not be well-suited to inductive learning. For example, in his connectionist model of beam-balance physics, McClelland suggests that the highest level of understanding — using the concept of torque to predict which way the beam will fall — cannot be learned from examples and requires explicitly transferring knowledge [McC89]. Second, many learning algorithms are often designed to extract previously unknown regularities from their environment. Thus the representations they develop may not be comprehensible to their users [BF88]. Finally (as we saw in chapter 3), if the relevant features are already known (as is the case with the Shepard citations mentioned earlier), it makes little sense to train an sub-symbolic representation when these relationships could be explicitly embedded in the architecture.

Efficiency. Sub-symbolic systems have had difficulty scaling up to large problems. In some cases, there may be computationally efficient ways to symbolically solve certain sub-parts of the problem. Also, simply decomposing the problem may reduce the overall complexity. (This has also been a factor in the growing use of modular connectionist systems such as the Meta-Pi network [HW90].) The information retrieval domain involves large databases; for example, SCALIR contains over 17,000 nodes just to represent approximately 4,000 documents. Although the system's rules for propagating activity and for learning *could* be implemented by a pure sub-symbolic system, it would require an order of magnitude more links, which would render it impractical for real-time use.

6.7 Problems with Hybrids

Hybrid systems face two problems not found, or found to a lesser extent, in their single-paradigm counterparts. First, the symbolic and sub-symbolic components in a hybrid system must be able to communicate. Second, if learning is to be supported, credit must somehow be assigned to each component.

The communication problem arises because the two paradigms use different representations. In most connectionist implementations of the sub-symbolic paradigm, the state of the system is contained in the real-valued activations of the units, whereas the long-term knowledge is embodied in the connection strengths, which can be expressed as a weight matrix. In contrast, state information in a symbolic system is contained in the positions and labels of a discrete set of tokens, such as the database of a production system or the markers in a semantic network. Long-term knowledge is represented as a set of static structures such as the production system rule base or the IS-A and other labeled links of the semantic net.

One solution to the communication problem is to subdivide the problem, delegating one set of tasks to each component. This would be an example of a loosely coupled system, as defined in Section 6.4. This approach might be appropriate for certain tasks, but it restricts the effectiveness of the hybrid; the components cannot benefit from each other's information when solving their individual tasks.

An alternative is to convert the representations of each component into a common language, or simply use one of the original representations for this purpose, reducing the amount of translation required. A variant of this is for each representation to operate on different aspects of the same medium. For example, Shastri's variable-binding network [SA90] mentioned earlier uses two properties of waves — phase and amplitude — to represent symbolic labels and sub-symbolic activation, respectively. Similarly, SCALIR uses amplitude for activity and vector dimension (viewed conceptually as *color*) for labels.

The credit assignment problem has haunted machine learning systems for many years: how to determine which part of the program should be rewarded (punished) when positive (negative) feedback is supplied. If a game-playing program loses, what parameters should be changed? Which ones were responsible for the loss? The problem can be largely solved by using a homogeneous representation and adjusting all "learning parameters" with a single mechanism. This is exactly the approach used in most connectionist systems; the learning parameters are link weights, and the single mechanism is a learning rule such as back-propagation. Thus each unit of the system can be modified in proportion to its contribution to the result. Homogeneous representations have also been used to facilitate learning in symbolic systems such as SOAR [LNR87].

However, hybrid systems are heterogeneous by definition. In addition to determining, for example, how much to change each weight in the connectionist network, one may need to know how much — or whether — that sub-symbolic representation played a role in that particular result, relative to the symbolic component. There are several possible approaches to this problem. The simplest is to restrict learning to only the sub-symbolic system. A more powerful but more complex approach is to train the individual components separately, fix their parameters, and then train the combination together. This is similar to the technique used on some modular networks. Unfortunately, it does not work in real-time learning domains such as SCALIR's. Finally, the systems can attempt to learn simultaneously. Though there is a risk of instability, the system can be damped by making the learning parameters from both components "compete" for the same resources. As chapter 9 explains, it is essentially this approach that SCALIR uses to assign credit to its connectionist and semantic networks.

6.8   SCALIR as a Hybrid System

According to the definitions of Sections 6.2, 6.3, and 6.4, SCALIR seems to qualify as a hybrid system. We now consider possible objections to this hybrid status. If SCALIR fails to qualify as either a symbolic or a sub-symbolic system, it cannot claim to be a hybrid. This section addresses these possibilities more closely. Alternatively, one might acknowledge SCALIR's hybrid status, but discount any advantages this might confer. This argument is discussed in the Section 6.9.

6.8.1   SCALIR as a Sub-Symbolic System

A challenge to SCALIR's sub-symbolic status would essentially say that even the connectionist component of SCALIR is really doing symbol manipulation. There are four grounds for this claim, each stronger than the previous ones.

Digital Computer as Symbol-Manipulator. The first point is that because SCALIR is written in a symbol-oriented language (Lisp) on a digital computer, it cannot claim to be doing *true* sub-symbolic processing.

This is an extremely weak objection (included here only for completeness). It applies, of course, to nearly all connectionist systems, which are designed with parallel connectionist hardware in mind. Even if the objection were valid, it would really apply only to *simulators* of the systems in question. A second issue is that the presence of symbol-manipulating abilities in a computer language — at least, any language that supports real arithmetic — do not preclude the construction of systems with continuous interchangeable entities. A last ditch attempt to salvage this objection might be to point out that digital computers are "fundamentally" discrete. Of course, this, too, is rejected by the fact that the transistors which constitute them are "fundamentally" analog, but that is missing the point. The entire objection is based on a misunderstanding of the levels of modeling. There is always an implementation level below the level of interest. An advocate of the physical symbol system hypothesis can acknowledge that sub-symbolic processing may exist at a lower, uninteresting level. Similarly, there is no incompatibility between the sub-symbolic nature of SCALIR's connectionist network and the symbol-manipulation that implements the program.

Lack of Hidden Units. The second point concerns the accessibility of all of SCALIR's units. If every node can be used for input or output, then SCALIR has no hidden units. Without hidden units, there is no way for SCALIR to develop internal sub-symbolic representations not anticipated by the programmer.

This argument presupposes a certain network architecture that SCALIR does not have. In networks with hidden units, such as layered feed-forward nets or Boltzmann machines, these units are not accessible from the environment in any way. In that sense, it is true that SCALIR has no hidden units. However, input units and output units in these other systems are manipulated and examined every time the network is used. In SCALIR, only a fraction of the network is activated by a query as input, and only a fraction becomes active as output. For the purposes of that query, all the remaining nodes in the network can serve as hidden units whose patterns of activity form a sub-symbolic representation. Furthermore, even if SCALIR had no way to represent "hidden" activity, this would not disqualify it as a sub-symbolic systems. Hidden units have added to the power of connectionist systems, but they are not required for sub-symbolic processing, as a Hopfield network demonstrates.

Localist Representation. The third point centers on the existence of a one-to-one correspondence between SCALIR's nodes and the objects it is representing (terms, cases, and statutes), as evidenced by the presence of labels. These are semantically meaningful concepts; a human observer can examine the system and tell what it is doing. Thus, the claim goes, there is nothing "sub-symbolic" going on. (Note that this is an indictment of all localist connectionist systems, not just SCALIR.)

This argument is based in part on the assumption that distributed representations are needed for sub-symbolic processing. This is incorrect for several reasons. As we have seen in Section 6.3.2, distribution is a relative concept. If SCALIR's cases are features of the law, then its terms are microfeatures. The fact that we can attach meaning to a term does not lessen its role as a microfeature of the law. Further, even if distributed representation were incompatible with symbolic processing (as van Gelder claims [vG89]), that does not imply that localist representation is incompatible with sub-symbolic processing. For this to be true "sub-symbolic" and "symbolic" processing would have to be mutually exclusive and absolute concepts, which (as Section 6.5 demonstrates) they need not be.[5]

The argument ultimately rests on the misapprehension that the presence of labels implies the absence of sub-symbolic processing. This is not the case, as Fodor and Pylyshyn explain:

> Strictly speaking, the labels play *no role at all* in determining the operation of the Connectionist machine; in particular, the operation of the machine is unaffected by the syntactic and semantic relations that hold among the expressions that are used as labels. To put this another way, the node labels in a Connectionist machine are not part of the causal structure of the machine. [FP88]

SCALIR's connectionist component, like the machine described above, ignores the node labels completely. If the labels were removed or scrambled, processing in the network would proceed exactly as before.

6.8.2 SCALIR as a Symbolic System

An argument against SCALIR's symbolic nature is simpler. Basically, it says that SCALIR uses "connectionist representations" — real-valued activities and weights on links — even in its symbolic component. It is true that all links are weighted, and that activation is the *lingua franca* used for communication between the subsystems. However, the processing of the symbolic component depends on matching the "colors" of activation (explained further in chapter 8) with labels on links. This is the "selective determination" of Definition 6.2. Again, the analysis of Fodor and Pylyshyn explains the distinction:

> ... [T]he state transitions of Classical [symbolic] machines are causally determined by *the structure ... of the symbol arrays that the machines transform*: change the symbols and the system behaves quite differently.

In SCALIR, the symbols being transformed are the symbolic components of activation at each node, and it is the symbolic links, by their filtering ability, that do the transformations.

---

[5]Of course, the validity of this statement, like those concerning localist and distributed systems, depends on one's definitions.

6.9   Avoiding One-Paradigm Reductionism

The last section has illustrated how SCALIR qualifies as a hybrid of symbolic and sub-symbolic mechanisms; whether hybrids are desirable is a
separate question.   One might argue that SCALIR's connectionist network, for example, can and should be replaced with a semantic network,
or alternatively that the system's semantic network should be replaced
with a connectionist network trained to emulate it.

These arguments are based on what might be called *one-paradigm re-
ductionism*, the belief that all AI systems can and should be reduced to
a single paradigm.   An ongoing area of connectionist research seems to
be focused on precisely this program: how to get a connectionist network to emulate various capabilities associated with symbolic systems.
This has led to connectionist expert systems [Gal88], production systems
[DS89, TH88], recursive structures [Elm89, Pol90, Smo90, Tou90], semantic networks [BM88], and connectionist and other sub-symbolic frame
systems [BF88, Der90].   Similarly, there has long been interest in adding
attributes such as graded combinations of evidence to symbolic AI systems (as in MYCIN [DBS77]); these might be viewed in retrospect as
attempts to capture some sub-symbolic properties in symbolic systems.

In a hybrid system, then, it *is* often possible to replace the symbolic
component (for example) with a sub-symbolic one trained to reproduce
the symbolic behavior.   Some may view this as an inherently desirable
substitution, because the resulting system is more uniform, easier to analyze, and — by some measures — simpler.   The challenge to the hybrid system designer, then, is to determine if and when this substitution
should be carried out.

If the designer of the system is engaged in engineering — that is,
an attempt to design the best solution for a particular problem — then
arguments based on "purity" or "plausibility" carry no weight.   If the
most effective system is a hybrid (because certain computations can be
performed more efficiently, for example), then there is no reason to try
to replace the symbolic mechanisms with sub-symbolic ones.

However, suppose the designer of the system is engaged in science,
attempting to investigate (but not necessarily model) certain phenomena.
Simplicity of explanation may indeed be a consideration, but which approach — hybrid or single-paradigm — provides this simplicity depends
on the phenomenon being studied.   The hybrid may still be appropriate if some of the other conditions from Section 6.6 obtain.   There may
for example be explicit constraints on the problem which must be represented; embedding these in an underlying sub-symbolic representation
may confound the analysis of the system.

Finally, one may be interested in a specific modeling task, in which the components of the connectionist system are meant to stand for components or groups of components in the actual system exhibiting emergent behavior and possessing no explicit symbol-manipulation capabilities. (Although the elements of the system being modeled are often neural, they need not be.) We would not be satisfied with a model that had an omniscient rule-based control mechanism intervening in the network's behavior. Under these circumstances, the success of the model can be established only by discarding the hybrid solution in favor of a purely connectionist approach.

The ultimate question for hybrid systems is whether the whole will be greater than the sum of its parts. As this chapter has shown, the answer is both yes and no. In one sense, any sufficiently powerful representational system can emulate the computations of another; sub-symbolic systems can be trained to duplicate the results of a hybrid. But as SCALIR demonstrates, the different strengths of the two paradigms *can* be combined effectively, resulting in a system with behavioral properties different from and better than a system constructed using only one approach.

Chapter 7

The Structure of SCALIR

Suppose one were asked to make a list of relationships between a given pair of court cases. The list might include some explicitly stated relationships, such as the fact that one of the decisions overturned the other, or cited it as controlling. It might include undeniably salient but implicit features of the cases, such as the fact that both involved, say, civil rights. The fact that the same judge wrote the two opinions might be on the list. There might be unusual but notable parallels, such as the fact that in both cases the defendant represented him or herself. Finally, it might include apparently trivial facts such as that in both cases the plaintiff was left-handed.

Some of the explicit associations can already be found in existing tools of legal research. For example, the nature of inter-case citations can be found in Shepard's Index. Similarly, digests (and in particular, the West key number system) indicate when two cases fall into the same areas of the law. It is clear how these sources could be incorporated into a legal IR system. One problem, though, is discovering and accessing the more subtle, implicit relationships — those based on what connectionists call the "microfeatures" of the cases.

Although some case relationships will certainly be irrelevant, it is hard to know in advance which ones. One case's important property characteristic might be another case's trivia. In fact, there are many subtle relationships which might be of interest to a potential legal researcher. For example, it might turn out that there was a pattern in the holdings of child-custody cases in which the judge was of the same sex as the parent awarded custody.

Ideally, a connectionist legal IR system would be able to represent all of the microfeatures of a case. In this way, unanticipated but important

149

relationships such as the one described here might emerge. However, there are several difficulties with this approach, not the least of which is that it would swamp a legal IR system with vast amounts of mostly irrelevant data. As a compromise, SCALIR represents what might be considered to be the most important microfeatures of the law: the words that occur in legal documents. Because legal statutes and cases constitute parts of the law (i.e., the texts *are* the objects of concern, rather than — as in science or medicine — being merely *about* the objects of concern), this text-based representation seems particularly appropriate.

This chapter describes the static structure of the SCALIR system: the components of the system and how they are constructed. The short-term dynamics of the system — how the actual retrieval process is implemented — is discussed in chapter 8; the long-term dynamics — that is, learning — are covered in chapter 9.

7.1   A Brief Overview

SCALIR is designed to represent and retrieve legal documents. Specifically, the prototype SCALIR system contains the full-text of approximately 4,000 documents on copyright law, including the 121 Supreme Court cases, the 1,240 Courts of Appeals cases, and the 2,625 District Court cases, as well as the 90 sections of Title 17 of the United States Code (the Copyright Act of 1976 and its amendments) and related statutes. In short, SCALIR includes all federal statutory and common law pertaining to copyrights.[1] The system is implemented on a Symbolics 3645 Lisp Machine.

The cases, statutes, and terms (words) used in them are represented as network nodes which form the substrate of the SCALIR architecture. Relationships between these objects are represented as weighted links. A quantity called "activation," is associated with each node; the activation at any given time is a function of the previous activation and the weighted sum of inputs to the node.

The fundamental postulate motivating the design of SCALIR is that *activity is proportional to relevance.* Thus it follows that a query takes the form of initializing the activity of nodes of interest to a high level, and retrieval consists of returning the most active nodes after this activity has been allowed to propagate. The implementation of this process is discussed at length in chapter 8.

---

[1]Note that it does not contain administrative law. Specifically, the regulations of the copyright office are not included.

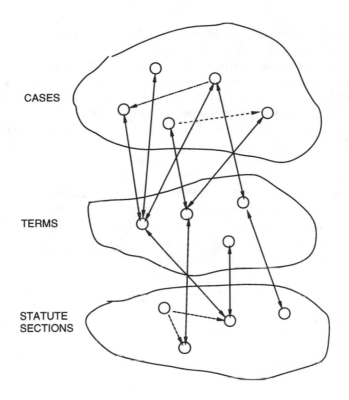

Figure 7.1: The general structure of the SCALIR network.

7.2 The Origin and Contents of SCALIR Nodes

There are three clusters of nodes in SCALIR, which roughly correspond to terms, cases, and statutes. These clusters are shown conceptually in Figure 7.1. The collection of documents (cases and statutes) was provided by West Publishing Co.; it includes all Federal cases judged by West's editors to be about Copyright Law, as of 1988. Thus the number of document nodes was fixed at the start of the SCALIR research. The terms, in contrast, were chosen automatically by a statistical analysis of the documents.

As discussed in chapter 4, research in information retrieval has led to many schemes for automatic indexing of documents. In SCALIR, the selection of index terms — that is, term nodes that are associated with documents — is based on a variant of the term frequency × inverse document frequency weighting scheme due to Salton and Buckley [SB88b].

151

Each term in the document is assigned a weight, and then the highest weighted terms are used to index the document.

The basic idea of the term weighting scheme is that two factors affect how indicative a term is of a document's content. First, there is a local factor: How often does each term occur in the document? All else being equal, the more often a word is mentioned, the more likely the document is to be about it. Second, there is a global factor: How common is the word in general? More specifically, in how many documents does the word occur? If a word occurs in every document in the corpus, then it will not be a useful index term. For example, "copyright" will not be a useful index term for any document in SCALIR's corpus, because it occurs in nearly all of them. If we want to increase the weights of a term j occurring often in a document i, the weight should be proportional to this term frequency, F_{ij}. Because we want to decrease the weights of a term j occurring in many documents, the weight should be inversely proportional to the document frequency, DF_j.

There are a few additional modifications that make the weighting scheme more useful. First, instead of using the inverse of the raw document frequency DF_j, we will use the inverse of its ratio to the total number of documents N in the corpus. Second, the expression should be normalized so that it is independent of the length of the document. This gives the following formula for the term weight TW_{ij} of term j in document i:

$$TW_{ij} = \frac{F_{ij} \times \log(N/DF_j)}{\sqrt{\sum_{k=1}^{N}(F_{ik} \times \log(N/DF_k))^2}}. \tag{7.1}$$

Note that this produces a result in the range [0,1].

In SCALIR, all documents were initially processed to determine all the unique words used in the corpus, and the number of documents in which each occurred. So-called "stop" words — non-content words such as articles and prepositions, as well as certain legal abbreviations like "S.Ct." (for the Supreme Court Reporter) were not included. Also, a very simple morphological analysis was performed to convert plural nouns to their singular forms. No other stemming was done; due to the nature of legal terminology (and statutory language in particular), it seemed inappropriate to equate terms like *originality* and *origin*, even though they have a common root. Furthermore, Belew's experience with AIR suggested that the system could learn morphological variants that proved useful.

There were 68,235 unique words used in the corpus, not counting the stop words. Table 7.1 shows some of the terms occurring in the most and the fewest documents. As a specific example, consider the term *video*.

Document Frequency	Term
3,820	court
3,793	defendant
3,774	judge
3,735	district
3,594	plaintiff
3,508	case
3,472	state
3,457	action
3,433	fact
3,422	held
⋮	⋮
1	aachen
1	aanestad
1	abailable
1	abajo
1	abandondoned
1	abarbanell
1	abard
1	abbeville
1	abbie
1	abbreviate
⋮	⋮

Table 7.1: Some terms occurring in the most and fewest documents. Obvious nonwords such as "aaabaab" have been omitted from the infrequent words; all but one of the infrequent words shown appear to be either proper names, foreign words, or misspellings.

This occurred in 150 of the 3,986 cases[2], or just under 4%. (In contrast, the word *infringement* occurred in nearly 84% of the documents.)

After the document frequency computations were completed, each document was processed again to determine the weight of each term. Terms with weights above a certain threshold were chosen to be used as index terms. The threshold was chosen empirically to identify approximately 10 terms per document.[3] Although more terms would generally make the system more powerful, the increase in connectivity would

---

[2]The 90 statute sections were not considered part of the corpus for the purpose of document frequency calculations.

[3]The network ended up with around 9.4 nodes per document. See Section 7.4 for details.

Term	Weight
vtr	0.4603
betamax	0.4149
respondent	0.2147
contributory	0.2142
congress	0.2133
sony	0.1952
recording	0.1391
access	0.1317
fair	0.1286
television	0.1284
home	0.1280
program	0.1265
use	0.1065

Table 7.2: The highest weighted terms in *Sony v. Universal*.

greatly degrade its performance. Altogether, 13,082 different terms were used to index the documents. Table 7.2 shows the highest weighted terms in one case, *Sony v. Universal*.

In addition to the nodes representing terms and documents, a few additional nodes were created for points in two treelike structures — the West key number taxonomy for copyright law, and the copyright statute. The 123 elements[4] of the West tree correspond to various topics and subtopics of copyright law; the leaves of the tree are the key numbers that are used in headnotes to classify the cases. The statute tree — unlike the cases, which have a "flat" structure — arises from the documents' division into chapters, which are further divided into sections. Nine "chapter nodes" were created, as well as an additional node representing the entire statute.[5] All of the hierarchical nodes were created semi-automatically. The structure of each tree was manually entered, and then the actual network nodes were created automatically by a program that traversed the tree. These tasks could be automated further in the future if the hierarchies were available on line.

The hierarchical structure nodes are viewed conceptually as special cases of term and statute nodes. That is, a node representing a key number topic is a kind of "metaterm," because, like ordinary terms, it

---

[4]I am avoiding the word "nodes" to avoid confusion with the nodes in the SCALIR network.

[5]This serves little purpose in the current database, but it would be useful if other statutes were available as well.

is descriptive of documents' content. Similarly, a node representing a collection of statute sections (a chapter) is clearly a "metastatute section."

In SCALIR's internal representation, nodes are represented as objects (flavors in Symbolics Common Lisp) with the following attributes:

- *System ID*. This is an integer uniquely identifying each node in a particular network. It is generated sequentially as the network is built.

- *Formal Label*. For a case or statute, this is the document's citation (e.g., "104 S.Ct. 774" for the *Sony* case mentioned above). The first number gives the volume, the abbreviation the reporter, and the second number the page on which the text of the case can be found.[6] For a term, it is simply the term itself.

- *Informal Label*. For a case, this is a listing of the litigants of the case as it appears in the text. For example, the *Sony* case is actually "Sony Corporation of America, et al. Petitioners v. Universal City Studios Inc., etc., et al." For a statute, it is the title of the section. (Term nodes do not use this component.)

- *Activity*. This is the level of activity of the node at a given time. The activity is actually stored as a list representation of a variable-length vector; this is discussed further in chapter 8.

- *Maximum Activity*. This is the maximum activity reached by the node during the current query. It is used to determine appropriate weight changes and is discussed in chapter 9.

- *Feedback* and *Maximum Feedback*. These are the feedback analogues to the previous two components; they are also explained in chapter 9.

- *Out-Links*. These are links from the given node to other nodes. They are sorted by weight from highest to lowest.

- *In-Links*. These are links from other nodes to the given node, also sorted by weight.

---

[6]Unfortunately, this type of citation does not *always* uniquely identify a case. In some instances — such as when a court refuses to hear an appeal — the case will consist of less than a page of text, and a second case will have the same citation.

- *Text Address*. This is an index into an array of file directories. When a user wants to view the text of a case, the system uses the text address to find the appropriate directory.[7]

There is a tradeoff between the desire to keep the size of the node objects small (so more can be fit in memory) and the need to have as much information as possible available immediately. For example, when case nodes are displayed on the screen, a short form of their name (the litigants) can be immediately shown, since that information is already stored as the informal label. The same information could have been obtained by simply storing the case's address and then locating the (tagged) names of the litigants from the disk file, but this would take significantly more time.

7.3   Multiple Link Classes

Links in SCALIR represent associations between the items represented by the nodes. Some of these associations are based on statistical inference, some on incontrovertible facts, and some on human judgments. Because there are three different types of associations, there are three different classes of links. These are known as C-links, S-links, and H-links, respectively.

   In most cases, when there is an association between two nodes, they are connected by *two* directed links (one in each direction), each with a different weight. In order to prevent any node from producing more activity than it consumes (thus risking an exponential explosion of total activity in the network), the sum of weights on all outgoing links from each node is constrained to be less than or equal to 1.0. This constraint is specialized to each of the three link classes, so that (initially) the sum of weights on outgoing links of each type must be less than or equal to 1/3. This uniform division was intended as a least-commitment decision about the relative importance of the various link classes; the distribution changes in response to user behavior.

7.3.1   C-Links

The first and most common type of link is the connectionist, or *C-link*. C-links represent weighted, unlabeled associations based on statistical

---

[7]Searching very large directories is a relatively slow operation on the Symbolics. The text address allows different cases to be stored in different, smaller directories. A larger system would probably need a more general file storage method, such as the use of B-trees.

inference. Almost all of the initial C-links correspond to associations between a term node and the documents it indexes.

These initial links between documents and terms are formed at the same time the indexing described previously is performed. The weight on a link from a document to a term is proportional to the term weight[8] TW_{ij} of Equation 7.1.

Because the sum of the outgoing C-link weights must be $\leq 1/3$, the term weights are scaled by a simple normalization. For example, suppose a document had three index terms with TW values of 0.3, 0.4, and 0.5. To convert these to document→term C-link weights, each would be multiplied by $\frac{1/3}{(0.3+0.4+0.5)} = 0.2777\ldots$ to produce link weights of approximately 0.0833, 0.1111, and 0.1389.

Note that the normalization will result in larger document→term weights for documents indexed by very few terms, and smaller weights for documents indexed by many terms. This is in fact the desired behavior, because the more terms there are, the less any individual one can be said to describe the meaning of the document.

The inverses of these links — that is, the term→document links — are given preliminary uniform weights, inversely proportional to the number of documents for which each term is an index. That is, if a term is linked to 10 documents, then each of the term→document weights will be one 10th of the total (one 10th of one 3rd). This uniform weighting scheme was used for all links in Belew's AIR system; it makes no assumptions about the relative importance of individual documents. Rather, it is based on a probabilistic argument similar to the inverse document frequency term used in IR: If a term indexes few documents, then interest in the term will very likely predict interest in those documents. As the number of documents increases, the power of that prediction weakens. Hence the weights are initially set to reflect this.

Although the vast number of C-links are found between terms and documents, there are a few additional links based on the presence of headnotes to cases. As mentioned earlier, there are nodes representing key numbers in West's taxonomy of the law; when cases have headnotes (indicating key numbers), a pair of C-links is created between each case and each of its key number nodes. The case→key number links are given weights equal to the mean of the case→term weights. This is intended to make the importance of a headnote equal to the average term indexing a case; SCALIR's learning mechanism will then increase or decrease its

---

[8]Note that there are two "weights" being discussed here, the term weight from the IR frequency analysis, and the link weight used by the connectionist network.

importance according to what users find valuable.[9] The inverse links —
from key numbers to cases — are weighted by the uniform scheme used
for the term→document links.

In SCALIR, the high out-degree of many nodes requires that in some
cases, not all links will be traversed every time. The choice of links
to traverse depends on weight; stronger weights are traversed first. In
the law, decisions by higher courts are (all else being equal) of more
interest than decisions by lower courts, and more recent decisions are
of more interest than older ones.[10] Because the initial term→document
links are uniformly weighted, there is no guarantee that the most useful
subset of these links — those leading to higher and more recent cases —
would be traversed. To solve this problem, the weights are given minute
adjustments; weights are increased according to court level and decreased
(an order of magnitude less) according to age. The resulting weights are
renormalized to preserve the 1/3 weight sum. The result of this is a list
of weights that is qualitatively unchanged, but sortable by age and court
level. (This technique is also applied to the key number→case links.)

Finally, C-links may be created by a learning mechanism described in
chapter 9. These new links may exist between any two nodes, regardless
of type.

7.3.2   S-Links

The second class of link in SCALIR is the symbolic, or *S-link*. S-links
form the semantic networks of the system; they represent static, a priori
knowledge. There are actually several types of S-link, each *labeled* with
its type, and given a *constant* weight.

Some S-links correspond to the factual relationships between court
decisions, the precedential history of the case. A typical S-link of this
kind would be one labeled *overturned-by*, indicating that the first case
was overturned on appeal by the second. These links were created from
the Shepard's citations described in chapter 5. Table 7.3 shows all of the
inter-case S-links used in SCALIR.

Due to a limitation in the way SCALIR's cases were identified and
represented, many of the Shepard's history citations are missing from the

---

[9]This decision may be somewhat controversial. Many legal researchers rely heavily on
headnotes to provide an accurate representation of the contents of a case. Others question
the accuracy of the headnotes and prefer to rely on searches of the decision itself. This
issue requires further study.

[10]Although Tapper has argued that citations to lower court decisions may be more important if the goal is to identify similarities between cases by examining the overlap of
decisions they cite[Tap80].

Shepard's Code	Corresponding S-link Labels
A	affirmed, affirmed-by
R	reversed, reversed-by
S	superseded, superseded-by
M	modified, modified-by

Table 7.3: Inter-case S-links. There are other Shepard's history codes, but they were either not applicable or did not occur in the SCALIR database.

Link Type	Example
contains, contained-in	(Chapter 1 contains §101)
refers-to, referred-to-by	"The works specified in §§102 and 103..."
subject-to, governs	"Subject to §§107 through 118..."
excepts, excepted-by	"Except as provided in §810 of this title..."
despite, ignored-by	"Notwithstanding the provisions of §106..."

Table 7.4: S-links representing statute dependencies.

SCALIR network. For this reason, these S-links played a smaller role in the system than originally anticipated. (This problem is discussed further on page 165.)

Another group of S-links is based on structural relationships among portions of statutes. The most obvious of these are the links labeled *contains* (and its inverse, *contained-in*) which occur between parent and child positions in the tree-like text of the statute. For example, if Section 301 is part of Chapter 3, then SCALIR would have a *contains* link from the latter node to the former. In addition, S-links are used to reflect dependencies between statute sections, such as "except where noted in section X" or "as defined in section Y." These dependencies were identified manually; this is the only phase of the SCALIR project in which additional[11] human expertise was used to analyze the case. Although currently a bottleneck in the process, this dependency-construction could probably be performed with fairly high accuracy by a simple pattern-matcher searching for phrases like those quoted above.

Figure 7.2 shows a small example of these relationships for part of the Copyright Act of 1976. A user interested in cases about national origin (§104) would additionally activate the terms associated with the previous sections referred to in §104. All S-links of this type are shown in Table 7.4.

A final group of S-links was used to join the topics of the West key

---

[11]Editors at West and Shepard's have, of course, already read and tagged the cases with headnotes and labeled citations, respectively.

Sec.104: Subject matter of copyright: National origin
(a) Unpublished works. -- The works specified by
section 102 and 103, while unpublished, are subject
to protection . . .

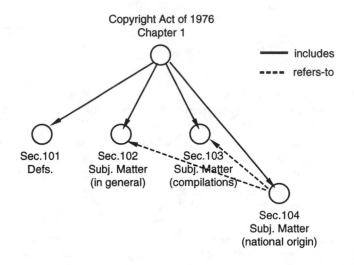

Figure 7.2: Dependencies between statute sections.

number taxonomy (also described in chapter 5). Like the links for the statute hierarchy, these S-links correspond to parent-child relationships in the tree. Unlike those statute links, however, these represent not physical composition (Chapter 3 is composed of Section 301, 302, etc.) but rather conceptual containment. Essentially, this is equivalent to the ubiquitous IS-A link found in most semantic networks.

The weights are set uniformly such that all outgoing S-links from a node sum to 1/3. This decision was the result of balancing two conflicting notions of S-link semantics.

On the one hand, an S-link was supposed to be characterized by its label; any instance of the link type *contains*, for example, should mean the same as any other instance. Indeed, one early idea was to give all S-links a "weight" of unity. They would thus serve as "wormholes," allowing activity to jump to distant parts of the network without loss of intensity. A variant of this idea would also have given all S-links the same weight, but it would have been a smaller value so that attenuation would occur.

On the other hand, the "activity is proportional to relevance" principle — and simple combinatorics — dictated that S-link weights should be small enough so that a node never creates new activity. As with the inverse document frequency idea, this approach suggests that if a node has many children (or out-neighbors), each one is less important than if the node had few. This second consideration ultimately won out; two occurrences of the same type of S-link may in fact have different weights depending on the out-degree of their respective source nodes.

S-links may be viewed as *definitional* in the sense of Brachman's analysis of semantic networks [BFL85]. That is, they correspond to the "physics" of the domain, the indisputable truths. The key number taxonomy S-links are especially definitional in the sense that each topic of law in the tree can be defined as the group of subtopics represented by its children. In any case, the S-links should not be defeasible; if one case reversed another, this cannot be undone. For this reason, S-link weights are fixed at creation and cannot be modified by learning.

7.3.3 H-Links

As originally designed, SCALIR contained just the two classes of links (C-links and S-links) already described; S-links were responsible for representing all explicit relationships between nodes. However, it soon became clear that not all explicit relationships have equal standing. For example, a Shepard's citation corresponding to the *history* of a case is qualitatively different from one corresponding to the *treatment* of a case. The former represents an indisputable fact about the world: Case X was reversed by case Y. In contrast, the latter represents the subjective opinion of an expert indexer — in AI terminology, a sort of knowledge engineer — working for Shepard's.[12] One cannot argue about whether a decision was reversed, but one can certainly disagree about whether a judge limited, questioned, or criticized another case. Also, the importance of citations varies considerably; the fixed weights of S-links would have prevented the system from adjusting their strength in response to user feedback.

As a result of these limitations, a third class of link was incorporated into the SCALIR network. Like an S-link, this new class has a label indicating the nature of the association, and thus enables logical inference. But like a C-link, it has an adjustable weight which can be altered with experience. This new class of link is called an H-link (for "Hybrid"). Because H-links are based on a priori knowledge but are learnable (and hence defeasible), they are similar to "assertional" links in Brachman's semantic network analysis. They correspond to facts that are probably true, or things that we believe when all else is equal.

By "overloading" the semantics of H-links, a more concise representation of citation relationships is possible. Rather than having a separate link type for every Shepard's treatment phrase, we can categorize the citations as points along various dimensions. This technique was also used by the CITES command in Hafner's LIRS system [Haf81]. A user could ask to see "positive" or "negative" citations, although there is no such dimension explicitly stated by judges (or by citators). The approach is also reminiscent of Ashley's use of Dimensions corresponding to various legal issues in representing trade secrets cases [Ash90], discussed in chapter 5.

In SCALIR, most treatment phrases are represented as points along one of two dimensions.[13] On one axis are those citations which deal with the rule or issue of law, from most dissimilar (OVERRULED) to most similar (FOLLOWED). On the other axis are those citations which focus on the facts of the two cases, also from most dissimilar (DISTINGUISHED) to most similar (PARALLEL). Although not every treatment phrase falls neatly onto one of these axes, it is a useful starting point for forming meaningful associations. The resulting space of case treatments is shown in Figure 7.3. The points were chosen in an attempt to capture the intensity expressed by Shepard's published descriptions of the treatment

---

[12]One might argue that the West key numbering system is the result of similar editorial decisions that have evolved over many years, but for the present it is treated as a fixed taxonomy.

[13]I am grateful to Andy Desmond of West Publishing Co. for suggesting this analysis.

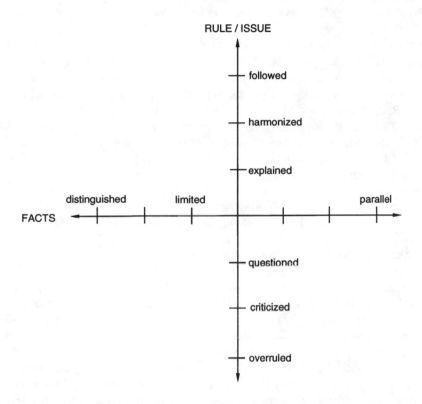

Figure 7.3: The space of Shepard's treatment phrases.

phrases.[14] Only two types of H-links are needed, one for each dimension; the links are then given different weights to correspond to the different positions on each axis. The result of this representation is that a user can ask queries of the conceptual form "what cases did the judge feel did not deal with similar issues?" rather than the syntactic form "what cases did the judge question, criticize, or overrule?"

There are two other types of H-links in addition to those representing the fact and rule dimensions. These correspond to two other citation relationships, one in which no Shepard's treatment phrase is given (an "unlabeled" citation), and one for citation in the dissenting opinion.

All H-links are based on citation information provided by Shepard's/-McGraw-Hill. The goal was to identify all citations joining cases in the SCALIR database. The Shepard's data is organized according to *cited* cases. That is, one looks in *Shepard's Citations* to find all the places (in other cases) where the current case is cited. For the purposes of use in SCALIR, the Shepard's data format presented two problems. First, the case of interest may have been cited as it appeared in a different reporter. For instance, the case *Sony v. Universal* is published both as 104 S.Ct. 774 in the West Reporter series, and 464 U.S. 417 in the United States reporter. If a judge in another decision referred to the *Sony* case by the West "address" and one tried to Shepardize it by looking up the U.S. reporter entry, the citation might be missed.

Because SCALIR's database was provided by West Publishing, the West reporter citations are the most reliable. Usually, the text of the decision lists the corresponding entries in other reporters. This information was used to create a lookup table of equivalent citations. This partially, but not completely, solved the first problem.

The second problem in incorporating Shepard's citations into SCALIR is that the citation listed gives the volume, reporter, and page where the citation occurred — not the page where the case begins. This is no problem for a human who can simply flip the pages (or screens) back until the beginning of the case. But the task is harder for the program trying to identify the citing case. It must know the starting and ending pages of the citing case.

Because of WESTLAW's "star paging" feature, SCALIR's database included the page numbers (and hence the ending page) of all its cases. This made it possible to identify many of the citing cases. Unfortunately, however, when the citation was from a non-West reporter, there was no way to determine which case was doing the citing, unless the citation oc-

---

[14]However, it should be noted that the Shepard's editors assisting this research denied that such an analysis was used in assigning treatment codes.

curred on the first page of the citing decision (a very rare event). For this reason, SCALIR may be missing many citations and thus many potential H-links.

To summarize, the Shepard's citations were converted into H-links by the following method: First, a table of SCALIR's cases was constructed giving the starting and ending pages of the canonical (West) edition as well as the equivalent starting positions for other editions. Then, for each citation in the Shepard's data file, the canonical form of cited and citing case was located (if possible). Finally, the nodes in the SCALIR network corresponding to these cases were identified and a link formed between them.

Each H-link was initially assigned a "proto-weight" corresponding to its position on one of the two dimensions discussed above. Unlabeled citations, and citations to the dissenting opinion, received proto-weights of 1.0. When all the H-links had been created, the weights were normalized to sum to 1/3. The purpose of the proto-weights was to insure that the semantics of the relative weight differences was preserved irrespective of the normalization process.[15]

7.4 Network Statistics

Table 7.5 gives some statistics about nodes in the network. For purposes of comparison, the table also shows the number of nodes used for an earlier, smaller database. Note that the ratio of term nodes to document (case and statute section) nodes decreases from 4.25 to 3.21 as the size of the corpus increases. This is due to the fact that fewer and fewer new words are encountered. This indicates some promise for scaling the system up to a larger collection of documents.

Information about the connectivity of the network is shown in Table 7.6. Note that each entry in the table actually corresponds to *two* link types, for example *refers-to* and *referred-to-by*. To find out how many of each individual type there are, this number should be divided in half. Figure 7.4 gives a general view of the network size and connectivity.

Because the number of edges in a completely connected directed graph is $n(n-1)$, the SCALIR network is less than 0.00035% "full." The mean out-degree of each node is 2.954. However, this is a somewhat deceptive figure. The most prevalent type of link in the initial

---

[15]Note that this method precludes the addition of any additional H-links to existing nodes later on. There are several possible ways to solve this problem, but all require some additional information to be stored in either links or nodes.

Type	Small Net	Large Net
terms	6,160	13,082
key numbers	0	123
Term Nodes	6,160	13,205
Supreme Court	121	121
Court of Appeals	1,240	1,240
District Court	0	2,625
Case Nodes	1,361	3,986
statute sections	87	90
statute hierarchy	0	10
Statute Nodes	87	100
Total	7,608	17,291

Table 7.5: Distribution of nodes in the network.

Link Type	Count
case-term	74,788
case-key number	14,378
statute-term	1,954
key number-term	630
C-links	91,750
unlabeled citation	7,580
dissenting opinion cite	294
rule/issue cite	932
fact cite	464
H-links	9,270
affirmed	16
reversed	8
superseded	128
modified	10
contains key number	244
contains statute	186
refers-to	238
subject-to	30
excepted-by	10
despite	14
S-links	884
Total	101,904

Table 7.6: Some link statistics.

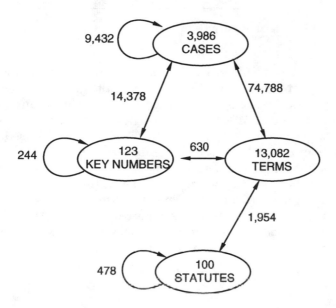

Figure 7.4: An aggregate view of the network statistics. The statute cluster includes the statute hierarchy nodes as well as the actual statute sections.

From	To	via	Out-Degree
term	document	C-links	2.91
key number	document	C-links	61.01
all term nodes	document	C-links	3.47
document	term	C-links	9.4
document	all term nodes	C-links	11.23
case	case	H-links	1.16
case	case	S-links	0.02

Table 7.7: Mean out-degree for various node types.

network occurs between documents and terms. It is thus more meaningful to compare the network's connectivity to a bipartite graph $K_{4086,13205}$, which (counting both directions) has $2nm$ edges. This still means that only 0.00094% of the possible term-to-document connections exist. Of course, this is largely an artifact of the term weight threshold used to determine which terms would be used to index the documents.

Table 7.7 shows the mean out-degree for nodes of various types. Note the large difference between the out-degree of terms (reflecting roughly the number of documents each term indexed) and that of key numbers (the average number of cases with that key number in a headnote). The distribution of term nodes (including key numbers) with various out-degree is shown in Figure 7.5; case node connectivity is shown in Figure 7.6.

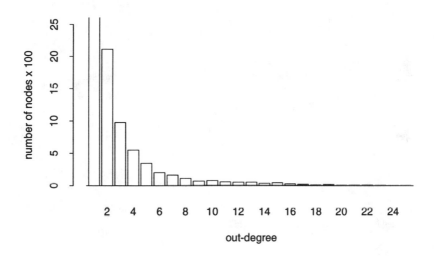

Figure 7.5: A partial histogram showing term node connectivity. The first column has height 79, off the scale shown. The right-hand tail of the distribution continues out to out-degree 336, with one node.

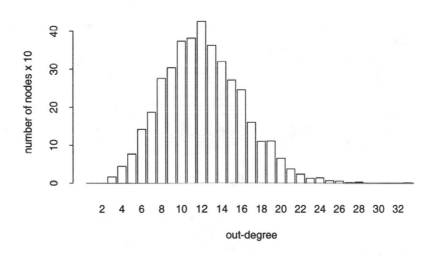

Figure 7.6: A histogram of case node connectivity. Cases were most commonly indexed by 12 terms.

Chapter 8

The Retrieval Process

This chapter describes the SCALIR "retrieval engine." In particular, it explains how the system's internal task of retrieving relevant documents is realized as a process of spreading activation. This explanation ultimately rests on the short-term dynamics of the system, where short-term means during a single query, as opposed to the long-term changes (learning) that occur over many retrieval sessions. The view presented here is necessarily narrowly focused. In particular, almost all discussion of how users actually engage in the retrieval process is deferred until Chapter 10.

8.1 An Activation-Based View of Retrieval

There are many ways to view the mapping from the document retrieval task to spreading activation in a network, several of which are introduced here. The basic idea — what chapter 7 described as the "fundamental postulate" — is that *activity is proportional to relevance*. The network has been constructed so that related objects are connected. By what is often called the *cluster hypothesis* in information retrieval [vR79], if we are interested in one item, we are probably also interested in others closely associated with it.

These two assumptions (the activity-relevance postulate and the cluster hypothesis) have some basic consequences. By the cluster hypothesis, documents are relevant if and only if terms that index them are relevant. (For simplicity, I use documents as items to be retrieved and terms as items to query. In fact, SCALIR allows both documents and terms to be queried and retrieved.) So our query becomes the list of relevant terms. By the activity-relevance postulate, if we want the system to treat the

171

query terms as relevant, we should give them large activity values. If the system does its job correctly — as described in the remainder of this chapter — this activity will spread to other "related" nodes. Immediate neighbors of queried nodes represent obviously related items. Those reached by longer paths of activation represent more subtle, indirect relations. Nodes that may not be strongly related along any specific path may become active through a gradual combination of evidence over several different paths. Ultimately, many (but far from all) nodes in the network will become active. Again applying the postulate, the most active nodes are the most relevant, and are returned as the response to the query.

A useful image of the system is of each node in the network being a bell, and each link being a spring from the top of one bell to the top of another. Differences in link weights can be viewed as differences in the stiffness of the springs. To "query" the system, simultaneously strike all the bells corresponding to the query terms. They will vibrate (and ring), and their vibrations will spread through the springs to their neighbors, their neighbors' neighbors, and so on. The bells ringing the loudest will be the "response."

This image makes clear a few of the design issues involved in SCALIR's retrieval mechanism. How hard should each bell be struck? Should we keep striking it as the vibrations die out? If there are many query bells, should each one be struck with the same force as if there are few? How can we prevent the whole network from ringing? How long should we wait to decide which bells are ringing loudest? If we wait too long, won't all the vibrations have died out? Each of these questions has an analogue in SCALIR and is discussed in the next section.

8.2   General Activation Issues

Many connectionist networks, such as those trained with the standard back-propagation algorithm [RHW86], have a simple feedforward structure, as shown in Figure 8.1. We generally assume instantaneous propagation of activity, even though in practice the activity levels are computed one layer at a time. The activations of the input nodes are set to the corresponding values of the input pattern. The activation a of each other node i is then set to a function f of the weighted sum $\sum w_{ij}a_j$ of its "upstream" neighbors.

Many functions can be used for f, but it is usually a differentiable nonlinear threshold function mapping to [0,1] or [-1,1]. The differentiability is needed for back-propagation. The nonlinearity is needed to represent functions such as exclusive-OR that are not linearly separable.

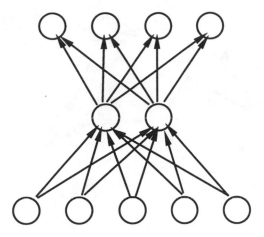

Figure 8.1: A standard feedforward network.

A commonly used f is the sigmoidal logistic function

$$f(x) = \frac{1}{1 + e^{-x/T}} \tag{8.1}$$

where T, the "temperature" parameter, determines the steepness of the slope. Low values of T make the function more step-like, whereas high values make it smoother.

In a feedforward network, there is no question about when the network is ready to produce a result. As soon as the activations of the output units have been computed, that is the result. There are, however, other types of networks with more interesting dynamics. In these settling networks, such as the one shown in Figure 8.2, activity is often binary, though it need not be [Hop84]. To activate the network, several units are *clamped* with input values. The activations of all the other units are then updated repeatedly until the network reaches equilibrium. The updates are often done in a random, asynchronous fashion. The new activation of a unit is generally 1 if the sum of the weighted inputs exceeds a threshold, otherwise 0. At equilibrium, the results are found by examining the states of the nonclamped nodes. Although this settling to equilibrium can in principle work in continuous time, the updates are usually done at discrete intervals.

How would each of these two approaches apply to the information retrieval problem? If we want to be able to query and retrieve both documents and terms, a feedforward network would have to contain both input and output units for each — twice as many as SCALIR —

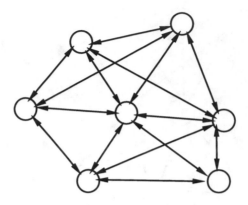

Figure 8.2: A settling network.

plus several hundred or thousand hidden units to represent higher-order associations. (Furthermore, it is not clear how the weights would be adjusted in response to the type of feedback signal available in SCALIR. This is discussed further in chapter 9.)

What might a settling network for IR look like? We can imagine a completely connected network in which all documents and terms were connected to all others. To query the system, we clamp the terms of interest. When it reaches equilibrium, all units whose activation is 1 would be considered retrieved. Unfortunately, there are several problems with this approach. First, it would require $O(N^2)$ connections for N items — around 10^8 in the case of the SCALIR database. Second, in order for the energy minimization analysis to go through, symmetric connections would have to be used. Because weights determine activity (all else being equal), this would violate the activity-relevance postulate; the association from a document to a term may be strong even if the association from the term to the document is weak (as in the case where the term indexes many documents, but the document has few index terms). Third, this type of network can store far fewer "memories" (no more than $\frac{N}{4 \log N}$, if we want all memories to be stable with high probability [MPRV87]) than the number of possible response sets (theoretically, $2^{\#\text{documents}}$). Finally, and most critically, we do not how long the system will take to reach equilibrium.

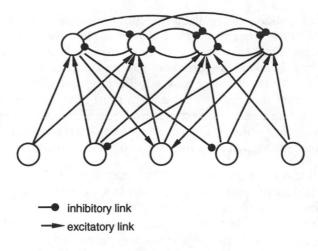

● inhibitory link
→ excitatory link

Figure 8.3: An interactive activation network.

8.2.1   Interactive Activation for IR

It would seem that a third, compromise approach is needed for the IR problem. We would like a network which supports interesting dynamics, allowing a gradual accumulation of evidence. But we want to avoid complete connectivity and the need to wait for equilibrium. Some of these attributes can be found in the interactive activation model of Rumelhart and McClelland [MR81, RM82]. In an interactive activation network, such as the one shown in Figure 8.3, the units are divided into layers, each unit generally inhibiting the others in its layer and exciting or inhibiting units in other layers.

The activity of a unit is updated by the rule

$$a_i(t + \Delta t) = a_i(t) - \Theta_i(a_i(t) - r_i) + n_i(t)(M - a_i(t)) \qquad (8.2)$$

where Θ is a decay rate, r_i is the resting level for node i, $n_i(t)$ is the weighted sum of the inputs to node i (net_j in common PDP parlance), and M is the maximum activity value for any node.[1] This final damping term is commonly used by Grossberg [Gro80]; it "slows down" the units as they try to approach activity extrema.

One important issue in the interactive activation approach is determining when the network has reached an answer. As Rumelhart and McClelland put it:

---

[1]Actually, this formula is correct only for the case in which the net input is positive. When it is negative, the final term is $(a_i(t) - m)$, where m is the minimum activity value allowed.

> Various options are available for monitoring readout performance of the simulation. First, it is possible to have the program print out what the result of readout would be at each time cycle. Second, the user may specify a particular cycle for readout. Third, the user may tell the program to figure out the optimal time for readout and to print both the time and the resulting percent correct performance. This option is used in preliminary runs to determine what readout time to use in the final simulation runs for each experiment. [MR81].

As we shall see, there are problems with each approach.

The suitability of an interactive activation-style model for information retrieval was demonstrated by Mozer [Moz84], in the work discussed earlier in Section 4.5.9. In Mozer's model, the two layers were documents and descriptors (terms). Each descriptor was connected to each document it indexed by an excitatory link. All such links had identical weights for all units. Each document unit was connected to each other document unit by an inhibitory link, also with a constant weight. The weights on the inhibitory links were low enough to allow many document nodes to be active simultaneously. In Mozer's system the query units were clamped on for the duration of processing, which continued until the network reached equilibrium.

Despite the promise of Mozer's model, it had several limitations. In addition to the equilibrium complications already described, Mozer's use of inhibitory connections between all documents runs counter to the clustering hypothesis; the fact that document X is relevant in no way implies that document Y is less relevant. In fact, there may even be a positive association between the two. The original Rumelhart and McClelland network was trying to model psychological data involving a forced-choice situation (trying to recognize letters in the context of words); thus it was appropriate for each choice to inhibit the others. No such motivation exists for the IR task. Although it may be argued that the mutual inhibition is necessary to prevent all nodes from becoming active, there are other alternatives, as Belew's AIR system [Bel86] demonstrated.

8.2.2   Activation in AIR

In AIR, the initial connections were only excitatory, and existed between documents and their descriptors (terms and authors). Thus connectivity was minimized. The query nodes were clamped for a fixed number of time steps, the network was allowed to update freely, and results were reported when certain termination conditions were met.

The activation rule of AIR's nodes also used a linear threshold function. It also included a decay term, expressed as a "retention" constant δ:

$$a_i(t+1) = f(\delta \cdot a_i + (1-\delta) \sum_j w_{ij} a_j(t)) \qquad (8.3)$$

The threshold function had an upper limit (saturate) and a lower limit (quiescent) for the absolute value of activity. By setting the quiescence level above zero, it was possible to "shut off" nodes with very small activations. Thus these nodes would not need to be further involved in the current computations.

The set of retrieved items was determined by using a varying significance threshold. At any given time, the nodes whose activity level exceeded this threshold were considered retrieved. Because all links out of a node summed to 1.0, the total activity in the network never increased, and the quiescence cutoff caused it to gradually "leak out" of the system. Accordingly, the magnitude of a node was likely to be smaller several links away from the query nodes. The significance threshold was reduced at each time step to compensate for this total activity loss.

The number of time steps to clamp the query nodes was determined empirically. Belew demonstrated that multiple iterations of clamping was desirable, because it allowed for "temporal integration" of activity traversing paths of various lengths, as shown conceptually in Figure 8.4 (after Figure 4.12 in [Bel86]).

There were four conditions used to stop propagating activity in AIR:

- *Equilibrium*. Propagation was halted if no changes were observed from one time step to the next. This never occurred in the full-scale network.

- *Quiescence*. This is really a special case of equilibrium; propagation halted when all nodes were quiescent. This also never occurred in practice.

- *Maximum Number of Nodes*. When a certain preset number of nodes had been retrieved (activated above significance), propagation was halted.

- *Significance Equal to Quiescence*. Because the significance threshold was reduced at each time step, it would eventually approach the quiescence threshold. When this happened, propagation was halted.

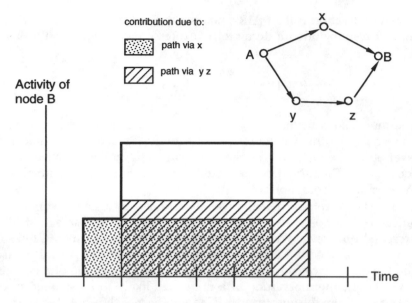

Figure 8.4: Belew's argument for clamping.

Belew reported that around two thirds of all retrievals halted due to the Maximum-Nodes condition.

8.3 SCALIR's Retrieval Algorithm

SCALIR adopted many of the AIR activation principles already described. Among these were the use of quiescence and decaying significance thresholds, clamping query nodes for a fixed number of iterations, and halting propagation when various conditions were met. However, there are several differences in SCALIR's approach. Many of the differences result from the different conception of a node's level of activity in SCALIR. This is discussed in Section 8.4.

8.3.1 Conservation of Activity

SCALIR's query nodes were clamped for a fixed number of time steps. Various amounts of time were tested; most of the experiments described in this work (including those used to evaluate the system, described in chapter 11) clamped for five time steps. The amount of activity pumped into the system is constant (as in AIR), independent of the query. This amount, internally called *pump-volume*, is distributed equally among all the query nodes. Thus the clamping value of each query node is higher for queries involving fewer terms.

Chapter 2 discussed the need for an IR system to provide a useful amount of information to the user. If a user is told that "no documents satisfy your request," the system is providing no guidance about what alternatives might be pursued. In contrast, if the system prints out a list of 5,000 retrieved items (or says "too many items, please narrow your search"), the user may be overwhelmed and will not know how to evaluate the response. Furthermore, all documents are relevant to some degree in any system which views relevance as a continuous, rather than binary, quantity. Thus the question is simply how far down the relevance ranking to go when presenting the user with the response.

In SCALIR (as in AIR), the user is assumed to be interested in about as much information as he or she can practically make use of. Thus every query retrieves at least a few documents, and no query retrieves more than a couple of dozen. On average, the number of retrieved items is constant.

If a user is interested in a constant-sized response set — that is, if he or she interprets the results as bearing a constant amount of total relevance — then by the activity-relevance postulate, a constant amount of activity should be pumped into the system, *independent of the query*. The response set will consist of nodes with various activities, but adding up to the same total. Perhaps it will contain 25 nodes that are equally relevant, or 10 that are very relevant and 30 that are less so. In any case, a good heuristic for producing this number of responses[2] is to pump in that same amount of activity — in this case, 25 units. This is accomplished by having a *pump-volume* of 5 for each of 5 clamping iterations.

Of course, the total activity "read out" of the system will only be equal to the activity pumped in if activity is neither created nor destroyed during the propagation process. To prevent the creation of activity, no node should output more activity than it takes in. This means that the sum of the weights on outgoing links must be less than or equal to 1.0, and that the activation function $f(x)$ must always be less than or equal to its argument x. Both of these conditions are strictly enforced in SCALIR.

To prevent the destruction of activity, no node should output *less* than it takes in. However, two factors make this an unrealistic assumption for SCALIR. First, in order to satisfy this condition and the previous one, the

---

[2]Because all the active nodes are relevant to some degree, it could be argued that the amount of activity pumped into the system is irrelevant to the number of items retrieved. However, the activation functions become less well-behaved for very small values, because small differences in weights become overly important.

outgoing link weights would have to always sum to exactly 1.0. But because 1/3 of this sum is reserved for each link class (see chapter 7 for details), nodes with no outgoing S-links will never have weights summing to more than 2/3. Second, in order to prevent unnecessary computations on infinitesimal values, nodes whose activity falls below a certain level are set to zero. This means that their activity is essentially destroyed.[3] Fortunately, the consequence of losing activity — retrieving fewer nodes — is easily correctable by simply adjusting the parameters so that propagation continues for a longer time. Even if fewer nodes are retrieved, this is a much less serious problem than the exponential explosion of activity that would result from violating the no-creation condition.

In addition to clamping the query nodes, the temporal integration effect was also achieved by allowing nodes to retain some of their previous activity. A retention constant, ρ, was used to determine how much of a node's activity was retained in the next time step; the rest was propagated to the node's neighbors.[4]

8.3.2   Significance and Quiescence

Two critical parameters controlling activation in SCALIR are the *significance threshold* θ_s and the *quiescence threshold* θ_q. The significance threshold is used to determine which nodes have high enough activity to be retrieved; it decays over time to compensate for the lowering of average node activity caused by the network's high fan-out. The quiescence threshold is the level below which nodes are considered inactive and removed from the current activity computations.

If the initial value of the significance threshold $\theta_s(0)$ is too low, then most of the query nodes' neighbors will immediately be retrieved. However, this may prevent more subtle and valuable associations from being presented to the user. In fact, the retrieval set would be very similar to the first few documents found in a standard vector model, because the query→document links are just those whose association was strongest. In contrast, if $\theta_s(0)$ is too high, then no documents will be retrieved until the threshold begins to decay. Accordingly, $\theta_s(0)$ was set to 0.1 for most of the experiments; this generally allowed some, but not all, of the query nodes' neighbors to be immediately retrieved.

---

[3] Belew experimented with the redistribution of this activity to the more active nodes, but found that it made no noticeable difference.

[4] In fact, SCALIR also implements a propagation constant π, which determines how much of the activity is propagated from a node. Although various values of both ρ and π were tested, π is normally set to $1 - \rho$ in accordance with the conservation of activation principle.

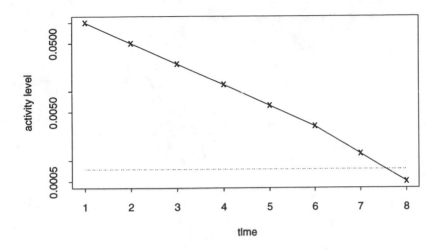

Figure 8.5: The significance threshold θ_s decaying over time. The dotted line is the quiescence threshold θ_q.

Unlike AIR, SCALIR begins to lower its significance threshold θ_s immediately, while the query nodes are still being clamped. The rate of decay is then increased when no more activity is being pumped into the network. By adjusting the initial threshold and the decay rates, the breadth and depth of the spread of activity can be controlled.

Varying the decay rate affects how nodes are retrieved as time progresses. If θ_s decays too slowly, then no additional nodes will appear until it nears the quiescence level, at which time many nodes will be retrieved all at once. This gives the user no indication that anything is happening for the duration of the search. If the threshold decays too fast, then — as with too small an initial value — the obvious associations will swamp the system, so that there is literally no room on the screen to present anything else to the user during the following time steps. Ideally, the system should find a few more relevant items at each time step.

Figure 8.5 shows the behavior of θ_s for several time steps. The change in slope occurs when the clamping phase ends; the rate of decay is then increased. (Note that the y-axis uses a logarithmic scale; the decay is actually exponential.)

To evaluate the effectiveness of the parameter settings, we can observe the proportion of activated nodes that become significant (that is, whose

181

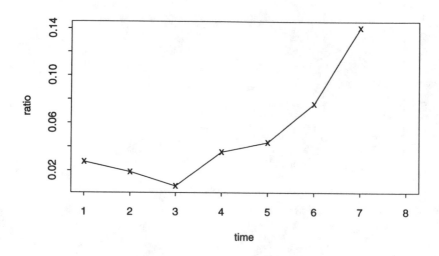

Figure 8.6: The ratio of newly significant nodes to all nodes activated.

activity exceeds θ_s) at each time step. Figure 8.6 shows this data averaged over five test queries. One reason for the large increase at the end is that the total number of activated nodes levels off while the significance threshold continues to decay. Nevertheless, the increase suggests that the decay rate was probably too rapid.

The quiescence threshold, θ_q, serves several purposes. First, it prevents real arithmetic errors by avoiding infinitesimal numbers. Second, it prevents the system from spending time on nodes that are unlikely to affect the retrieval. Third, it serves a pruning role, cutting down on the effective fan-out. When θ_q is too low, the system bogs down and irrelevant material is retrieved near the end of propagation. When it is too high, nodes which are important but have not yet exceeded the significance threshold are removed before their activity gets a chance to accumulate (during successive clamping time steps).

The "culling" action of the quiescence threshold gives SCALIR (like AIR) the ability to exclude many nodes from further computation. Unlike the situation with a typical connectionist network, *only those nodes directly involved in a particular retrieval require computation.* In practice this means that nodes with no activity need not be updated. Initially, only the query terms and their neighbors are active, so this is a great saving of computational resources. During propagation, however, the list of

182

nodes requiring computation increases exponentially. The value of the quiescence threshold is that it provides a mechanism for shrinking this list.

The SCALIR implementation stores all currently active nodes in a priority queue, sorted by activity level. This makes the retrieval (reporting nodes with activities above θ_s) and culling (removing nodes with activity below θ_q) operations more efficient. Many active nodes do not need to be examined at all. (Sorting, however, is itself an expensive operation.)

8.3.3 Tapered Search

Earlier versions of SCALIR, such as the one reported in [RB91a], relied on the quiescence threshold to avoid an impractically large set of active nodes. However, once the larger network was installed — and particularly, once all of the key number associations were in place — the fan-out from many nodes increased dramatically. The quiescence threshold proved too crude an instrument for controlling this combinatorial explosion; setting it higher eliminated documents known to be relevant.

The solution was to introduce a *tapered search* mechanism. In a tapered search, similar to the tapered forward pruning technique used in some game-playing programs [GEC67], only a subset of a node's neighbors are visited. Furthermore, the number of neighbors to visit — the "beam width" — decreases in proportion to the distance from the starting point.

To implement a tapered search efficiently in SCALIR, the links out of each node were sorted in decreasing order of weight. When propagating activity, the system would consider only the first b neighbors of each node. At the next time step, the beam was made narrower by a "focusing" factor ϕ. Various values of beam width and focus were tested. Because the beam width affected the combinatorial explosion of the system — and hence its speed — most directly, it was found to be a useful parameter for adjusting the degree of responsiveness. Initial values of 15 or higher resulted in more "batch"-like sessions, taking several minutes. Values of 10 or lower produced more "interactive" sessions, generally taking less than one minute for a retrieval. Because the mean out-degree of even document nodes was less than 12 (see Table 7.7), these b values typically cause little loss of recall. The nodes affected most are the key number nodes, which often index dozens or hundreds of cases. For these nodes, the tapered search effectively restricts activity propagation to more recent cases and those decided by higher courts.

Table 8.1 summarizes the parameters used in SCALIR retrievals, and gives typical values for each.

Name	Symbol	Value	Comments
`*pump-volume*`	–	5	Amount of activity to pump while clamping
`*pumps*`	–	5	Number of time steps to clamp query nodes
retention	ρ	0.4	Proportion of activity retained by node
propagation	π	$(1-\rho)$	Proportion of activity propagated by node
quiescence threshold	θ_q	0.00075	
significance threshold	θ_s	0.1	(This is actually the initial value $\theta_s(0)$.)
clamping decay	d_{clamp}	0.5	Rate at which θ_s decreases during clamping
free decay	d_{free}	0.4	Rate at which θ_s decreases after clamping
beam width	b	15	Initial number of neighbors to propagate to
focusing factor	ϕ	0.75	Amount b is reduced at each time step

Table 8.1: A summary of the SCALIR retrieval parameters.

8.3.4   Evolution of the Activation Function

The initial design of SCALIR called for a sigmoidal activation function such as the one given in Equation 8.1. It was originally believed that the changes in slope had the desirable effect of pushing the state of a unit toward 0 or 1. Once the system was built, however, it became clear that this assumption was incorrect. Due to the use of a decaying significance threshold, the same activity value might initially correspond to an irrelevant item, and later to a relevant item. The "forced choice" behavior of the sigmoid function had the effect of shutting off nodes with small activities which might later prove significant. One solution would have been to adjust the temperature (T) parameter dynamically, but this seemed like an unnecessary complication.

Rather than trying to correct the forced choice behavior, a linear threshold function, similar to the one used in AIR, was tested. The lower cutoff region corresponded to the quiescence threshold, and the upper cutoff was supposed to prevent the unbounded growth of activity. Both thresholds would produce a nonlinearity that would enable the composed functions to represent problems that are not linearly separable.

After observing the system in operation, however, it was discovered that *the upper-bound thresholding never actually occurred*. The link weights were small enough, and neighboring items dispersed enough, that the level of activity never exceeded 1.0. This was verified over several queries. As a result, the thresholding was removed, making the activation function simply a linear identity map (not counting the quiescence threshold for very small values).

Due to this change and modifications to the clamping procedure, there are certain cases in which a node may have an activity level greater than 1. In particular, when fewer than five[5] nodes are queried, each query node will be "supersaturated" — that is, will have activity greater than 1 — during the clamping phase. Because the link weights are constrained such that total activity is nonincreasing, as explained in Section 8.3.1, this does not cause any instability. Furthermore, the supersaturation has never been observed in any nodes besides those queried, and then only during clamping.

The use of a linear function for f does prevent SCALIR from being able to represent certain associations such as XOR. Fortunately, this is not a serious limitation in information retrieval. A XOR B is equivalent to $(A \wedge \overline{B}) \vee (B \wedge \overline{A})$; few people ask a retrieval system for, say, all documents about apples but not oranges, and oranges but not apples. If a user did

---

[5]Assuming the total amount of activity input at each clamping step (the `*pump-volume*`) is 5.

want this set, he or she could simply ask it in two successive queries. Other nonlinear functions correspond to similarly improbable queries.

Whereas typical IR methods compute first-order relationships between terms and documents, SCALIR computes a local approximation of all associations (first and higher-order) between all items. This was first noted by Belew in his analysis of AIR [Bel89]. The computation is equivalent to repeated multiplication of a sparse matrix with both terms and documents on both dimensions, and nonzero entries on the diagonal to provide the gradual accumulation of evidence. SCALIR's retrieval process computes just the needed multiplications at run time. In contrast, the Latent Semantic Indexing technique [DDF+90] described in chapter 4 essentially precomputes all the associations.

8.3.5 The Retrieval Algorithm

Figure 8.7 gives a general view of SCALIR's retrieval algorithm. The θ_s, θ_q, and b parameters have been discussed before. Decaying these parameters simply means setting them to the decay factor times their old value (e.g., $b(t)$ becomes $b(t-1) \times \phi$). Recall that there are actually two decay rates for θ_s, one during clamping and one after.

The variable names shown in all capital letters represent sets. QUERY--NODES contains all the nodes chosen by the user during the query. ACTIVE-NODES is the set[6] of nodes from which activity continues to propagate. RESPONSE-SET contains all nodes which have passed the significance threshold. They are displayed on the screen.

As is clear from the test at the end of the loop, SCALIR has four termination conditions. In decreasing order of likelihood, they are:

- *Search Beam Width Zero.* When b is reduced to the point that nodes are no longer spreading activity to their neighbors, the propagation loop stops.

- *Significance Decays to Quiescence.* When $\theta_s \leq \theta_q$, no more nodes will ever be retrieved, so there is no sense continuing propagation.

- *Response Set Reaches Maximum Size.* SCALIR has an adjustable parameter that sets a maximum on the number of responses to retrieve. This is currently set at 60, and is based on the approximate maximum number of items that could be displayed on the screen if all node clusters (terms, cases, and statutes) filled their portion

---

[6]Because this is ordered, it is technically a priority queue. But like a set, it contains at most one instance of each element.

Set θ_s **to initial value.**
Set b **to initial value.**
Set ACTIVE-NODES **to** QUERY-NODES.
Repeat {
    If still clamping, set activities of nodes in QUERY-NODES.
    Set RESPONSE-SET **to all nodes in** ACTIVE-NODES **whose activity is above** θ_s.
    Remove from ACTIVE-NODES **all nodes whose activity is below** θ_q.
    Add first b **neighbors of nodes in** ACTIVE-NODES **to** ACTIVE-NODES.
    Update activities of all nodes in ACTIVE-NODES.
    Sort ACTIVE-NODES.
    Decay b.
    Decay θ_s.
} **Until** $(b = 0)$ **or** $(\theta_s \leq \theta_q)$ **or** $(|\text{RESPONSE-SET}| = \textbf{maximum})$ **or** $(\text{ACTIVE-NODES} = \emptyset)$.

Figure 8.7: SCALIR's retrieval algorithm. Names in all capitals are sets.

of the display. In practice, terms and cases are more likely to be retrieved than statutes, so some retrieved items will not be visible.

- *No More Active Nodes.* This is a weak equilibrium condition. Because the activity of all nodes begins to decay at least as soon as the clamping phase ends, the active nodes will eventually become inactive.

Note that there is no stronger equilibrium condition ("stop when no new nodes get activated"), because the net is so large that this never occurs before other factors halt the propagation. Typically about 500 nodes, or just over 3% of the network, are involved over the course of any retrieval, with 100-200 of these active at any one time.

The remaining issue from the algorithm is to define "update the activity of a node." For now, we will consider nodes connected only by C-links. Recall that each node retains ρ times its old activity and passes on $(1 - \rho)$ to its neighbors. Thus the new activity a_i of a node i is

$$a_i(t+1) = \rho a_i(t) + (1 - \rho) \sum_j w_{ij} a_j(t) \qquad (8.4)$$

where the j are all the nodes which have links to node i. Because all nodes pass on $(1 - \rho)$, we can simply put this factor on the "receiving end." More generally, we might say that $a_i(t+1) = f(x)$, where x is the entire right hand side of Equation 8.4. But because the identity function $f(x) = x$ is used (see Section 8.3.4), this term is unnecessary. Note that the thresholding operation is done separately in the algorithm.

8.4 Hybrid Activity Propagation

If neighboring documents are those that share many of the same terms, we can view C-links as the "streets" that connect them. But if C-links are streets, S-links are like interstate highways; they provide a direct path between two disparate parts of the network. This is shown conceptually in Figure 8.8.

So far, SCALIR's activity and retrieval mechanisms have been discussed as though all activity propagates uniformly through the system. However, this is not the case. Because SCALIR's network is heterogeneous (or, alternatively speaking, because SCALIR's nodes are part of more than one network), this simple model cannot capture all of the processing.

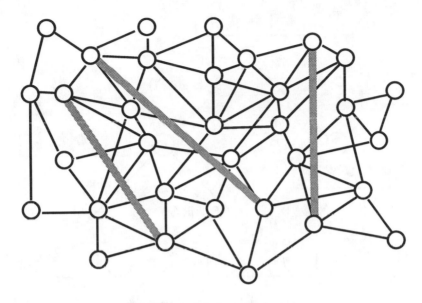

Figure 8.8: S-links as highways.

The purpose of SCALIR's labeled links (H-links and S-links) is to give the system the ability to pass activity selectively. That is, an S-link[7] should be able to "decide" whether or not to pass "markers" depending on their "tags." In contrast, C-links — fulfilling their role in the inter-changeability property of activations in connectionist networks — must pass all activity equally well.

In order to provide a mechanism for hybrid learning, it is necessary to use a common medium for the S-link markers/tags and the C-link activities. Conceptually, this is accomplished by viewing C-links as modulators of quantity and S-links as modulators of quality of the same substance. Perhaps the best way to envision this relationship is to view activity as light. Active nodes "glow," propagating light to their neighbors. C-links are like grey filters; they pass all wavelengths of light, but with attenuated intensity. S-links are like colored filters, passing only a single color (a small band of wavelengths).[8] When a node is queried, it glows with white light — all wavelengths are present. However, *the activation "color" of a node's neighbor depends on the type of link between them.*

Note that once the light has been colored by a filter, it stays colored.

---

[7]For the remainder of this section, I use S-links as examples of labeled links, though H-links are equally valid.

[8]Actually, colored filters may also reduce intensity, as S-links may reduce activity.

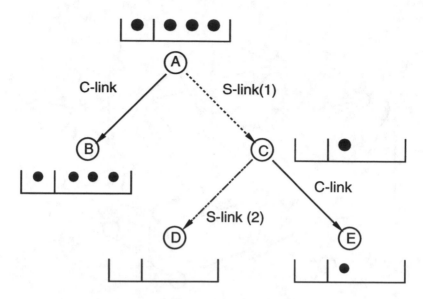

Figure 8.9: Hybrid activity propagation.

This means that the entire network can be made to pass only a certain kind of activation, *without the need for any global information*. This makes the system especially amenable to future implementation on a parallel message-passing architecture.

To implement the "colored light" properties, SCALIR represents activity as a *vector* rather than a scalar quantity. The initial component of the vector, indexed zero, corresponds by convention to miscellaneous unfiltered light containing all wavelengths — that is, to white light. The symbol μ (for "miscellaneous") is used to signify this component. Each other component of the vector corresponds to a specific type of wavelength — to a specific color. These components are associated with the symbol τ (for "typed"); a specific type may be labeled τ_1, τ_2, etc.

Figure 8.9 shows an example of the hybrid propagation scheme. The large circles in the figure represent nodes in the SCALIR network; the different arrows represent different kinds of links. C-links are shown as solid arrows, S-links (of various types) as arrows with various shadings. The rows of dots represent the activity vectors; the single dot at the left of each represents the miscellaneous activity, while the others are all the typed components. Suppose the node A at the top of the figure is activated with all colors. Because the link to node B is a C-link, it passes all of A's colors of activation to B, attenuated by the weight on

190

the link. In contrast, the link to node C is an S-link of type 1, so only the corresponding component of activity gets passed along. Finally, note that node D gets *no* activity, since the type of the link from C to D does not match the type of activity present at C.

Because SCALIR has 28 different labeled link types (8 H-links and 20 S-links), each activity vector must have 29 components, the extra representing the miscellaneous activity. Vector storage and manipulation is computationally expensive, particularly when we consider that most of the components will be zero for most nodes most of the time. For this reason, the vectors are represented internally as lists of tagged values. For example, the vector [0.0, 0.3, 0.0, 0.0, 0.0, 0.7] would be represented by the list ((1 0.3) (5 0.7)). This more concise representation allowed more of the network to reside in memory, more than offsetting the extra cost of performing the pseudo-vector operations.

Throughout this chapter, I refer to the "level of activation" of a node as a scalar quantity. For example, I said that nodes whose activity levels were greater than the significance threshold were retrieved. It should now be clear that the "level of activation" of a node is not equivalent to the activation itself. Rather, the level, or intensity, of activation, is a *function* of the node's activation vector, basically equal to the length (norm) of the vector. (See Section 8.5 for details.) This allows negatively activated components to make positive contributions to the overall activity level of a node.

The vector representation of activity requires a refinement of the activity update rule given in Equation 8.4. The set of links between two nodes can be viewed as a vector of weights, where the zeroth component is the C-link and the others are the typed links. Some of the new terms are simply the vector equivalents of the terms in the previous equation; others are more complex. The new rule is:

$$\mathbf{a}_i(t+1) = \rho \mathbf{a}_i(t) + (1-\rho) \sum_j [a_j^\mu(t)\mathbf{w}_{ij}^* + (\mathbf{a}_j^*(t) \diamond \mathbf{w}_{ij}^*) + \mathbf{a}_j(t)w_{ij}^0] \quad (8.5)$$

where the superscripts indicate components; $*$ means "all but the initial component" (that is, all but the miscellaneous component of the activity vector, and all but the C-link of the weight vector). The "$\diamond$" symbol represents the component-wise vector product. The propagation of activity can be broken into three steps corresponding to the three terms in the sum:

1. Activity flows from the miscellaneous component of node j (a_j^μ) across all typed (labeled) links to the corresponding typed activity components of node i (a_i^τ). This is a one-to-many process.

2. Activity flows from the typed components of node j through the typed links to the corresponding typed components of node j. This is a one-to-one process, and activity of a certain type only flows when that link type is present.

3. Activity flows from all components of node j through a single C-link to the corresponding typed components of node i. This is a one-to-one process, but all types participate.

These different operations are shown conceptually in Figure 8.10.

The propagation of activity from one SCALIR node to another can be viewed as the flow of activity through a little feedforward network with only some connections specified, as shown in Figure 8.11. This in turn can be represented by the appropriate matrix algebra, and the elements of the matrix which get filled provide another perspective on the nature of hybrid propagation.

Consider two nodes, j and i with activities [0.2, 0.2, 0.2, 0.2] and [0.0, 0.0, 0.0, 0.0], respectively. Imagine an H/S-link of type 1 from j to i with weight 0.4, and another connection of type 3 with weight 0.6. Also assume that j is the only neighbor propagating activity to i. As the four-dimensional vector indicates, there are three possible types of activity, plus the miscellaneous component, in the example.

We can write the activity of i (or at least, j's contribution to it) as follows:

$$a_i = Wa_j. \qquad (8.6)$$

By following the first two steps of the the propagation procedure (we can omit the third since there is no C-link), we can fill in the weight matrix and get the following equation:

$$
\begin{bmatrix} 0.0 \\ 0.16 \\ 0.0 \\ 0.24 \end{bmatrix} =
\begin{bmatrix} 0 & 0 & 0 & 0 \\ 0.4 & 0.4 & 0 & 0 \\ 0 & 0 & 0 & 0 \\ 0.6 & 0 & 0 & 0.6 \end{bmatrix}
\begin{bmatrix} 0.2 \\ 0.2 \\ 0.2 \\ 0.2 \end{bmatrix} \qquad (8.7)
$$

There are two important things to notice about the weight matrix (aside from the fact that it's lower triangular). First, the only diagonal entries are those where an H- or S-link is present. Second, the only nondiagonal entries are those in column 0, where activity flows from a miscellaneous component to a typed component. These two sets of entries correspond to the second and first "steps" of hybrid propagation, respectively.

What about nodes connected by C-links? Because all components of activity get modulated by C-links, the weights on these links serve as

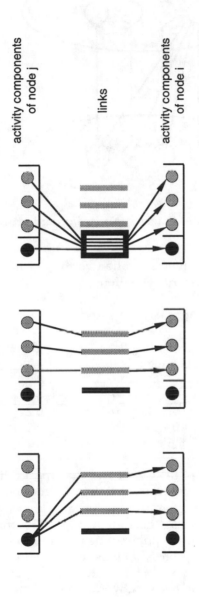

Figure 8.10: A conceptual view of activity propagation. Each of the three activity flows depicted corresponds to one of the sum terms in Equation 8.4. The solid circles are the miscellaneous activity components; shaded circles are the typed components. Similarly, solid bars are C-links; shaded bars are H- and S-links.

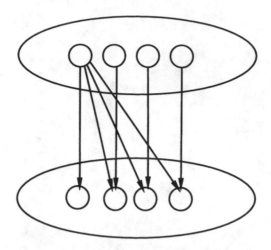

Figure 8.11: Two SCALIR nodes as a feedforward network.

scalar multiples for the incoming activation vector. For nodes with both C- and H/S-links, we can rewrite Equation 8.6 as

$$\mathbf{a_i} = \mathbf{W}\mathbf{a_j} + w_{ij}^0\mathbf{a_j}. \tag{8.8}$$

But this is equivalent to simply adding the C-link weights to the diagonal of matrix $\mathbf{W}$ (assuming C-link weight is 0.2):

$$\begin{bmatrix} 0.04 \\ 0.20 \\ 0.04 \\ 0.28 \end{bmatrix} = \begin{bmatrix} 0.2 & 0 & 0 & 0 \\ 0.4 & 0.6 & 0 & 0 \\ 0 & 0 & 0.2 & 0 \\ 0.6 & 0 & 0 & 0.8 \end{bmatrix} \begin{bmatrix} 0.2 \\ 0.2 \\ 0.2 \\ 0.2 \end{bmatrix} \tag{8.9}$$

(Note that $W_{1,1}$ is the sum of the C-link and the type 1 S-link. The fact that the sum is the same as the type 3 S-link is a coincidence.)

One possibility is to treat the propagation and learning in SCALIR as occurring at the level of these "micro-networks." This might possibly allow for easier analysis, but it would not be practical to implement the system in this way. The reason is that the connectivity of the micro-networks is an order of magnitude higher than the actual connectivity of the SCALIR network. The micro-network would *always* need at least $2k$ connections between any two "macro-nodes" (where k is the number of possible activity components), even when the actual SCALIR network contained only a single link between those nodes.

8.5   Antirelevance and the "But Not" Operator

Many information retrieval systems make use of a BUT NOT operator; a user may be interested in, say, birds but not waterfowl. In traditional Boolean terms, A BUT NOT B is equivalent to $A \wedge \overline{B}$. Clearly, users of SCALIR should be able to formulate queries of this type. Furthermore, during the browsing stage (described in chapter 10), the system should have a way to process negative as well as positive feedback from the user.

Initially, it might appear that the best way to handle negative feedback as well as BUT NOT queries would be to clamp the negative query nodes with negative activity. However, this would overload the meaning of negative activity. Recall that many H-links correspond to negative or positive citations between cases. These are represented by negatively or positively weighted links *of the same type*. Thus a given component of a node's activity vector may contain negative values. This doesn't mean "this case is irrelevant," but rather "this case became active through a negative citation path." These cases certainly aren't irrelevant; a lawyer wants to know what decisions criticized the one he or she is examining.

The solution to the negative overloading problem was to introduce an additional "antirelevance" component into the activity vector, selected by the index[9] -1. Negative query nodes divide up several units of antirelevance (*pump-volume*/2) just as positive query nodes share several units of relevance. Antirelevance is treated as a typed (as opposed to miscellaneous) activity component with no matching links. This means it propagates only across C-links. This is desirable in some instances (if I'm not interested in this case, that doesn't mean I'm not interested in anything it cites), but not in others (if I'm not interested in this chapter of the statute, I'm probably not interested in any of the sections in it). Thus this is not a completely satisfactory solution.

We can now be clear on precisely what "level of activation" means. With respect to a node's status as active — that is, continuing to propagate activity, and not quiescent, the level of activation is simply the length of the vector:

$$\text{level}_{\text{act}}(\mathbf{a}) = \|\mathbf{a}\| = \sqrt{\sum_{k=-1}^{n} a_k^2}. \qquad (8.10)$$

(Here the subscript refers to the vector component, and the superscript to exponentiation, as in traditional notation; n is the highest vector com-

---

[9]Negative indices are possible in this implementation, because the vectors are represented as tagged lists.

ponent index.) With respect to determining relevance, however, the level excludes — and subtracts off — the antirelevance component:

$$\text{level}_{\text{rel}}(\mathbf{a}) = \sqrt{\sum_{k=0}^{n} a_k^2} - a_{(-1)}. \qquad (8.11)$$

By using these two different measures for quantifying levels of activity, SCALIR is able to handle the concept of nodes that are "very active but not relevant." If only the former measure (8.10) were used, then antirelevant nodes would be retrieved, because they might be significantly active. If only the latter measure (8.11) were used, antirelevant nodes would be culled as quiescent, thus preventing antirelevance from propagating.

8.6 "Symbolic" Queries

The most common queries a SCALIR user might ask are general ones: "What documents are about this topic?," "What documents are like this one?," or even "What is this document about?" In none of these examples does the user specify the type of association to examine. The queries are implemented by simply setting the miscellaneous activity component of the query nodes and letting activity propagate according to the rules given previously.

Suppose, however, that a user is interested in a query such as "What cases criticized this decision?" SCALIR's hybrid representation supports this type of query, but it is more complicated — and somewhat less effective — than the general type. The activation vector makes it easy to restrict the type of activation that gets passed. We simply activate only the typed component of the vector, and the activation rule insures that only the matching links will propagate this activity. For a query like "What key numbers fall under this general topic?," the system works quite well.

These "symbolic" queries are less precise when they involve document nodes, however. The reason is that because C-links pass all vector components, restricting the propagation to a specific type of *labeled* link does not prevent propagation through *unlabeled* links. Consider the small network shown in Figure 8.12. In this figure, the user has issued a general query to the case *A v. B*. The case node is given miscellaneous activity, which propagates through all links and is filtered according to their type.

Now consider the same network activated by a "symbolic" query, as shown in Figure 8.13. The user has asked for cases that disagreed with

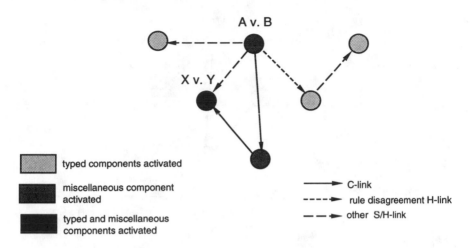

A v. B

X v. Y

typed components activated

miscellaneous component
activated

typed and miscellaneous
components activated

C-link

rule disagreement H-link

other S/H-link

Figure 8.12: Propagation of miscellaneous activity from a general query.

the rule of *A v. B*. Those nodes that were associated through chains of H- and S-links of other types are no longer activated, but those connected by C-link paths (like *X v. Y*) still are. Thus SCALIR does not support "pure" symbolic queries, at least as currently implemented.

One simple solution that would alleviate this problem is to change the way symbolic queries are initiated. Rather than placing the "colored" activity at the query node itself, SCALIR could execute a special first-pass local propagation, "manually" placing the correct activation components on just those neighbors of the query node that were joined by the correct type of labeled link. However, this would simply defer the problem; it would not prevent the C-linked-neighbors of the query node's neighbors from becoming active.

Alternatively, a more extreme solution would be to simply disable propagation through C-links for the duration of the query. This would be relatively easy to do in the current implementation of SCALIR. However, all other facets of the system have been designed to require only local computations, to facilitate future porting to parallel hardware. The disabling of C-links would violate this "local information" policy, and may thus be undesirable.

A final issue concerning the propagation of symbolic activity is the transitivity of certain associations. There are some instances where transitivity is almost certainly desirable, such as the subsumption relationships in a hierarchy. For example, if I want to know what key number topics fall under a certain topic, I certainly want to know what subtopics

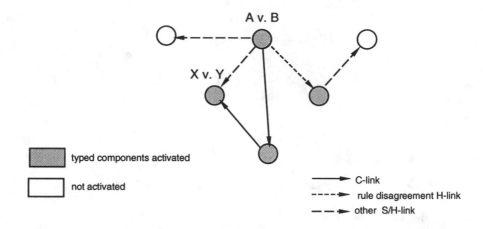

A v. B

X v. Y

typed components activated

not activated

C-link
rule disagreement H-link
other S/H-link

Figure 8.13: Propagation of typed activity from a "symbolic" query.

fall under those as well. There are other cases where transitivity really doesn't make sense, such as in dissenting opinion citations. If I want to know if a case B cited the dissenting opinion of case A, that doesn't mean I want to know if anyone cited the dissenting opinion of B. In this case, propagation should stop after crossing one link. Finally, there are examples where the answer is ambiguous: If I am interested in cases that criticized this one, it is not clear whether I should also be interested in cases that criticized *those* cases.

As currently implemented, all links in SCALIR are transitive. This could be altered by having a more complex activation rule for each type of labeled link. For example, if we are interested in finding cases that cited the dissenting opinion of A, the H-link could cause a sort of Doppler effect, changing the "color" of the light to, say, a general citation. This would allow the system to retrieve cases that cited the dissenting opinion, and any cases that cited those.

A related effect already occurs along the fact and rule dimensions of H-links. If case C criticized case B which criticized case A, and we ask about cases that criticized A, the negative weights on the criticized H-links will repeatedly invert the activity. This is consistent with the semantics of negative citation links. These "phase shifts" also support cancellation of conflicting evidence; a case is unlikely to be retrieved if one chain of evidence suggests agreement on facts and another chain suggests disagreement.

Unfortunately, because the calculation used to determine relevance

198

involves the norm of the activity vector, SCALIR cannot currently distinguish between negative and positive citations. This is a serious limitation. The problem might be overcome by modifying the "level of activity" calculations, but this requires further study.

Chapter 9

Feedback and Learning

In addition to the short-term dynamics that occur during retrieval, the SCALIR network also exhibits long-term changes — in the form of weight modification and link creation — that affect its behavior over many queries and many users. This learning occurs at run time, in response to users' browsing behavior. This chapter includes a range of discussions about learning issues, from a general examination of learning strategies for information retrieval to the tuning of specific parameters in candidate learning rules. Although they differ in scope and detail, they can all be viewed as successively refined versions of the question "how can SCALIR learn?"

The most general answer suggests a learning strategy appropriate for this type of system in this problem domain, providing a kind of template for a learning rule. The next level of detail attempts to instantiate the template with specific properties of the system (activation of queried nodes, level of feedback received, saturation of various weights, and so on). Simulations are performed to narrow the set of relevant terms. Finally, the learning rule is specialized to handle SCALIR's vector-valued activation, refined to behave more effectively, and demonstrated on some simple examples.

9.1   Choosing a Learning Approach

A primary virtue of connectionist systems is their ability to learn from experience. There are three general types of learning: supervised, unsupervised, and reinforcement. (A more detailed survey may be found in Hinton's review of connectionist learning methods [Hin89].)

In a *supervised* regime, the system designer presents the system with a set of training inputs and the "target" outputs for those inputs. The system learns to produce the correct outputs for the training set, and then hopefully can generalize this solution for new data. If we know what output the system should produce for each input, we can measure the error in the actual response, and then sum the errors for all input-output patterns. (Generally the sum of squared target-output deviations is used, for various reasons.) The learning algorithm simply has to change each weight in proportion to its effect on reducing the error. Specifically, if the only connections in the network are from input units directly to output units, the weight change on a link from i to j is:

$$\delta w_{ji} = -\eta \frac{\partial E}{\partial w_{ji}} \tag{9.1}$$

where E is the total error and η is a constant known as the *learning rate*. If error is viewed as a function of all the weights, this learning rule, due to Widrow and Hoff [WH60] corresponds to a "steepest descent" of the error surface. The back-propagation algorithm [RHW86] extends the Widrow-Hoff idea to the case of multilayer networks, providing a mechanism for adjusting weights that do not directly receive a target. There are other supervised learning procedures for other network architectures.

At first glance, it might seem that supervised learning is not particularly useful, because we are simply training the system to reproduce an answer we already knew in the first place. There are two reasons why supervised learning is in fact beneficial. First, a supervised learning system can usually generalize to novel cases, or provide error-correcting capability. Second, we may be interested in using the representations the system develops, as in the case of Cottrell's work on image compression [CMZ87].

In an *unsupervised* regime, the system learns to detect regularities in the data, without being given an a priori set of "right answers." For example, the competitive learning procedure studied by Rumelhart and Zipser [RZ85] (but similar to several earlier approaches) finds clusters of similar input patterns. This is accomplished by having hidden units compete for the right to become active when that pattern is present. As Hinton points out [Hin89], this is equivalent to trying to minimize the error between the input pattern and its representation by a single active hidden unit. Alternatively, an unsupervised learning procedure may try to optimize a general constraint. Kohonen, for example, has used topographic constraints [Koh82], whereas Durbin and Willshaw's elastic net [DW87] tries to minimize a distance function.

In a *reinforcement* regime, the system is trained by getting a single, global, scalar-valued "reward" in proportion to the correctness (according to some domain-specific metric) of its outputs, without being told what the right answer should have been. Connectionist reinforcement schemes are often based on stochastic automata, in which each unit is viewed as an automaton whose weights determine the probability of producing a certain response [BA85]. As Hinton points out, reinforcement learning is useful in complex systems where computing derivatives of an optimization function is difficult. However, reinforcement can be extremely slow:

> Even in the trivial case when all the local variables contribute independently to the global reinforcement signal, $O(NM)$ trials are required to allow the measured effects of each of the M possible values of a variable ... [with] N other variables. ... It is as if each person in the United States tried to decide whether he or she had done a useful day's work by observing the gross national product on a day by day basis. [Hin89]

None of these approaches is quite suited to the information retrieval domain. As discussed in chapter 4, IR does not have an analogue to absolute right and wrong answers. If a user is retrieving a set of documents, some may be more relevant than others, but this is user- and task-dependent. Even if we believe that a perfect relevant and non-relevant set exists, the set is not known, and thus could not be used for training. A small number of input-output pairs (queries and "correct" responses) could be manually prepared, but this will be so much smaller than the number of possible queries and responses for even modest-sized corpora that generalization is unlikely. All these reasons suggest that supervised learning is not appropriate.

Unsupervised learning is a possibility, but it is not clear what the network should be trying to learn. One can imagine optimization functions (perhaps based on word co-occurrence statistics) that attempted to alter the representation of documents or terms to form useful clusters. However, such functions could probably be used more efficiently by algorithmic clustering methods. In any case, they would not take user preferences into account.

Reinforcement learning is perhaps most plausible, but it requires knowing how good a retrieval set is, and expressing this as a single number. Although such measures exist in IR [SM83], they require a priori knowledge of which documents are relevant.

Because of the different character of IR tasks, Belew's AIR system used an unconventional (by connectionist standards) adaptation mechanism. AIR used a *localized* reinforcement rule in which the "rewards" were supplied dynamically by users during each search session. Users responded to queries by optionally indicating, for each of the system's responses, how relevant the document was to them. This relevance feedback is incorporated into the process as a browsing mechanism. From the user's perspective, he or she is simply asking the system to push the search farther in one direction or prune it in another. But the AIR system uses this feedback to change the weights on the links, altering the representation of the documents themselves. This differs significantly from the more common type of adaptation in IR systems such as [SK86], in which relevance feedback is used only to formulate new (and hopefully better) queries.

9.2   Hybrid Learning and the Credit Assignment Problem

Chapter 6 described the credit assignment problem: determining which part of a program should be rewarded or punished for its role in an action. This problem was originally identified by Minsky [Min63] and received much attention in Samuel's work on teaching a program to play checkers [Sam63]. As noted earlier, connectionist learning algorithms address the problem by relying on the homogeneity of the representation. Through learning algorithms such as back-propagation [RHW86], the weight on each link in a network can be modified in proportion to its contribution to the result.

In SCALIR — indeed, in any hybrid system — the credit-assignment problem resurfaces. In a SCALIR retrieval, how much of the "goodness" of the answer depends on the S-links, how much on the H-links, and how much on the C-links? In theory, we can determine this by tracing activity back in time through the network, and computing the role each link played in the final result. However, because of the size and complex connectivity of the network, this is extremely difficult and costly. Furthermore, existing solutions for simpler networks [WZ89] require vast amounts of space as well as nonlocal computations. Thus this approach is not well-suited for the IR problem, in which connections between tens or hundreds of thousands of documents are used.

Conceptually, SCALIR's solution to credit-assignment is to provide a mechanism for *competition* between the heterogeneous components. Each H-link type competes with others to maintain its share of the total weight, and H-links collectively compete with C-links. This competition mechanism ultimately lets users apportion credit and blame to the different components. If a node retrieved through links of particular types is found useful, these links will become stronger at the expense of the untyped connectionist links. To achieve this, SCALIR's links are modified only by relevant activity components; this mechanism is described in Section 9.5.

In a sense, the competition between link classes may be viewed as the learning of a meta-parameter indicating the relative importance of the connectionist and symbolic components of the system. The value of this parameter, rather than being set or learned explicitly, emerges as a result of the many symbolic and sub-symbolic interactions that occur any time a node is activated by more than one mechanism.

9.3 Learning Rules that Use Feedback

To narrow our search for a learning rule, we need to examine exactly what information is available — both from the user and from the system — and then determine how to use if most effectively. Because learning corresponds to changes in weights (the system's "long-term memory"), we need to decide which weights to change, and by how much.

In trying to improve its performance through learning, an IR system has only two pieces of information: what it did and how the user responded. In SCALIR, the system's action takes the form of the activations of the nodes (especially those retrieved), and the user's response consists of a list of nodes to pursue further ("expand") and a list of nodes to suppress ("prune"). The nodes to expand (marked with a plus sign in the display) will be referred to as *positive feedback* nodes; the ones to prune (marked with a minus) will be called *negative feedback* nodes.

Consider a node i receiving input from another node j by a connectionist link with weight w_{ij}. (This analysis will treat all activities as scalar quantities as in a simple connectionist network; it will be generalized later on.) If node i receives positive feedback, how should the weight be changed? If j was active and w_{ij} was positive, and i being active was beneficial (since it received positive feedback), then clearly w_{ij} should be increased. Table 9.1 considers the other possibilities (negative feedback, negative weight, etc.); note that it is impossible for i to have had negative activity, because it would not have been retrieved in that case.

Once we know how to change the weight qualitatively, we need to decide *how much* to change the weight. We could just move the weight a small constant amount. However, this ignores some information that might help to learn more efficiently. The activity of node j is clearly important; if j was barely active, than the link really played little role in activating i (especially relative to other links from more active nodes).

Case	Weight	j	i	Feedback	Desired Change
1	+	+	+	+	↑
2	+	+	+	−	↓
3	−	−	+	+	↓
4	−	−	+	−	↑
5	+	−	+	+	↓
6	+	−	+	−	↑
7	−	+	+	+	↑
8	−	+	+	−	↓

Table 9.1: How weights should change under various conditions.

In that case, w_{ij} should be changed less. Feedback may also be non-binary, in which case we would like to change the weight more for strong feedback than for weak.

AIR relied on both sources of information to adjust the weights. AIR's learning rule treated weights as correlations between presynaptic[1] activity (at node j, in our j-to-i example) and postsynaptic feedback (at node i). Thus the new weight[2] of a node after feedback was:

$$w'_{ij} = \frac{\sum a_j f_i - \frac{1}{N} \sum a_j \sum f_i}{\sqrt{\sum a_j^2 (\sum a_j)^2} \sqrt{\sum f_i^2 (\sum f_i)^2}} \tag{9.2}$$

where f_i is the feedback at node i, a_j is the activity of node j, and N is the number of times this event has occurred.

A simpler reinforcement rule that uses the same information says simply to change the weight by a small amount proportional to both the presynaptic activity and the postsynaptic feedback:

$$\Delta w_{ij} = \eta f_i a_j \tag{9.3}$$

where η is again a constant *learning rate*.

In contrast, a typical supervised learning rule makes use of three sources of information — the presynaptic activity, the postsynaptic "feedback" (the target), *and* the postsynaptic activity:

$$\Delta w_{ij} = \eta (t_i - a_i) a_j \tag{9.4}$$

---

[1]This terminology is borrowed from neuroscience; the link from one node to another is being viewed as the synapse between two neurons.

[2]Unlike most connectionist learning rules, AIR's rule is not defined in terms of a change made to the old weight.

Can this approach be used for the IR domain? Intuitively, we would like to make larger weight changes when the node receiving feedback has "farther to go." It might be argued that when a user gives positive feedback, he or she is indicating a desire to make that node as active as possible. Thus we might use the feedback signal as a kind of "pseudo-target," resulting in a kind of "activation scaled" learning rule like this:

$$\Delta w_{ij} = \eta(f_i - a_i)a_j. \qquad (9.5)$$

In fact, there is a continuum of learning rules between Equation 9.3 and Equation 9.5. For positive feedback, both previous equations are special cases of the rule:

$$\Delta w_{ij} = \eta(f_i - \gamma a_i)a_j \qquad (9.6)$$

where γ, which ranges from 0 to 1, indicates how strongly to factor in the activity of the postsynaptic node. For negative feedback, the rule

$$\Delta w_{ij} = \eta[(1 - \gamma)f_i - \gamma a_i]a_j \qquad (9.7)$$

is used instead. When γ is 0.0, no activity scaling takes place; the same weight change is made regardless of how far node i was from its maximum level. When γ is 1.0, scaling dominates reinforcement completely, so that no weight change would occur when node i's activity approached a maximum (or approached zero, for negative changes).

9.4   A Simulation of Learning from Feedback

The ultimate test of a learning rule comes when it is used in a system with thousands of documents and dozens of users. But although the rules are still being refined, it is useful to try them out in a simpler, simulated IR environment. The particular simulation described in this section demonstrates the behavior of the learning rules under different conditions. In particular, the results of the simulation suggested that the concept of "activation scaling" (represented by the γ parameter), introduced in the last section, was not helpful.

The simulation was necessarily simplistic. Not only did it assume that a total relevance ordering existed over all the documents, it actually used those relevance ranks as its only source of information about them. What made the simulation worthwhile, however, was that it mimicked the "noisy" relevance judgments one might expect from a group of actual users.

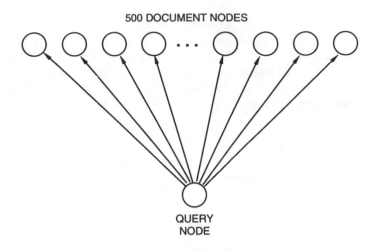

500 DOCUMENT NODES

QUERY
NODE

Figure 9.1: The simple network used for testing learning rule ideas.

The model was based on a simple feedforward network consisting of one "term node" connected to 500 "document nodes," as shown in Figure 9.1. Each imaginary document had a zero-based index indicating its relevance (i.e., document 0 was most relevant and document 499 least); the top 10 of these were considered "relevant" and the rest "nonrelevant."

To simulate retrieval, activity was placed on the query node and propagated to the document nodes. A sigmoidal activation function was applied, and the 10 most active nodes were considered to be "retrieved," and had a certain probability of getting feedback. Whenever any node received feedback, its incoming weight was updated according to the current learning rule. The process was generally repeated for 5,000 iterations.

Simulated feedback attempted to capture the subjective and context-sensitive relevance judgements of real users. Because real users may disagree about whether they like a given document, and a single individual may not give the same feedback response at different times, a stochastic model was used. The assumption of the model is that there are two reasons why a document might receive positive feedback. First, the user could feel that the document is relevant in an absolute sense, and want to find more like it. Second, the user could feel that the document was among the best retrieved (though perhaps "the best of a bad lot"), and want to steer the search toward this more promising direction. A corresponding argument holds for negative feedback.

Thus two factors were taken into account in deciding whether feed-

208

back was given to a retrieved node: The document's *absolute* "relevance" over the set of all documents (this was just the document's index), and its *relative* goodness over the set of retrieved documents. The two factors were defined as follows:

$$\text{abs\_fb\_factor} = \frac{i + 1.0}{N} \tag{9.8}$$

(i is the index and N is the total number of documents), and

$$\text{rel\_fb\_factor} = \frac{\text{rank\_in\_RET}_i}{|\text{REL}|} \tag{9.9}$$

where REL is the number of relevant documents, and rank_in_RET is the rank of the given document among all those retrieved.

These two factors (absolute and relative) were combined to form a weighted average "feedback factor":

$$\text{feedback\_factor} = \beta \times \text{abs\_fb\_factor} + (1.0 - \beta) \times \text{rel\_fb\_factor} \tag{9.10}$$

where β controlled the relative contribution of the two factors. A high β value simulated users who gave feedback according to a document's absolute relevance, whereas a low value corresponded to users caring only about how a document compared to others that had been retrieved. β was set to 0.5 for most of the experiments; high values produced little learning, whereas low values were extremely unstable. Ideally, we would like to determine β from empirical studies of user feedback behavior. However, such an experiment would be extremely difficult, because it would require a relevance ranking of all documents agreed upon by all users.

Actual feedback was determined by one of two tests: If the value of a random number over [0,1] was greater than the feedback factor, the node received positive feedback. If the value of a (different) random number was less than the feedback factor, the node received negative feedback. Otherwise the node received no feedback. Because a node cannot receive both positive and negative feedback, the second test occurred only if the first failed, with the order of the two tests (negative and positive) determined each time by a third random choice.

To evaluate the success of the learning rule, the *normalized recall* of the system was recorded at each time step. Normalized recall is a variant of the recall measure (defined in chapter 4) which takes ranked relevance into account [SM83]. It is defined as

$$\text{RECALL}_{\text{norm}} = 1 - \frac{\sum_{i=1}^{\text{REL}} \text{RANK}_i - \sum_{i=1}^{\text{REL}} i}{\text{REL} \times (N - \text{REL})} \tag{9.11}$$

where RANK$_i$ is the rank of the document in the entire corpus. The measure ranges from 0 to 1, and the goal of the learning rule is to maximize it over time. Note that normalized recall depends *only* on the positions of the relevant documents (specifically, if they are retrieved, and if not, how far they are from being retrieved). This means that normalized recall remains constant when the order of retrieved relevant documents is permuted, as well as when nonrelevant, nonretrieved documents are permuted.

An additional variable in the model was the distribution of the initial weights. If the weights were given random values between zero and one, the initial ranking would be completely random. However, SCALIR starts with "plausible" weights based on analysis of the text, not random weights. To simulate this, the link to each document i was set to the document's "relevance ratio" $(N - i)/N$ plus a uniform random value from [0.0, 0.5].

The results of this experiment were somewhat dissatisfying. Performance varied widely depending on the various parameters.[3] It was also highly dependent on the initial weights, which varied depending on the seed used for the random number generator.

Figure 9.2 shows six sample runs. In each case, $\beta = 0.5$, $T = 1$, and $\eta = 0.1$. The lower group of curves were run with random initial weights, the upper group of curves with the "plausible" weights described above. The three curves in each group correspond to γ values of 0.0, 0.5, and 1.0. The most notable aspect of the graph is that the ordering of the curves is completely different for the two groups. In one case, the lowest value of γ performs the best, while in the other, higher values seem to work better. Simply redoing the same condition with a different random start was often enough to change the order of the curves.

Why were the results so unpredictable? One reason was that for larger values of γ, negative and positive feedback had varying effects. (For example, a large weight change resulted when a highly active node received negative feedback, but only a small change when the same node received positive feedback.) This is consistent with the goal of making changes proportional to how far off a node is from its "target," but it conflicts with the expectation that negative and positive feedback should be equally strong statements of preference by the user.

Activation-scaling might even lead to incorrect learning. If the total feedback pumped into the system is constant independent of the number of nodes involved (as with activation), then the feedback at a given node

---

[3]In addition to γ, the learning rate η and the "temperature" T of the squashing function (from equation 8.1) were varied.

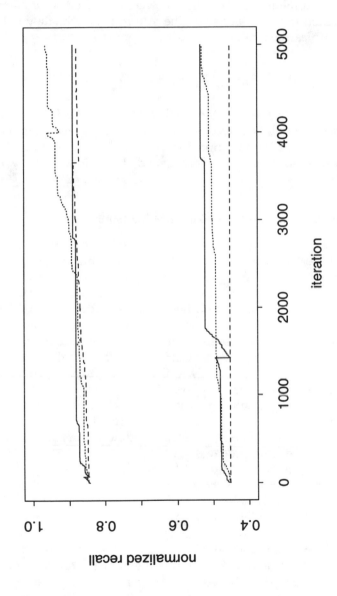

Figure 9.2: Normalized recall for different values of γ. The upper group of curves were tested with "plausible" initial weights, the lower group with random weights. In each case the solid line is the result for $\gamma = 0.0$, the dotted line for $\gamma = 0.5$, and the dashed line for $\gamma = 1.0$.

could be very small. Thus it is conceivable that a positively activated node receiving positive feedback could actually get a weight decrease, if the level of feedback was below the level of activation. Because the results of these preliminary experiments were inconclusive, and activation-scaling added to the risk of error, the γ term was ultimately not used in the SCALIR learning rule.

9.5 SCALIR's Learning Rule

The learning rule used in the final version of SCALIR is essentially based on the simple localized reinforcement rule given in Equation 9.3. However, several modifications are required to support the multiple link types, vector-valued activation, and dynamic activity levels used in SCALIR.

9.5.1 How Activity and Feedback are Measured

The simple learning rule is based on knowing the activity of a presynaptic node and the feedback of a postsynaptic node. But these quantities are dynamic in SCALIR. The activity of a query node is constant during clamping and then decays; the activity of most other nodes gradually increases during clamping and then decreases afterwards. What value, then, represents the "absolute" activity of a node for a given retrieval?

There are several possibilities. One is to simply use the activity level present at the end of the retrieval. However, this is misleading, because most nodes decay quite severely at the end of propagation. Ideally, the value used should reflect the node's total importance or contribution to the retrieval. This might be measured as the integral of the node's activity over time. Because all nodes are active for the same number of time steps, this can be approximated (modulo a constant factor) by the *average* activity during propagation.

The average activity is still problematic, however. The most important contribution of a node to the overall retrieval occurs when the node becomes significantly active. The period before and after this is less important. Thus SCALIR uses the *maximum* level of activity reached by the node during propagation. This technique was also used successfully in AIR. The maximum activity level is stored as one of the attributes of the node, and gets updated whenever the node's activity is updated.

For nodes that directly received a "prune" or "expand" signal from the user, the feedback value is easy to calculate. These nodes are initially clamped with a certain feedback and then allowed to decay; their maximum feedback will simply be the clamped value. The feedback is divided up among the vector components in proportion to how large each component was in the activity vector (or in the case of negative feedback, the negative of this component).

But what about neighbors of these feedback nodes? By the cluster hypothesis described in chapter 8, if the user liked one item, he or she would probably like others closely associated with it (all else being equal). Thus feedback should "spill over" to neighboring nodes. Furthermore, a node may have become active due to a chain of propagations; to reward or punish nodes at the start of the chain, those nodes must have access to some part of the feedback signal at the end of the chain.

For these reasons, feedback is allowed to propagate through the SCA-LIR network just like activity. In fact, the algorithm used for feedback propagation is identical to the one used for activity, except for two small differences. First, the link directions are reversed so that feedback flows "backwards" through the network. Second, since the purpose of feedback is not to retrieve anything, there is no concept of "significance" or "response set," and hence there can be no "maximum size of response set" termination condition. This occasionally makes feedback propagation somewhat slower than activity propagation.

Readers familiar with back-propagation (BP) may see some similarity in SCALIR's learning algorithm. However, the similarity actually lies only in the idea of "reversing" the propagation of activity. The differences are more striking: BP works for layered networks with scalar-valued activity and a single link type. BP also approximates gradient descent to any desired degree, and is guaranteed to find error minima, though possibly local. SCALIR's learning procedure works for unlayered, (potentially) fully recurrent networks with vector-valued activity and a multiplicity of link types, some symbolic and some connectionist. Furthermore, since relevance judgements cannot be made for all possible future queries, we have no way to measure a "correct answer," and thus there is nothing analogous to convergence to a globally minimum error. SCALIR's learning rule is a heuristic that, based on empirical evidence and previous experience with AIR, seems to produce the desired behavior.

As with activity, the maximum feedback at each node is recorded and updated during feedback propagation. When propagation is complete, the maximum values of feedback and activity at each node become the a_j and f_i of Equation 9.3.

9.5.2   Extensions for Vector-Valued Activity

The purpose of the learning rule is to reward or punish weights that caused beneficial or harmful action. But because activity does not propagate uniformly through SCALIR's different link types, the simple learning rule is not sufficient. In fact, two different learning rules are needed, one for C-links and one for H-links. S-links do not learn, so no third learning rule is required.

C-links pass all components of activity and feedback, so only a simple modification is needed. (Recall that SCALIR represents hybrid activity as a vector of different components, one corresponding to "miscellaneous" activity, the rest corresponding to different link types.) Substituting vectors for activation and feedback for the a_i in Equation 9.3 yields the following rule:

$$\Delta w_{ij} = \eta \mathbf{f}_i \mathbf{a}_j \tag{9.12}$$

Thus the inner product of the two vectors is used to determine the weight change.

This rule has correct properties with respect to hybrid activity and feedback propagation; it changes the weight in proportion to the overlap of the two vectors. This means that if, for example, the presynaptic node contained activity of type 1 only, and the postsynaptic node contained feedback of type 2 only, no weight change would be made. This is the correct action, because the presynaptic node played no role in what the user liked about the postsynaptic node.[4]

Each H-link passes only a single type of activity. Thus the change to an H-link weight should only take into consideration those components of the activity and feedback vectors that are allowed to pass through the link:

$$\Delta w_{ij} = \eta f_i^\tau (a_j^\tau + a_j^\mu) \tag{9.13}$$

where the superscript τ indicates the specific type of activity passed by that link, and μ indicates untyped ("miscellaneous") activity.

9.5.3   Damping, Normalization, and Learning Rate

The primary goal of the learning rule is to make long-term changes to the weights such that the system's performance improves. However, it should also meet some secondary goals: balancing the roles of different link classes, maintaining the conservation of activity, and providing steady yet stable weight changes.

---

[4]Note that this situation is only likely to arise when the feedback at the postsynaptic node is present due to propagation back through H- or S-links of a certain type.

As discussed in chapter 7, all weights out of any node must sum[5] to 1.0 in order to conserve activity. Furthermore, 1/3 of this sum is initially reserved for each of the three link classes (C-, H-, and S-links). Because S-links do not learn, they maintain their 1/3 share of the totally outgoing weight. C-links and H-links, however, compete for the remaining 2/3. Thus the maximum weight any (positive) link can attain is 2/3. This maximum value will be called M.

As a weight approaches the M boundary, it causes the other weights from the node to approach zero. This means that their contributions to other parts of the retrieval set are limited. To dampen this effect, positive weight changes are scaled by the weight's distance from M:

$$\Delta^+ w_{ij} = \eta \mathbf{f}_i \mathbf{a}_j (M - w_{ij}). \qquad (9.14)$$

The same term is analogously added to the H-link rule. In other words, if activity and feedback are constant, a small weight will receive a larger increase than a large weight. Note the difference between this new term and the γ parameter used in Equations 9.6 and 9.7. Both scale the magnitude of the weight change, but γ makes the change depend on the *activity* of the node — which is highly variable and dependent on the query — whereas the new term plays a damping role according to the *weight*.

Recall that initially negative-weighted links in SCALIR correspond to negative citations such as "criticized" rather than to inhibition or dissociation between nodes. Accordingly, positive weights should not be allowed to become negative (and vice versa). This means that the minimum weight of an initially positive link is zero. This results in a similar rule for negative weight changes:

$$\Delta^- w_{ij} = \eta \mathbf{f}_i \mathbf{a}_j w_{ij}. \qquad (9.15)$$

In practice, the prescaled weight change is computed (as in Equations 9.12 and 9.13) and then the appropriate scaling is done once the sign of weight change is known.

Irrespective of the damping term, additional normalization is usually necessary to keep the weight sum constant. During learning, all nodes whose links' weights were changed get checked for renormalization. If the new weight sum is greater than 1.0, the weights are all multiplied by the inverse of the sum. This is a fairly simple operation that adds a relatively insignificant amount of time to learning.

The only remaining parameter is the learning rate η, which controls how much change the system is willing to make each time a user expresses a preference. If η is too small, the network's improvement will

---

[5] Actually, it is the sum of the absolute values.

be very slow, and may appear unresponsive to user feedback. If it is too large, casual feedback may cause large unwanted changes. Large η may also cause oscillations when users disagree. Instead of gradually moving toward the mean of user preferences, some nodes may bounce in and out of the retrieved set. Finally, in certain circumstances large η values can override the damping term, especially with negative weight changes, allowing positive weights to become negative. For all these reasons, it is important to set η carefully.

The only real error condition is the negative weight situation, thus this is the only hard constraint. To prevent this, it is necessary that the magnitude of the negative weight change always be less than the weight itself (i.e., $\Delta^- w_{ij} < w_{ij}$). The maximum inner product occurs when both nodes i and j have activity/feedback of a single type. Thus we can drop the vector notation. Using Equation 9.15 and rearranging terms, this constraint amounts to the following:

$$\eta < \frac{1}{f_i a_j}. \tag{9.16}$$

The maximum activity in the network occurs at the clamped query nodes, the maximum feedback at the clamped feedback nodes. Furthermore, the greatest clamping value will occur when only one node is queried, and when only one retrieved node receives feedback. Because the total amount of negative feedback is half the amount of activity (known internally as the *pump-volume*), this yields the constraint

$$\eta < \frac{1}{\frac{1}{2}(*pump\_volume*) \times *pump\_volume*} \tag{9.17}$$

which is just

$$\eta < \frac{2}{(*pump\_volume*)^2} \tag{9.18}$$

For the usual *pump-volume* of 5, this gives an upper bound of 0.08 on η.

A heuristic way to set η to a reasonable level below this upper bound is to ask, "How many people should be required to give this node negative feedback before the weights that led to its retrieval approach zero?" (This is only a general approximation, because the damping term will slow convergence toward the asymptote considerably. Also, this envisions a extreme-case scenario in which only one node was queried and only one node, adjacent to it, received feedback.) Presumably, this will depend on the size of the user community and the frequency with which they give feedback, but it suggests η values on the order of 0.001 to 0.005 for a hypothetical SCALIR installation in a law firm with between 10 and 50 users.

9.5.4   Negative Feedback and Anti-Activity

When a user wants to prune a node, this normally causes the components of the feedback vector to be set to the negative of the corresponding activity components. However, there is one special case in which this is not the desired action. Consider a node A given anti-activity by the user, connected by a positively weighted link to a second node B. B gets some anti-activity from A and some normal activity from other sources. Now a user gives B negative feedback. We would like to *strengthen* the link from A so that A's anti-activity suppresses B's retrieval.

If the normal feedback procedure is used, however, the anti-activity component of the feedback vector will be set to the negative of its activity counterpart. The effect will be to *weaken* the link. To handle this case, the sign of the anti-activity component is *not* inverted when negative feedback occurs.

9.6   Demonstrations of Learning

To illustrate the behavior of the learning rule under various conditions, three experiments were performed on very small (three to five nodes) networks. (Learning tests on the full-scale network are discussed in chapter 11.) Each experiment measured a network's responses to positive and negative feedback. The simplest network had only one "layer," no recurrence, and only one link type; the other networks successively relaxed these conditions.

In each of the test networks, the following procedure was used:

1. One or two nodes were queried (i.e., clamped with positive activity).

2. Activity propagated through the network. Due to the small size of the network, there were only as many iterations as necessary to activate all nodes.

3. One node was marked for positive feedback and one for negative feedback.

4. Feedback was propagated through the network.

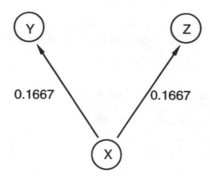

Figure 9.3: The **learn3** network.

5. All weights were adjusted according to the learning rule.

This process was generally repeated 20 times. Note that this is not the situation that would normally occur with actual users, because users' feedback signals automatically generate new queries with the items they wanted to expand on.

In all cases, the *pump-volume* was set to 1 and the learning rate (η) was set to 0.1. This high value of η is consistent with the η constraint described in the previous section, given the low value for *pump-volume*. Nevertheless, it is higher than would be appropriate for an actual use situation.

9.6.1 A Very Simple Network

The first network, called **learn3** (for the three nodes), is shown in Figure 9.3. This network consists of a node X connected by C-links to two other nodes Y and Z. As is the case with any initial network in SCALIR, the C-link weights (which in this case are all the weights) from each node sum to 1/3. Node X was queried, Y received positive feedback, and Z received negative feedback.

The activation-feedback-learning cycle was repeated 25 times. The resulting weight changes are shown in Figure 9.4. The upper curve represents the weight on the X→Y link; the lower curve is for the X→Z link. The former weight grows toward the maximum value M (2/3), whereas the latter approaches a minimum value of zero. Note that the slope of both lines decreases as the weight nears its asymptote; this is a direct result of the damping terms of Equations 9.14 and 9.15.

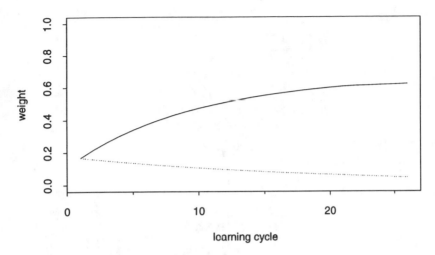

Figure 9.4: Weight changes for the **learn3** network. The solid line represents the weight of the X→Y link; the dotted line is for the X→Z link.

9.6.2 A "Two-Layer" Recurrent Network

A slightly more complicated example is the four-node recurrent network shown in Figure 9.5. In this network, both the feedback and the activity must propagate through two layers in order to have an effect. Again, the outgoing links of each node initially sum to 1/3 and will be allowed to range up to 2/3. Node W is queried, and nodes Y and Z are given positive and negative feedback as before.

Figure 9.5 also shows the link weights before learning and after twenty learning cycles. As expected, the X→Y weight increases and the X→Z weight decreases. By the end of the twenty learning cycles, node Y is over four times as active as initially, and over five times more active than node Z. These changes in activity level are shown in Figure 9.6.

Initially, the feedback effects from Y and Z roughly cancel when they reach X. But as the X→Y link gets stronger, more of Y's feedback than Z's reaches X. Thus the link from W to X also gets strengthened.

All of the weights on "inverse" links have also been increased. This is only slightly surprising at the link from Z to X. Because X eventually receives positive feedback (as explained earlier), it must be desirable to cause X to become active. Because Z is positively active (though decreasingly so) and has a link to X, Z can help increase X's activity by strengthening the link.

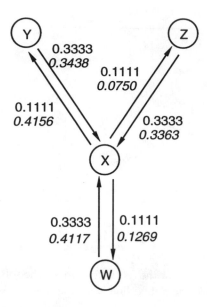

Figure 9.5: The **learn4rec** recurrent network. Weights before and after learning are shown.

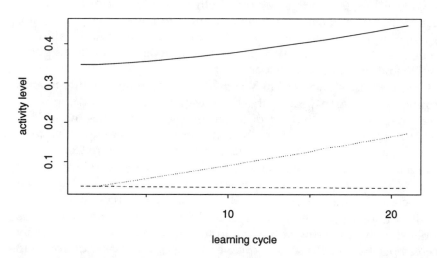

Figure 9.6: Activity levels for nodes X (upper curve), Y (middle), and Z (lower) in the **learn4rec** recurrent network.

220

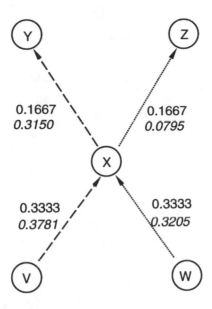

Figure 9.7: The **learn5h** network. Two types of H-links are used; weights are shown before and after learning.

9.6.3 An H-Link Network

The third network, shown in Figure 9.7, demonstrates the H-link learning rule. The network includes two types of H-links. Both nodes V and W are activated (with miscellaneous activity) as query nodes. Node Y receives positive feedback and Z negative feedback as before. Because feedback is apportioned according to how active each component was, Y's feedback and Z's are of two different types.

Figure 9.8 shows the activation levels after various amounts of learning. The activity levels shown for node X are actually the norms of the activity vectors; two vector components (one for each link type) are active. The results show the benefits of the hybrid propagation and learning rules. Node X is able to propagate both activity and feedback with no "crosstalk." This means that rather than cancelling out, the conflicting feedback can be channeled back to the previous layer. Thus the V→X link can be strengthened and the W→X link weakened simultaneously. This is evident in the before-and-after weights shown in Figure 9.7.

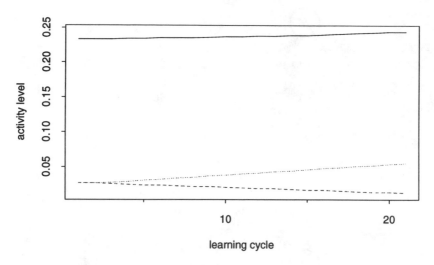

Figure 9.8: Activity levels for nodes X (upper curve), Y (middle), and Z (lower) in the **learn5h** network.

9.7 One-Shot Learning

In addition to learning by weight modification, SCALIR is also capable of "one-shot" learning under certain circumstances. For each node marked with positive feedback, SCALIR creates a new link from each query node to the marked node, unless the link exists already. The weight on each new link is set to the median of the existing weights from the presynaptic node. These new links can serve as relations for a kind of user-generated thesaurus; if users employ one term in a query and a related term gets retrieved and marked with positive feedback, the two terms will be associated from then on. The strength of the association is still subject to weight-adjustment learning subject to its later utility.

Whenever SCALIR encounters a previously unknown term, it creates a new node. The combination of this and the link-creation mechanism allows the SCALIR lexicon to grow dynamically. The new term may be of no value in its first retrieval, but it can be immediately connected to the rest of the network.

This one-shot learning technique is similar to one used in AIR. However, AIR's link-creation scheme was more extreme: Every node receiving positive feedback was joined to every other positive feedback node, as well as to every query node. Furthermore, negatively weighted links were created between every positive feedback node and every negative

222

feedback node.

There are several reasons why SCALIR modified this scheme. First, SCALIR includes a larger network with a substantially higher out-degree. It seemed impractical to create new links so often. Second, the motivation for associating all positive feedback nodes was less clear; users might be simultaneously pursuing different paths of interest, both related to the initial query but unrelated to each other. Third, negative links for dissociation would have been inconsistent with SCALIR's use of negative links for negative citations. Negative link creation also seemed to be responsible for the "miscellaneous cluster" problem described by Belew in his analysis of the AIR experiments [Bel86].

One disadvantage of SCALIR's more conservative approach is that compound terms do not get formed as easily. For example, if the query "database" retrieves the terms "data" and "base," and both receive positive feedback, their new association will be indirect (through the query term) rather than via a link between them.

9.8 Micro- and Macro-Experiments

This chapter has described two sets of experiments: a simple model of retrieval used to develop the learning rule, and some tests with small networks deliberately constructed to evaluate that rule. These experiments have been useful and successful. The simulation model of Section 9.4 demonstrated that a system can learn to improve its documents' representations, and thus improve normalized recall, even in the face of a noisy relevance feedback signal. It also revealed the sensitivity of learning to factors such as activation-scaling. The network tests described in Section 9.6 illustrated the correct behavior of the learning algorithm with respect to positive and negative feedback, asymptotic convergence on weight maxima and minima, and (perhaps most importantly) the ability to handle conflicting learning signals among multiple link types.

Experiments of this kind play an important role in the development of a system like SCALIR. They highlight problems or unnecessary complications relatively early in the design process. They can be used to demonstrate concept feasibility. In particular, the success of the learning rule for the test networks is a necessary condition for its ultimate success at the legal IR task.

Nevertheless, the models used in these experiments are far removed from this real-world task. This is perhaps most obvious for the simulation model. The simulation leaves out everything that gives SCALIR its power — spreading activation, accumulation of evidence, and hybrid representation, among others. Its model of user feedback behavior is based on unproven assumptions, and its distribution of hypothetical document relevance bears no relation to any real-world text corpus.

The tests of the actual SCALIR learning rule, however, are no less divorced from the real IR task. First, the actual networks for which SCALIR's learning algorithm is designed are thousands of times larger than the test networks. The real networks exhibit dynamics not found in the simple cases. Second, real user feedback automatically causes a new query to execute, thus a real net would never get the same activity-feedback sequence on successive searches. The intervening browsing search might well result in "unlearning" the previous feedback. Third, real users are unlikely to do the same search repeatedly, and different users doing the same search are unlikely to give the same feedback.

Thus although the "micro-experiments" of this chapter show promising results, they provide no guarantee that SCALIR's learning mechanism will work as intended. For this reason, "macro-experiments" are needed as well; the system must be tested with an actual text corpus and actual users. A study of this type is described in chapter 11.

Chapter 10

Interacting With SCALIR

This chapter returns to the user-system interface issues raised in chapter 2. A user's interaction with SCALIR is described in detail, the origins of the interface are discussed, as is user testing of the system. Finally, I attempt to assess how well SCALIR meets the design goals outlined at the conclusion of chapter 2.

10.1   How SCALIR Looks to the User

The SCALIR interface discussion begins by examining the initial layout of the screen. Figure 10.1 shows how SCALIR looks when the user starts the system. The screen is divided into three main nonoverlapping fixed-sized panes. The largest of these, the *network pane*, is the center of interaction. The network pane is used both to query the system and display results. The network pane initially displays three "dummy nodes" representing an imaginary case, term, and statute section. To the right of the network pane is the *text pane*, which is used to display the text of documents selected by the user. Below the network pane is the *command pane*. This provides an alternate (non-mouse-based) method for entering commands. It is also used to display messages describing the system's current action.

·A "noun-verb" syntax is used for most commands. Objects are normally selected by positioning the mouse pointer over the object so that it appears boxed, then pressing the left mouse button. The appropriate action is then chosen from the menu at the top of the screen.

The menu contains seven commands:

- *Clear* — Erases the existing display from the network and text panes,

225

226

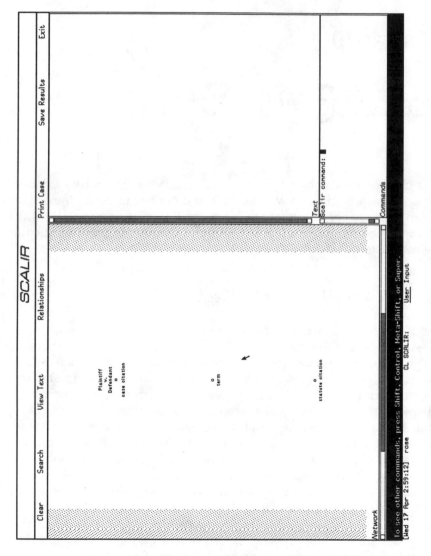

Figure 10.1: The SCALIR screen at the start of a session.

clears any current activation in the network, and displays a new set of dummy nodes for a new query.

- *Search* — Begins a new search using the marked query nodes. Nodes marked with a minus are considered **BUT NOT** terms and are clamped with anti-activity.

- *View Text* — Displays a pop-up menu of titles of recently viewed documents; selecting a title causes that document to reappear in the text pane.

- *Relationships* – Never implemented, this was to have provided a kind of "dialog box" to allow the user to choose which links to display (e.g., only links from query nodes, or only links of a certain type). This would have controlled the complexity of the display.

- *Print Case* — Sends the text of the selected case to the printer. This was deliberately left disabled due to copyright restrictions on SCALIR's database.

- *Save Results* — Saves a textual listing of all cases, terms, and statute sections queried and retrieved during the current query session.

- *Exit* — Performs cleanup operations and exits the system.

Two final screen regions, provided as a standard part of the Symbolics environment, provide status information. The thick black bar is the *documentation line*; it describes context-dependent information about the result of pressing each mouse button. For example, if the mouse pointer is over a menu item, the documentation line describes that command. Below this line is the *status line*. In addition to general Symbolics system information, the status line contains a progress indicator — a thin line under a text string at the lower right edge of the screen. This is used to show users how far a current operation has progressed.

10.1.1 Initial Queries

To formulate an initial query, the user selects one of the three dummy nodes. When the node is selected, a small window appears in which the user types a single descriptor. For term nodes, the descriptor is simply a word or a key number. This situation is shown in Figure 10.2, in which the user has just finished typing the word *chip*. For statute nodes, the descriptor is the official citation for the statute section in the *United States Codes Annotated* (e.g., 17 USCA 101). For case nodes, the

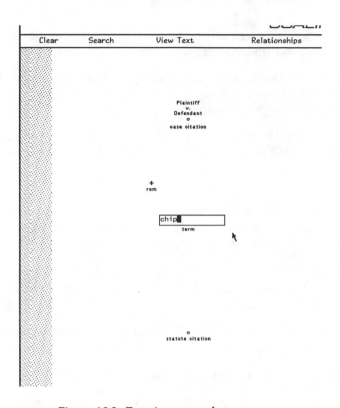

Plaintiff
v.
Defendant
o
case citation

+
rom

chip

term

o
statute citation

Figure 10.2: Entering a search term.

descriptor is the name of a litigant. After pressing return, a pop-up menu of case titles in which either the plaintiff or the defendant match the user's descriptor appears; the user then selects the desired case. This is shown in Figure 10.3.

After a descriptor has been entered, it appears as the label on a newly displayed node. Each descriptor is initially marked with a plus sign, indicating that the user wants to expand the search with that item. By selecting any node with a descriptor (i.e., not a dummy node), the user can cycle through three possible states: positive, negative, and neutral. Clicking on a positive node makes it negative (marked with a minus sign). Clicking on a negative node makes it neutral (marked with a dot). Clicking on a neutral node makes it positive. This allows users to correct any errors they may have made (because neutral nodes are not used in the query), or to change their minds about query terms.

The positive-negative-neutral cycle may not seem like an obvious

228

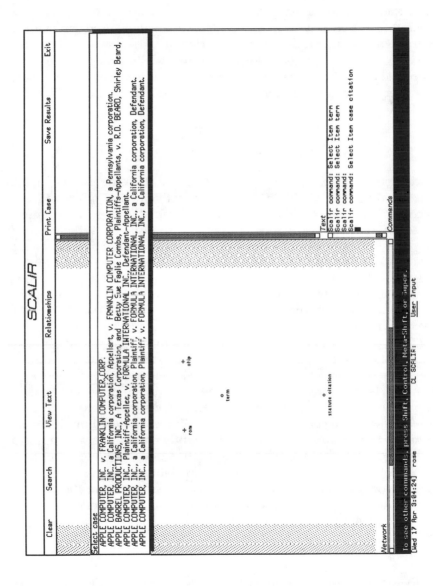

Figure 10.3: Choosing a case to be included in the query.

mapping of actions to states, but the alternatives were even less appealing. Some users were expected to be unfamiliar with using the mouse for input; restricting mouse use to a single button reduced this adjustment.[1] Furthermore, a natural mapping (negative left, neutral middle, and positive right — as on a number line) contradicted widely used conventions for three-button mice (select left, menu right).

The use of dummy nodes for initial queries eliminates the need for a separate query language.[2] Initial queries, like feedback queries, take on a query-by-example character; the user is asking for items "like this one."

10.1.2   Specifying Symbolic Relationships

In addition to indicating items to search on (by choosing positive query nodes) and those to avoid (by choosing negative nodes), users can also specify specific relationships of interest. (Internally, these were implemented by restricting activation at that node to a specific activity vector component.) This is done by pressing the middle mouse button when a node was highlighted. (This was a substantial violation of the one-button convention, but it seemed preferable to requiring that the user first mark the node and then select a menu command.) This action causes a small window to appear in front of the text pane, showing a "palette" of link types to choose from.

Link types on the palette are differentiated by shading (solid for positive, grey for negative), arrowheads (pointing to node for incoming links, away from node for outgoing links), and various dashed line types representing H- and S-link associations. The dashed lines proved difficult to distinguish (especially in the network pane, where they were much thinner), and would ideally be replaced with different colored lines. Colors could also be used to show activation from different sources, as suggested by the color metaphor for hybrid propagation described in chapter 8.

When the user selects a link from the palette, a matching link is be drawn to or from the selected node, as illustrated in Figure 10.4. This is intended to convey a sense of qualification: "find me all nodes such that this one is connected to them by this kind of link." Several link types can be added to the same node selection, thus the palette is "modal" and requires pressing an **END** key to be dismissed.

---

[1] However, this constraint was violated in two instances, the symbolic relationship command described later, and the Symbolics scroll bars.

[2] One might, however, consider the sequence of mouse selection operations a gestural language of sorts.

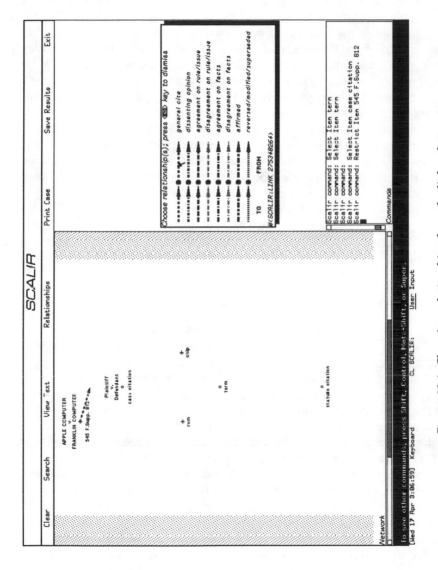

Figure 10.4: Choosing relationships from the link palette.

As initially envisioned (see, e.g., an earlier paper on SCALIR's interface [RB91b]), this process was viewed as letting the user *draw* the query. The palette was intended to be used to "select a drawing tool," so that any links drawn would come out with the chosen dashed line type. This idea was ultimately rejected because of problems in conceptualizing where the line would be drawn *to*. If users were permitted to draw the line from the selected node to any other node, it would convey the incorrect idea that activity would flow from the source node to the target node. It would be possible to require drawing the line to a dummy node, but users would probably be unclear on the reason for this. Furthermore, the next query term would turn the dummy node into a real node, reducing this to the previous problem. A third alternative was to have the users draw lines to or from arbitrary points in space. However, the drawing action would then no longer play any significant role in the process, only the palette selection. Thus in the current system, the user makes the palette selection, and the system draws the link.

It is important to note that the link palette is only needed for "symbolic" queries. As noted in chapter 8, there were problems in maintaining the "purity" of symbolic queries during activation. Thus they were not presented to users as a standard part of the system.

10.1.3   The Retrieval Display

Users can create any number of nodes for the initial query; when the user has finished entering items to be queried, he or she selects the **Search** command from the menu. The network pane is cleared and the (positive) query nodes are redrawn at the center. Immediately afterward, as activity spreads through the network, additional nodes (those that are significantly active) begin to appear, each one farther from the center than those previously displayed. This is shown in Figure 10.5. Items in the center are perceived by the system as being most relevant; those farther to the sides are increasingly less relevant.[3] Within a term, case, or statute cluster, the position of the next node displayed alternates between the left and right sides and between the upper and lower rows.

Nodes representing cases are displayed in two rows at the top of the network pane, those representing terms in two rows at the center, and those representing statute sections in two rows at the bottom. The purpose of the two rows is simply to fit more items into a smaller horizontal

---

[3]The relationship of relevance to distance is not linear, however; there are discrete positions for the next most relevant node at any time. Belew used a continuous logarithmic scale in one of AIR's optional display modes [Bel86].

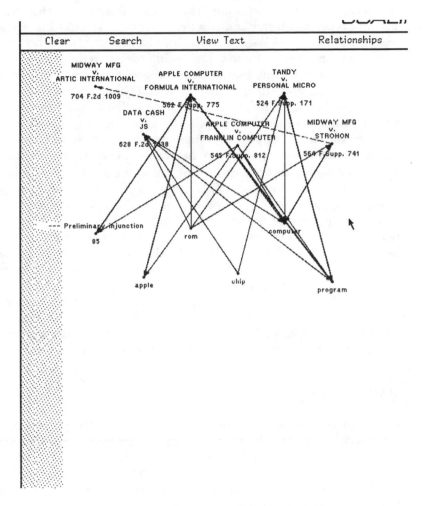

Figure 10.5: Incremental display of the network during activity propagation.

space. The diameter of each node indicates the node's activity. How-ever, due to the limited space, the range of possible diameters is highly constrained, and thus this feature is rarely distinguishable.

Whenever a new node appears on the screen, any links to it from previously displayed nodes are drawn. Line dashes and shading indi-cate link type, as on the link palette; connectionist links are shown as undifferentiated solid lines. Although links almost always occur in to-from pairs, only one of these is shown in order to reduce screen clutter. For C-links, arrowheads indicated the direction of activation flow that caused the later node to appear. For H- and S-links, arrows correspond to the semantics of the link (e.g., a "criticized" link would have the arrow from the citing case to the cited case.) Because links joining two nodes in the same row might appear to connect any intervening collinear nodes, a small random skew is added to the vertical position of each node.

To read the full text of a document, the user double-clicks on its node with the left mouse button. This causes a new scrollable window to appear in the text pane, with the title of the document at the top of the window. A portion of the text (currently 25 paragraphs) is read in from disk and displayed in the window. This is shown in Figure 10.6. When the user reaches the end of the currently displayed portion, he or she can select a hypertext-style text string "click here to see more of document."

The document windows are actually stacked in front of the original text pane. As a result, the user can switch back and forth between sev-eral documents simply by double-clicking their nodes. To prevent too many files from being left open, only the last 25 document windows are preserved. A least recently used strategy prunes the list of windows.

10.1.4   Browsing

Except for the initial query using dummy nodes, the system operates in "browsing" mode. The user looks at the retrieved items and decides which ones should be pursued further and which should be eliminated. Because the titles of cases are not very informative, the user will often spend a fair amount of time reading the text of selected documents before deciding whether to pursue them further.

The system displays retrieved nodes as small filled circles. When a user wants to expand the search further at a node, he or she selects it with the mouse, causing the circle to be replaced by a plus sign, as with the initial query. In fact, the browsing/feedback mechanism is identical to the initial query mechanism, except that there is no need to enter the descriptors.

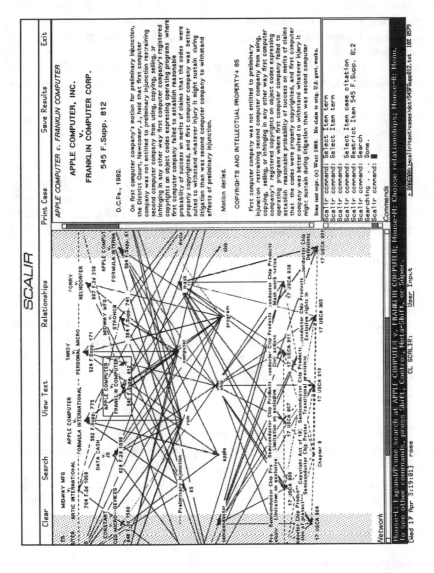

Figure 10.6: Viewing the text of a retrieved document.

235

Because there are more nodes than fit on the screen at once, the network pane scrolls horizontally. A potential danger of this scrolling is that the user would "get lost" and no longer be able to tell where the most important nodes (the initial center of the display) were. To avoid this problem, the sides of the network pane are shaded progressively darker, as shown in Figure 10.7. This serves two purposes. First, the shading makes the relationship of the current position to the center clear. Second, the shading makes it increasingly difficult for users to read the names of items farther from the center. This gives a physical representation to the conceptual notion of documents at the fringes being less salient, and discourages their overuse. (Users can always highlight the nodes and read their titles from the documentation line at the bottom of the screen.)

When the user is finished marking nodes for expansion or pruning, he or she selects the **Search** command and the retrieval process repeats. Typically a user will do two or three of these browsing "probes" following each initial query. To start an entirely new search, the user presses **Clear**.

In its normal mode of operation, SCALIR uses the browsing probes as a feedback signal for learning. As described in chapter 9, feedback must be propagated through the network, weight changes must be made, and links resorted. During the feedback propagation, the message "Processing user preferences . . . " appears in the command pane, while a progress indicator is used in the status line. Feedback propagation usually takes at least as long as the initial search. But unlike the initial search phase, the user does not get any visual representation of the system's actions, except for the progress indicator. This issue will be discussed later on. Messages also appear during the weight-changing and link resorting operations, but these generally take only a few seconds.

10.2   User Testing

Evaluation of users' experience with SCALIR focused on both low- and high-level issues. The low-level issues include the physical attributes of the interface, such as what mouse click was required or how a menu item was labeled. In fact, some of these applied not only to SCALIR but to graphical interfaces generally, a confounding factor inherent in SCALIR's graphical design. The high-level issues related to the general functionality provided by SCALIR, such as query formulation.

To evaluate the effectiveness of interaction with SCALIR, two groups of users tested the system. The first group consisted of four attorneys, one of whom was currently teaching a course on legal research. All of the lawyers had at least some practical experience with copyright law.

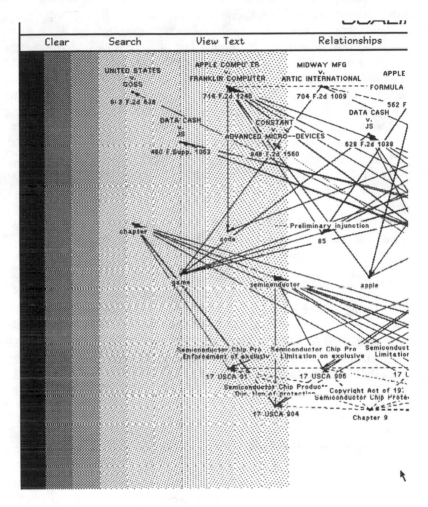

Figure 10.7: Shading conveys decreasing relevance.

Three were familiar with traditional computer-assisted legal research systems. Only one had used a computer with a mouse. These users were
encouraged to describe what they were doing and make any comments
they desired, and audio recordings were made of their sessions. Unless
noted otherwise, user comments will be from this first group.

The second group consisted of fourteen computer-science graduate
students, one of whom also had a law degree and had done legal research in the past. Although specific data were not collected about their
information retrieval experience, most reported that they used the university's on-line bibliographic retrieval system. All were experienced
computer users familiar with mouse-based windowing systems.

Users were given a brief demonstration of an initial query, a retrieval,
and a browsing probe. They were then asked to choose from a list of hypothetical research questions about copyright law and then use SCALIR
to try to find any documents relevant to the question. All users spent at
least one hour on the system and attempted two to four research questions.

Users' reactions to the system were mixed. One user, for example,
seemed to relish the qualitative differences of interacting with SCALIR
as compared to a traditional system:

> I'm just fascinated with the use of the system. One of the
> reasons I say this is that I think sometimes WESTLAW, in
> trying to get [people] to use it, they get so caught up in the
> terms. I just say "use it." Play with the machine so you feel
> comfortable with it. This [SCALIR] makes it so that someone,
> makes it exciting. You just want to sit here and play with
> the thing, so that once you get past that fear, then it becomes
> something that you use; it becomes a tool.... Instead of a toy
> it becomes a tool.

In contrast, another user felt that the system was too limited for practical
use as a legal research tool:

> You picked a limited area of expertise, and I suspect that most
> lawyers in that area are already familiar with the cases that
> are here.... In terms of use we would need something much
> broader to be commercial....
>
> But because of the graphics and the ability to bring up the
> cases and such, I'd be interested in how it might be used as
> a teaching tool.

In addition to these general reactions, users had many specific suggestions and comments, described as follows.

10.2.1 General (Non-SCALIR) Interface Issues

Some of the users' comments pertained to features of the Symbolics system, or mouse-and-windows systems generally, rather than to SCALIR per se.

Using the Mouse for Input. All of the lawyers were required to fill out a small on-screen form before starting, which required mouse selection, in order to give them some familiarity with its movement. Only one had previously used a mouse. However, this proved more of a handicap for some than for others.

One user in particular seemed to feel that the mouse limited the appeal of the system. "I don't like mouses," the subject reported, "They may be useful to you, but a lot of lawyers, because they don't use the Apple type [computer], may not like a mouse." Later on, the same user explained that pressing a single key (a menu shortcut available on many MS-DOS applications) was preferable to clicking a menu button. This user also remarked that SCALIR was "like a computer game." In contrast, another user said, "I really like using the mouse.... I find it really convenient to just move around and get where I wanted." In general, most users seemed relatively adept at selecting screen items after a few minutes.

Scrolling. Many users (including the computer science students) had difficulty with the scroll bars used with the Symbolics windows. First, users found the commands for left and right movement to be counterintuitive: to view an object to the right of the display, the left-hand mouse button must be pressed[4], and vice-versa. Second, the left and right movements are asymmetrical: clicking left makes the current mouse position the new left edge of the screen, whereas clicking right moves the old left edge of the screen to the current mouse position. Third, the farther right (or down, for vertically scrolling windows) the mouse pointer is, the larger the left and right movements are. Users continually pressed the wrong button, or tried to move to the next screenful of text by repeatedly scrolling a tiny amount. One user suggested replacing the scroll bars with **Page Up** and **Page Down** buttons.

10.2.2 Low-Level Interaction Issues

Users had several comments about the mechanics of interacting with SCALIR. These were fairly low-level issues, many of which could be easily corrected.

---

[4]Presumably this action is intended to be interpreted as "scrolling the paper to the left," rather than "looking to the right."

An Early Design Flaw. In a early version of the system seen by one user, the command **Retrieve** appeared in the menu instead of **Search**. This somewhat comical example illustrates the confusion that can result from what turned out to be a simple interface flaw:

> Subject: [Puzzled over why no text is appearing in the text window.] What did I say?
>
> Experimenter: Well, you said that you wanted to see these two cases.
>
> S: Oh, I thought I would get to see them.
>
> E: You just wanted to look at the case? Then you shouldn't have said "retrieve."
>
> S: Oh.
>
> E: That's what you do when you want to do another search.
>
> S: I thought that would get me the cases. To me "retrieve" means "get the case," so I did that wrong. . . . So how did we get this? I should have said "Read Text."
>
> E: No, "Read Text" just lets you read the text of any of the cases you've already read.
>
> S: So if I just wanted to read the text of this . . . case, what should I have done?
>
> E: Click twice on it . . .
>
> S: Oh. . . . We can't . . . interrupt the search?

"Extra Steps." Another aspect of the interaction which annoyed users was the need for what they perceived as extra steps to enter a query. In a traditional system, the user types a search term on a command line and presses the return key. In SCALIR, users must first select a dummy node, enter their descriptor in the box, press return, and then press the **Search** command in the menu. Users commonly made the mistake of typing without selecting a dummy node (which caused their descriptor to appear in the command pane), or pressing return after entering a descriptor and expecting the system to start searching. Sometimes users had to be led through the process step by step:

> Experimenter: [M]ove up and press "Clear" . . .
>
> Subject: Left?
>
> E: Yeah. Now . . . select "term" and type in a word. . . .
>
> S: Left again?

E: Yes.

S: [Types word.] Click?

E: Return. Okay, now click again. [Subject types another word.] Return.

S: And then, "Search"?

E: "Search."

This exchange took place nearly 45 minutes after the user sat down at the system.

One solution to the "extra steps" problem would be to use the initial mouse click to select an editable string already displayed on the screen, rather than popping up a box in which the term had to be entered. That way, no "return" would be needed, and the user would not be misled into thinking that he or she had already told the system to start searching. However, this approach would not work well for cases, because it is not clear how the matching-case menu selection could be incorporated.

Although it is true that SCALIR's interface requires more mouse clicks or keystrokes than a traditional CALR system for some operations, it is important to note that it requires far fewer for others. As an example, displaying a retrieved case in LEXIS or WESTLAW requires the entry of one command to show the list of retrievals and then the typing of the case's rank to display it, both operations requiring a return to execute. In contrast, a SCALIR user can simply double-click the desired case node with the mouse.

Momentary Menus. A final low-level problem was the decision to use "momentary" menus for case selection. (This situation occurs both when entering a case descriptor and when executing the **View Text** command.) Momentary menus are dismissed when the mouse pointer moves off the menu, rather than requiring a mouse click. This prevents users from having to choose an item if they don't like any of the choices. However, one user kept accidentally moving the pointer off the menu and complained that some positive action should be required to dismiss the menu.

10.2.3 Major Design Issues

The most important user comments concerned conceptual problems, enhancements, or suggestions for changing the nature of the interaction.

Single Descriptors versus Phrases. A common complaint among users was the restriction that only one descriptor could be entered at a time. Several pointed out that WESTLAW and LEXIS allowed phrase searches. Although it would be easy to let users enter phrases and then convert them to multiple query nodes, this might give users the mistaken impression that the retrieval takes phrase associations into account. Another approach might be to create a "phrase node" and link it to the nodes for each of its constituent terms. This might encourage users to enter their entire query as a phrase, which would result in the creation of many nodes that might never be used again.

Perhaps the most promising idea is to allow users to enter phrases, convert them to constituent term nodes, and then immediately create links between the constituents if they do not already exist. This would allow the system to add compound terms to its lexicon without having to wait for one constituent to appear in a query and the other to be given positive feedback.

Wild Card Characters. A related complaint was SCALIR's lack of support for wild card expanders. Both WESTLAW and LEXIS allow wild card searches; in WESTLAW, for example, a query term ending with an exclamation point will match any terms in the text with the same root. This could be addressed by storing the terms in a hierarchical data structure such as a trie (rather than a hash table), so that all matching terms could be found with very few probes.

Adding Search Terms. Perhaps the most serious limitation with the current interface was the system's inability to add new query items to existing searches. After doing an initial search, the users often thought of additional terms that would have helped to broaden or narrow the search. Unless those terms appeared in the response set, they were forced to choose between browsing with the existing responses or starting from scratch with a new query. This was especially problematic from the system's point of view, because it only learns when browsing occurs.

There are at least two ways to overcome this limitation. There could be a menu command called something like **Add Query Item** that would prompt the user for new search descriptors, perhaps using dummy nodes. Alternatively, the dummy nodes could always be displayed. In either case it is unclear where the new items should appear, especially when the screen is already full. If they were added to the fringes of the network display, they might not be visible to the user. One possibility is to put the new nodes between (vertically) the existing clusters.

Interestingly, none of the users suggested a need for an **Undo** feature. Such a feature was considered until very late in the design process; it would have allowed users to return either to the previous state (before the last browsing probe) or to the initial retrieval state (before any browsing probes). Yet users seemed to feel that they could "correct mistakes" by adding or subtracting terms through feedback — if only additional terms, not visible on the screen, could be included. Although this does not imply that **Undo** is unnecessary, it does suggest that users can accomplish a similar goal — improving their query — without invalidating the current retrieval.

Network Complexity. Any additional complexity in the network display would probably be unwelcome, however. Users already had difficulty distinguishing the different link types; one remarked:

> There ought to be a way to suppress those lines, because I feel like I'm inundated. . . .

> It's gotten so cluttered. See, that's what I'm saying, it just gets so cluttered . . . You should really suppress some of these lines.

In fact, a **Show Relationships** command, which was never implemented due to time constraints, was intended to allow users to choose a less complex network display.

Text Searching. Many users suggested enhancements for manipulation of documents in the text window. The simplest of these was to highlight words in the document that matched search terms, and have a KWIC (keyword in context) search mode that automatically scrolls to the next term occurrence. As users frequently pointed out, this operation is quite easy in WESTLAW and LEXIS. There are two alternatives for determining which terms to highlight. Either only the particular case's index terms could appear, or any word matching a significantly active term. A related suggestion was to support general string searching in the text.

Hypertext Extensions. An extension of these ideas, suggested by other users, was to be able to perform browsing probes by clicking on the highlighted index terms in the text. This would cause the same action as clicking on the corresponding term node itself (e.g., a previously unmarked node would get labeled with a plus sign). An extension of this suggested by one of the computer science students would allow users to mark *any* term (or phrase) in the text and have the system add that node to the network pane, whether it was previously present or not. This seems like a very promising idea, although it would add to the complexity of the interface. As with adding search terms, the question of where to display these new nodes is unresolved.

As currently implemented, SCALIR may be viewed as the "dual" of a hypertext system. In an ordinary hypertext system, the user manipulates documents which are linked together as a network. The documents dominate the interaction, though some hypertext systems allow users to view a kind of map showing the documents they have visited and the connections between them. In SCALIR, the network of links dominates

the interaction, and users may intermittently view the documents connected by the network. User testing seemed to suggest an increased role
for the documents in the interaction.

10.2.4   Preconceptions and Misconceptions from CALR

One interesting finding of the user testing was the conflicting and often
erroneous ideas users had about traditional CALR systems. For example,
users disagreed strongly about the importance of headnotes. One user
firmly stated that headnotes were more often wrong than not, and thus
the "conceptual searching" in WESTLAW provided no advantage over
LEXIS. In contrast, another user said, "I think WESTLAW [is better],
because it's just keyed into everything; they're using the key system. I
don't know, WESTLAW is just ..., you get more support than you do
with LEXIS."

One user's objection to SCALIR was its topical database:

> Subject: The thing that's a little bit fake is that you're already
> in copyright [law]. I would have had to put in a query to get
> me to that, and that's sometimes the harder part.
>
> Experimenter: In WESTLAW, you can at least get down to the
> Intellectual Property Database.
>
> S: Not just by picking a database.... Mostly, you go into a
> database of case books — supreme court as a database, or
> ... — and then to do a topic you have to use the key system,
> but their key numbers are partly the problem, because of the
> fact that they [West editors] decide how it goes.

In fact, both WESTLAW and LEXIS have topical databases. This user
clearly was unaware of this feature despite several years of experience
with traditional CALR systems. (The user also appeared not to believe
that this feature existed after being told.)

One of the clearest lessons to emerge from the study was that traditional CALR users, like those who have learned any complex system,
are creatures of habit. In using SCALIR, they were more likely to look
for operations analogous to those with which they were already familiar, and find fault when they were implemented differently. In contrast,
the other users were more likely to take advantage of features unique to
SCALIR, and suggest further enhancements. An interesting experiment
would be to train first-year law students initially on SCALIR, and then
get their reactions to a traditional system.

10.3   Assessing the Interface

User studies of the kind described in the previous section are extremely useful in discovering flaws in a user/system interface and getting suggestions for improving it. However, they do not tell the whole story. Users can only respond to the features they encounter, not to the space of possible alternatives.

Thus it is useful to assess the success of a system's interface by examining its attributes and comparing them to the initial design goals. This section does this for SCALIR.

10.3.1   Summarizing SCALIR Interaction Attributes

The following list summarizes the central properties of user interaction with SCALIR. Many of these features were also present in AIR, as described in an earlier interface analysis [RB91b].

No Query Language. Initial searches are conducted by selecting dummy nodes and filling in their attributes. Users do not have to learn a specialized command syntax to begin using the system.

Network Displayed as Visibly Weighted Associations. The user actually sees the representation being manipulated by the system, rather than simply getting a textual list of responses.

Response Presented Incrementally in Time. This keeps the user occupied during wait time. Perhaps more importantly, it provides a feeling of "direct engagement": prod the system and watch waves of activity flow outward.

Spatio-Temporal Position and Shading Indicate Conceptual Distance. The user gets three cues to relevance: the order in which the documents appear, their closeness to the center of the display, and the brightness of the background.

Learning Takes the Form of Browsing. The user's browsing behavior is used as a learning reinforcement signal, in addition to generating the next query. Thus the system improves while placing no additional burden on the user.

Generalized (non-Boolean) Relationships Queried. In addition to obviating the need for users to understand Boolean algebra, SCALIR's conceptually simpler mechanism provides a wider (and continuous) range of possible match criteria.

Logical Relationships can be "Drawn" from Palette. Rather than having to generate a quantifier or other logical restriction, users can simply select the relations of interest from the link palette. Again, this shortens the learning curve; the space of choices is evident from the palette and need not be memorized or looked up in the manual.

Wider I/O Channel than Conventional IR. Any type of node (document or term) can be used in a query or a retrieval. Searching with documents supports a "query-by-example" mechanism ("find me the documents like this one"); retrieving terms provides suggestions for further searches.

10.3.2   Direct Manipulation Revisited

It is argued in chapter 2 that the direct manipulation paradigm is well-suited to the information retrieval problem as long as the resulting systems are not limited to simply recreating existing manual techniques on a computer screen. It is now useful to compare the results of the SCALIR interface design decisions with Shneiderman's three criteria for the direct manipulation paradigm. (Again, much of this analysis also applies to AIR [RB91b].)

"Continuous representation of the objects and actions of interest." The first question one must consider is, "what are the objects of interest?" In SCALIR, the objects of interest are not the retrieval tools (file drawers and index cards), but rather the documents being retrieved, features which they have in common (e.g., terms, key numbers, etc.), and the relationships between them. All of these are graphically displayed as long as they are active.

What about the representation of objects not currently active? In SCALIR, these are not visible. There is no analogue to a closed file drawer or other indication that there are more items available than those currently being examined. One might argue that only those active enough to be displayed are "objects of interest." However, users' requests for additional terms not displayed on the screen suggests that this is not entirely the case.

"Physical actions or labeled button presses instead of complex syntax." In SCALIR, query formulation is incorporated into browsing; the user moves a mouse pointer to select nodes, and clicks to indicate a desire to expand or prune the search further in those directions. Initial queries are performed the same way, by selecting dummy nodes, though an additional descriptor-entering step is required. SCALIR also allows users to "open" a document by double clicking on its node. Thus this aspect of the system is consistent with this criterion. This principle is not carred to its logical conclusion, however; the text cannot currently be selected.

"Rapid incremental reversible operations whose impact on the object of interest is immediately visible." These are really two distinct features; each will be considered separately. All operations in SCALIR produce immediate

visible feedback. Those operations which concern user specification of the task (query formulation, relevance feedback) are reversible.

In general, however, the primary IR task operation — retrieval — is neither incremental nor reversible. There are three reasons for this. First, because the system learns from experience, the user cannot "undo" a search the way one might undo a deletion in a text editor or an update in a spreadsheet. Second, because the IR task is viewed as the continual refinement of an ongoing exploration of the space of documents, there isn't really anything to undo.[5] Third, relevance in new searches depends on activity accumulated from previous searches. For these reasons, the system is largely incompatible with the reversibility feature of a DMI.

Thus the primary tension between SCALIR's design goals and the principles of direct manipulation lies in the directionality of time. In a spreadsheet, there is no temporal dependence; one can change the numbers back and forth with no effect. But once SCALIR's network learns, its world is changed forever. The current search would have come out differently had the user not just responded to the results of the previous one.

Of course, it is possible to imagine undoing learning as well as retrieval. However, this would require a great deal of additional storage (state information about the previous weights). Furthermore, SCALIR's learning mechanism depends on getting a statistically meaningful sample of browsing from all its users. If users constantly "covered their tracks," the system would never learn at all. In fact, a similar phenomenon occurred during user testing; one user executed the **Clear** command after every initial search, never using the browsing feature at all.

10.3.3 Instantiating the Framework

Finally, let us return to the framework for IR interaction offered at the conclusion of chapter 2, and see how each principle has been instantiated in SCALIR. SCALIR was designed to incorporate these features (though they had not been articulated in precisely this way), so it is uninformative to note that the system possesses them. Yet as chapter 2 demonstrated, this framework itself can be grounded in an analysis of the IR task. Thus SCALIR may be viewed as an attempt to convert observations about human information finding into architectural features of a working IR system.

> *The information retrieval task consists of meeting the information need of the user. Accordingly, the user should be a participant in all*

---

[5] As noted previously, however, users must be able to add or delete search items.

*aspects of the task, and the system's behavior should be responsive
to the behavior of the user.*

It is difficult to say what "all aspects of the task" would mean in various
systems. Although SCALIR does not, for example, show users which
weights are getting changed, it does convey a better sense of how it
works than many experimental IR systems. As one user explained, "It's
sort of showing you what it's doing."

On the other hand, the method by which SCALIR retrieves some
nodes and not others is not apparent to users; it requires an understanding of the text indexing and the activity propagation mechanism.
This might be a drawback for users familiar with the easily understood
Boolean response sets.

In particular:

1. *The expression of a user's information need (the query) and
   the system's attempts to fulfill it (the retrieval) should use the
   same representation. This gives the user a sense of perspective
   and supports both query-by-example and retrieval-by-example.*

In SCALIR, both queries and retrievals employ a graphical representation of network nodes. The "sense of perspective" was in fact described
by one of the subjects in the experiment: "I like the idea that it gives
you more of a perspective, and you can start playing with ideas and
relationships. That's useful."

2. *The query process and the retrieval process should be intertwined and incremental, so that the user can browse and
   change the search goal during the search process.*

This is instantiated in SCALIR by allowing repeated browsing probes on
successive sets of significantly active nodes. However, there are also negative aspects to this feature. It is this interleaving of query and retrieval
that makes "undo" such a difficult concept to implement.

3. *The user should participate directly in the model world, both by
   directly manipulating the objects and perceiving the processes
   (e.g., retrieval) in it, all at the appropriate level of abstraction.*

As discussed in the previous section, most of SCALIR's interaction attributes are compatible with the direct manipulation approach. SCALIR's
model world is the space of copyright case law; the user can explore the
space by following chains of association. It is difficult to assess whether

this is the "appropriate" level of interaction, but it seems natural for the legal research task.

> 4. *Chains of association should emerge from the user's behavior, without requiring explicit commands. In particular, when two or more items are reported to be relevant to the same query, the system should permanently associate them. The more often this happens, the stronger the associations should be.*

SCALIR's link creation mechanism (described in chapter 9) causes new associations to form. They are strengthened whenever subsequent users employ them to find useful items.

> 5. *The system should exhibit adaptation to the user's behavior, i.e., it should alter its representation of documents as the users' knowledge becomes incorporated into the system.*

The weight modification procedure (also described in chapter 9) is driven by users' browsing choices. If a document is viewed as being represented by its associations — particularly the terms that best represent its content — then users indeed add their knowledge to the system by causing the strengths of these associations to become modified.

This adaptive behavior is extremely controversial, however. There may well be users who are uncomfortable with the idea of a system whose responses differ from day to day (even though a human researcher, such as a reference librarian, also changes). It remains to be seen whether an adaptive system would gain user acceptance in an actual use environment.

> 6. *Adaptation should be global, so that each user may benefit from the experience of other users.*

SCALIR implements this by providing only a single set of weights, shared by all users. Thus the knowledge incorporated by any individual becomes available to all.

Clearly, the implementation of these design principles has involved some tradeoffs. Some of the principles have only been partially realized; others may have been instantiated in ways that cause other problems for the user. Nevertheless, the user study suggests that SCALIR has been largely successful in demonstrating how a system that embodies these principles can work.

Chapter 11

Performance Evaluation

The SCALIR system was designed to provide many capabilities not found in traditional legal research services or even in most experimental IR systems. These include the interactive, browsing nature of the interaction (and the system's ability to learn from it), the integration of a priori domain knowledge and statistical indexing, retrieval of both terms and documents by a gradual combination of multiple sources of evidence, and so on. Accordingly, evaluating SCALIR's performance presents somewhat of a challange. Many of its features are simply incommensurate with those of other systems, so there are no benchmarks or standards of comparison. Developing techniques for measuring these features is a major research project of its own. In the mean time, we can get some partial results by letting users exercise those new capabilities, and by examining the system's behavior to see if the capabilities achieve their intended goals. The results of applying the former method are described in chapter 10; this chapter focuses on the latter.

An alternative strategy is to strip out many of the features which make SCALIR unique until what remains can be compared more directly with a traditional IR system using standard evaluation techniques. However, these techniques have many problems of their own, as chapter 4 indicates. They make many simplifying assumptions about the nature of relevance; one or more experts determines the relevant set for some predetermined queries, and systems are essentially evaluated by how well they match the expert's opinion. Obviously, this technique is ineffective for testing systems designed for different text corpora where no relevance judgements are available. Furthermore, they are limited (as noted already) to the lowest common denominator of functionality. Most importantly, traditional evaluation methods ignore the user entirely. They make no attempt to measure the satisfaction of actual users performing actual research tasks.[1]

Unfortunately, the alternatives to traditional evaluation are extremely difficult and often expensive. For example, as Blair and Maron (referring to the study described in chapter 4) reported:

> [O]ur experiment took six months; involved two researchers and six support staff; and, taking into account all direct and indirect expenses, cost almost half a million dollars. [BM85]

With obstacles like these, it is not surprising that so few user evaluations are performed.

This chapter describes some techniques used to evaluate SCALIR; they represent an attempt to provide a more naturalistic view of IR evaluation. Three evaluation approaches were employed. The first involved a qualitative assessment of SCALIR by itself, designed to learn whether its features were successful. The second was a comparison of SCALIR with a traditional system — WESTLAW — designed for the same domain; users were asked to compare the results of the two systems. The third evaluation compared the SCALIR system before and after a series of interactive query sessions with actual users whose browsing caused changes to the SCALIR network. Each of these is described in the following sections.

11.1   SCALIR Alone

A large part of evaluating SCALIR in isolation involved judging users' satisfaction with the system. That study — in which subjects were observed attempting to use the system for various research tasks — was described in chapter 10. This section focuses instead on judging whether SCALIR lived up to its design criteria.

During earlier stages of SCALIR'S design, there were many specific behaviors which the system was intended to perform. Some of these were responses to problems with traditional systems, such as evidenced by the VTR/VCR example discussed in chapter 4. Specifically, it was argued in an earlier paper [RB89] that SCALIR would be able to make three kinds of important inferences not possible with a traditional IR system.

First, SCALIR should be able to retrieve relevant documents even when they do not contain any of the query terms. This intended behavior is shown in Figure 11.1, taken from the 1989 paper. As we described it then:

---

[1]Blair has made similar observations about existing recall/precision studies [Bla90].

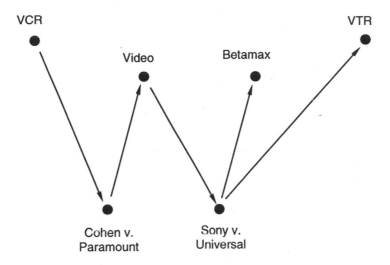

Figure 11.1: The predicted set of associations for retrieving the *Sony* case.

How would SCALIR find *Sony v. Universal*? Figure [11.1] shows a possible chain of associations. As we saw earlier, the term VCR appears in other (less relevant) cases, such as *Cohen v. Paramount*, which shares the term video with the *Sony* case. As a result, both *Sony* and the terms it uses are displayed. [RB89]

Figure 11.2 shows the result of the actual VCR query on the completed SCALIR system. The *Sony* case is in fact retrieved, though not quite in the manner expected. *Cohen v. Paramount* is the first case activated by VCR. But instead of activating *Sony* through the term video, SCALIR used a combination of evidence through the shared terms home and television.[2]

Second, user feedback was intended to create new associations which would provide more direct paths from queries to relevant responses:

The nodes marked for positive feedback are considered to be "co-relevant" and are joined by new C-links. Those which receive negative feedback have their connection strengths reduced. In the future, a query to the term VCR would retrieve

---

[2]This retrieval is different from another shown in an earlier paper [RB91a]; the earlier one was the result of a previous version of SCALIR with a smaller database and a somewhat simpler search mechanism.

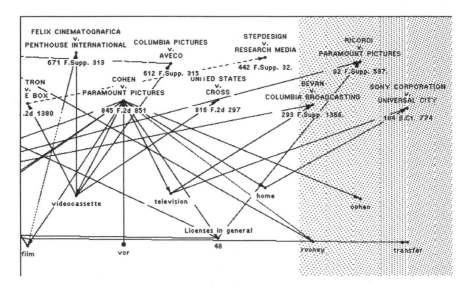

Figure 11.2: The actual *Sony* retrieval.

Sony directly, while the less relevant cases would no longer be displayed. [RB89]

Figure 11.3 shows how this intended behavior would look. Because this behavior involves learning, SCALIR's actual performance at the task will be discussed later in Section 11.3.

Third, it was hoped that SCALIR could take advantage of symbolic relationships such as citations, incorporating them into ordinary retrievals without the need for a separate explicit request:

> For example, suppose that a user is interested in whether the formats used in a computer program can be copyrighted. In one of the relevant decisions (*Whelan v. Jaslow*[3]) the judge cited another case (*Synercom Technology v. University Computing*[4]). ...SCALIR can pass activity along the citation chains, retrieving a third case (*Broderbund Software v. Unison World*[5]) which cited *Synercom*. Though not superficially relevant to the query, *Broderbund* — which deals with the related topic of whether menus and displays in a program are subject to copyright — would still be retrieved. [RB89]

---

[3]797 F.2d. 1222.
[4]462 F.Supp. 1003.
[5]648 F.Supp. 1127.

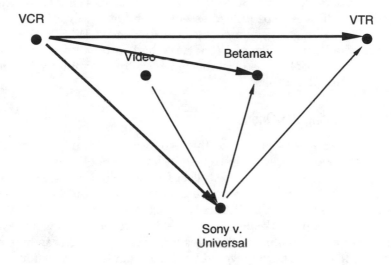

VCR

VTR

Video

Betamax

Sony v.
Universal

Figure 11.3: Desired result of incorporating user feedback.

Although the citation information for these particular cases was not present in SCALIR's database, there were actual examples of cases retrieved
by this combination of citation and term association.

11.2 SCALIR v. WESTLAW

Comparing the performance of SCALIR with a traditional IR system
such as WESTLAW is highly problematic. Queries in WESTLAW cm
ploy Boolean and proximity operators and wild card expanders, whereas
SCALIR queries rely on browsing and the gradual combination of evidence. In an ideal study, actual users might be given a fixed or unlimited
amount of time to use each system and find as much relevant material
as possible.

A more practical comparison would be to simply do similar searches
on both systems and find out which one had the better responses. But
what is a "similar search," and how will "better responses" be judged?
For the purposes of comparing the two systems, "similar" searches contain the same search terms and require approximately the same effort or
intervention on the part of the user. In Section 11.2.4, we return to the
question of judging responses.

In order to prevent the comparison from being biased toward SCALIR,

255

aspects of interaction with SCALIR not available in WESTLAW were omitted; SCALIR was to be judged essentially by how it would respond to a WESTLAW query generated by an experienced WESTLAW user. Accordingly, all capabilities of WESTLAW had to be allowed to make those queries plausible. It is important to keep this asymmetry in mind while examining the results.

11.2.1   Generating the Queries

To generate the queries on which the two systems would be tested, a sampling of issues appearing in copyright law casebooks, treatises, and articles was generated. From these, a list of 36 hypothetical research questions on copyright law was constructed. Each research question was expressed in English (e.g., "Can fictional characters be copyrighted?"). This list was given to a pair of experienced legal researchers[6] who were asked to first rate the plausibility of the question. That is, the researchers assessed how likely an attorney would be to research such a question. The researchers also constructed two forms of WESTLAW queries they might use for each question. One set of queries represented "basic" searches, the other represented "expert" searches, where the latter were distinguished primarily by their use of key numbers as query constituents. The "basic" searches were used for comparison with SCALIR.

Of the 36 suggested research questions, 9 were given the highest "plausibility" rating, 13 the second highest. These 22 queries became the basis of subsequent evaluation, and the rest were discarded.

Each WESTLAW query was then converted to its SCALIR analogue. First, terms restricting the search to copyright (from among the topics in the intellectual property database) were omitted, because all of SCALIR's cases deal with this subject. Second, Boolean and proximity operators were omitted, as were phrase delimiters (quotation marks). This left just the set of constituent terms used in the WESTLAW query. For example, the query

```
"unclean hands" /p infringe!
```

would become

```
unclean hands infringe!.
```

Next, each term containing a wild card expander was replaced by all matching terms with a corresponding node in SCALIR's network. This resulted in the list

---

[6]Editors from Shepard's/McGraw-Hill generously provided their services for the "legal consulting" tasks involved in the experiment.

`unclean hands infringement infringer infringing.`
Note that the term *infringe* was not included, because no case in SCALIR's network was indexed by it. This is probably due to the term's high document frequency (it occurred in over 1,000 cases), which assured a low term weight. Table 11.1 lists 10 of the questions used, and their WESTLAW and SCALIR forms.

In order to insure that the two systems were searching the same database, the researchers writing the WESTLAW queries were also instructed to add an additional term restricting the search to the database of copyright law cases. In addition, a date restriction was added, preventing the retrieval of cases decided since the cases in SCALIR's database were obtained, in Fall of 1988. Thus all WESTLAW searches were run with the additional query constituents & `topic(99)` & `date(< 1989)`.

11.2.2 Performing the Searches

To replicate the effect of the wild card expander, SCALIR's query mechanism was modified so that the collection of terms generated from the wild card (e.g., `infringement, infringement, and infringing`) would share the activity of a single term when the query nodes were clamped. To adjust SCALIR's search parameters, 6 of the 22 queries were randomly chosen. The system was "tuned" to produce plausible results for these 6 queries, resulting in the parameter values shown earlier in Table 8.1. Ten queries were then chosen from the remaining 16 to be used in the experiment. This number was chosen to balance the desire for a broad sample of copyright law with the need to maintain a tractable number for evaluation. Each of these was then run on SCALIR and WESTLAW.

Cases in WESTLAW can be retrieved using one of three orderings. The most commonly used is reverse chronological order; a less common variant is based on order of publication. The third choice, ordering by terms, presents the documents in decreasing order of number of search terms. That is, the document with the highest number of search term matches is presented first, then the one with the next highest number, and so on. Although ordering by age is the default for most case law databases, the term ranking was chosen for this experiment. This provided a more commensurate set of responses for comparison with SCALIR.

One additional difficulty was the fact that WESTLAW divides its corpus into separate databases for cases before and after 1945. Thus the queries had to be run twice. However, the result was two separate rankings of retrieved cases, with no way to merge them. Accordingly, only

1. What constitutes "fair use" of copyrighted material?
   WESTLAW: `"fair use" /s copyright!`
   SCALIR: `fair use`

2. Can the look and feel of a computer program be copyrighted?
   WESTLAW: `computer /10 program & look feel & copyright`
   SCALIR: `computer program look feel`

3. Does giving a speech constitute publication?
   WESTLAW: `speech spoke! /s publication /p copyright!`
   SCALIR: `speech publication`

4. Has the "unclean hands" doctrine been used to defend against charges of copyright infringement?
   WESTLAW: `"unclean hands" /p copyright! /p infringe!`
   SCALIR: `unclean hands (infringement infringer infringing)`

5. Can receiving a radio broadcast be copyright infringement?
   WESTLAW: `radio /s broadcast /p copyright! /p infringement`
   SCALIR: `radio broadcast infringement`

6. Can computer databases be copyrighted?
   WESTLAW: `computer /s database /s copyright!`
   SCALIR: `computer database`

7. Can fictional characters be copyrighted?
   WESTLAW: `character /p copyright!`
   SCALIR: `character`

8. Who owns the copyright on letters sent from one person to another?
   WESTLAW: `own! /s letter /s copyright!`
   SCALIR: `(owner ownership owning) letter`

9. If a book is copyrighted, is a translation an infringement?
   WESTLAW: `translat! /p copyright! /s infringement`
   SCALIR: `(translated translation translator) infringement`

10. Can blank forms be copyrighted?
    WESTLAW: `(blank /3 form!) (business /3 form!) (generic /3 form) (blank /3 chart) /s copyright!`
    SCALIR: `blank forms business generic chart`

Table 11.1: The research questions and their WESTLAW and SCALIR query equivalents.

258

the newer WESTLAW response set was ultimately used, and all cases prior to 1945 were dropped from SCALIR's ranking.

11.2.3 Specific Comparisons

Looking at individual retrievals, one can find many instances where both systems retrieved irrelevant[7] cases. For example, WESTLAW retrieved the recent "look and feel" case *Lotus v. Paperback Software*[8] in response to the question about fictional characters (Query 7). (WESTLAW escaped being penalized for this, however, because the case was too new to be included in SCALIR's database.) SCALIR, on the other hand, retrieved a case about Look Magazine (*Rosemont Enterprises v. Random House*[9]) in response to the "look and feel" question (Query 2).

Far more important, however, are the many relevant cases retrieved by one system and not the other. These are, after all, the cases that a lawyer might miss in his or her research. In general, it appeared that the cases missed by SCALIR were the result of two factors: lack of full-text indexing, and lack of phrase or proximity control.

The first problem occurred, for example, in the query involving copyrights on computer databases (Query 6). No cases in SCALIR's corpus were initially indexed by the term *database*; the term was not weighted highly enough even in relevant cases. Thus SCALIR's responses for the query dealt with computers generally, rather than computer databases. Two possible solutions exist: the term weight threshold for indexing could be lowered, or an alternate weighting procedure could be used.

The second problem was evident in the "blank forms" query (Query 10). Here, SCALIR retrieved cases strongly connected to the terms *blank* and *generic*, such as *Elektra Records v. Gem Electronic*[10], which is concerned with a machine used to record copyrighted music on blank tapes. The combination of evidence from the constituents of the term *blank form* was not enough to outweigh the strong connection from *blank* to *Elektra*. These irrelevant cases took the place of better ones that would have otherwise been retrieved. Indeed, four of WESTLAW's top six responses to this query were also found by SCALIR, but were "bumped out" by cases like *Elektra*. This situation is sensitive to several constraints; simply adjusting the retrieval parameters might alleviate the problem. In general, though, compound terms seem a worthwhile addition to SCALIR; chapter 10

---

[7]I am basing these judgments on my own familiarity with copyright law, resulting from my experience participating in a course on intellectual property.

[8]740 F.Supp. 108.

[9]256 F.Supp. 55.

[10]360 F.Supp. 821.

discussed a few ways in which this feature might be incorporated into the existing system.

WESTLAW, on the other hand, seemed to suffer most from the standard IR problems described in chapter 4. Any time the exact combination of query terms did not occur in the case, WESTLAW failed to retrieve it. In addition, a few serious omissions seemed to result from overly restrictive connectives or key number restrictions. For example, WESTLAW failed to find two critical cases about copyrights on fictional characters (Query 7) that SCALIR found. The first of these, *Columbia Broadcasting v. Victor DeCosta*[11] concerned a copyright claim on the television character "Paladin"; the second, *Warner Bros. v. Columbia Broadcasting*[12] dealt with the copyright status of the Dashiell Hammett's Sam Spade character.

These comparisons illustrate the different character of the WESTLAW and SCALIR approaches to retrieval. WESTLAW's Boolean and proximity search mechanism prevented that system from making some of the mistakes make by SCALIR. At the same time, SCALIR's more complex combination of evidence procedure could often generalize a search to include documents in which variants of a query term were used. This suggests that the two approaches may be complementary; each has advantages and disadvantages.

11.2.4   A Quantitative Evaluation Procedure

Although the comparison of individual responses is illuminating, it is also desirable to assess overall performance through a more quantitative measure. Because a real-world text corpus was used, no a priori relevance judgments were available. Instead, the relative effectiveness of each system's responses was assessed by means of a questionnaire which asked subjects to rate each case on the basis of its relevance with respect to a given research question. These research questions were the same English sentences used by the legal researchers to generate the WESTLAW queries.

In designing the questionnaire, several factors had to be considered. First, how much of the document would need to be included in order for a subject to adequately judge its relevance? This had to be balanced with the need to have enough cases to get an accurate measure, without requiring too much of the subject's time. Based on early estimates of the time required, it was determined that approximately the first 200 words of the judge's opinion — usually two or three paragraphs — was

---

[11]377 F.2d. 315.
[12]216 F.2d. 945.

sufficient. A lawyer examining a sample of the questionnaire agreed that relevance judgments were possible for text samples of this size.

Another consideration was whether the subjects would be asked to rank cases, choose between side-by-side SCALIR and WESTLAW responses, or rate the cases. Ranking was judged too time-consuming; it is also extremely difficult for subjects when many items are involved. The forced-choice approach seemed to confound the rank ordering with the absolute relevance of a document, because only equally ranked documents could be compared. Thus it was decided to have subjects rate the relevance of individual cases from both systems, and then compare the aggregate ratings of the two groups.

The highest ranked cases from each system's response set were thus selected, excerpted, and placed in random order on the questionnaire. Instead of comparing response sets, subjects would simply rate the case on a 7-point scale from 1 (marked "totally irrelevant") to 7 (marked "vitally relevant"). The following instructions were included:

> For each case, read the excerpt and decide how relevant you think the case is to the copyright research question at the top of the page. Then put a check mark in the circle you think best rates the relevance of the case. Use whatever criteria you think are important.

Figure 11.4 shows a typical questionnaire entry.

To provide adequate end anchors for the scale, subjects were given examples of cases at the extremes, accompanied by the following instructions:

> The question at the top is "Is home videotaping of television programs an infringement of copyright?" The first case, *Sony v. Universal*, deals with precisely this issue and has been decided by the Supreme Court. Thus the circle numbered 7 has been checked, indicating that the case is vitally relevant to the question. The second case, *Merriam v. United Dictionary* has to do with the publication of a high school dictionary. Neither the fact situation nor the legal issues of this case appear to have anything to do with the question, so it has been judged totally irrelevant, and 1 has been checked.

An additional example case was provided for practice. In order to alleviate order effects, each subject received the questions in a different random order.

Based on the estimates of the amount of text that could be read in a reasonable time, the top six cases were considered "highest ranked."

WHAT CONSTITUTES "FAIR USE" OF COPYRIGHTED MATERIAL?

Katrina MAXTONE-GRAHAM, Plaintiff-Appellant, v. James Tunstead BURTCHAELL, Andrews & McMeel, Inc., and Harper & Row Publishers, Inc., Defendants-Appellees.

803 F2d 1253 (C.A.2 (N.Y.),1986.)

IRVING R. KAUFMAN, Circuit Judge:

(1) Nearly half a century ago, a distinguished panel of this Court including Learned Hand called the question of fair use "the most troublesome in the whole law of copyright," Dellar v. Samuel Goldwyn, Inc., 104 F2d 661, 662 (2d Cir.1939) (per curiam). That description remains accurate today. Since Judge Hand's time, the common law doctrine has been inscribed into the Copyright Act, but the fair use inquiry continues to require a difficult case-by-case balancing of complex factors. The purpose of fair use is to create a limited exception to the individual's private property rights in his expression–rights conferred to encourage creativity–to promote certain productive uses of existing copyrighted material. Fair use has been defined as "a privilege in others than the owner of the copyright to use the copyrighted material in a reasonable manner without his consent, notwithstanding the monopoly granted to the owner (by the copyright)." n1

1. Rosemont Enterprises, Inc. v. Random House, Inc., 366 F2d 303, 306 (2d Cir.1966), cert. denied, 385 U.S. 1009, 87 S.Ct. 714, 17 L.Ed.2d 546 (1967), (quoting Ball, The Law of Copyright and Literary Property 260 (1944))....

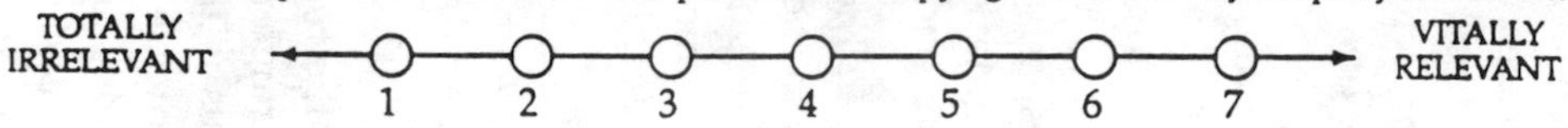

TOTALLY IRRELEVANT — 1 2 3 4 5 6 7 — VITALLY RELEVANT

Figure 11.4: A sample questionnaire entry.

What if both systems retrieved all the same best cases? Then there would be no basis for comparison, even if all responses after the top six were totally distinct. Even if the overlap was smaller, it seemed that for the comparison task, duplicates conveyed no information about which system was better. Thus to increase the discrimination value of the questionnaire, only non-overlapping cases were used. For example, if two cases in the top six of one set occurred in the top six of the other, the two cases would be removed from both sets and replaced with the next (seventh- and eighth-highest ranked) cases. This was repeated until the two sets had empty intersection.

11.2.5 Questionnaire Results

The questionnaire was originally intended for a class of law students who had recently completed a class in intellectual property. After attempts to get several different groups of law students and then paralegals to participate failed, undergraduate students studying information retrieval had to be used. Eight of 10 returned the questionnaire. These subjects thus based their responses on a general understanding of English, rather than any legal knowledge. This undoubtably made their relevance judgements less refined.

A two-factor within-subjects analysis was intended so that variance due to individual subject differences could be factored out of the system comparison. This type of experiment generally requires fewer subjects to detect significant effects, since each subject essentially serves as his or her own control.

Unfortunately, the undergraduate subjects, with no legal experience, were unable to complete the questionnaire in the allotted time. On average, each subject finished only 4 of the 10 questions. Because the sequence of questions had been randomized, each subject completed a *different* 4 questions, only partially overlapping others. Because the subjects neither completed all test conditions nor reliable subsets, the within-subjects analysis could not be used.

Instead, the data were treated as in an ordinary two-factor design; each subject's response to a given query and system was considered a data point for that treatment condition. These results are shown in Table 11.2. The column marked "Overlap" lists the number of (discarded) overlapping cases from each system's highest ranked set.

At first glance, it appears that subjects marginally preferred SCALIR; SCALIR's responses received higher scores for 6 of the 10 questions, and a slightly higher score overall. SCALIR's higher rating is maintained when queries with missing data points are omitted, as well as when only those

	Overlap	Scalir	Westlaw	Mean	N
Query 1	1	**5.70**	4.63	5.17	5
Query 2	1	3.04	**4.29**	3.67	4
Query 3	5	**2.83**	1.67	2.25	2
Query 4	1	**6.50**	2.20	4.35	2*
Query 5	2	**4.43**	4.13	4.28	5
Query 6	0	1.17	**3.08**	2.13	3*
Query 7	2	4.10	**4.77**	4.43	5
Query 8	1	**3.71**	3.25	3.48	4
Query 9	4	**4.33**	2.30	3.32	5
Query 10	1	1.92	**4.13**	3.02	4
Mean		**3.77**	3.45	3.61	

Table 11.2: Results of the SCALIR v. WESTLAW comparison. Numbers in **sans serif** type show higher rated system; asterisks indicate one less response for WESTLAW on that query.

Source	SS	df	MS	F
Query	53.53	9	5.95	0.7758
IR System	0.84	1	0.84	0.1093
Q × I	54.25	9	6.03	0.7862
S/QI	429.37	56	7.67	

Table 11.3: Analysis of variance summary for the SCALIR v. WESTLAW comparison.

questions with the highest values of N are used. However, an analysis of variance[13] reveals that these differences are statistically insignificant ($\alpha = 0.05$). Table 11.3 summarizes these results.

What conclusions may be drawn from the data, given that we have no evidence for rejecting the null hypothesis that subjects are equally satisfied with both systems? Although there simply may be too few — and too ill-trained — subjects to tell, SCALIR's equal performance was nonetheless promising. As noted earlier, SCALIR was judged on only a subset of its capabilities, whereas WESTLAW's were exploited fully. Thus there were several factors in the traditional system's favor. For instance SCALIR was forced to use all terms from WESTLAW queries, without the benefit of enclosing them in phrase or proximity restrictions. These are not necessarily the queries that a SCALIR user would have chosen. Neither did users get to see the additional term suggestions that SCALIR

---

[13]The unweighted means solution [Win71] was used to compensate for unequal cell sizes.

routinely provides as part of its retrieval.

Having established that a stripped-down version of SCALIR is capable of emulating or complementing a traditional system, we now turn to the question of how its most prominent additional feature, learning, affected its retrievals.

11.3 SCALIR Before and After Learning

Although SCALIR's learning rule produced desired results on small test cases (as shown in chapter 9, it was unclear whether the learning mechanism would lead to actual improvements under real usage situations. To test this, a group of subjects agreed to use the system for at least an hour and attempt to research various copyright questions. These sessions were also used to evaluate user interaction with the system, as described in chapter 10.

Fourteen subjects participated in the learning phase of the experiment: 2 lawyers and 12 computer science graduate students, one of whom also had a law degree. Each subject was given the same list of ten research questions used to generate the queries in the SCALIR v. WESTLAW comparison described in the previous section. He or she was instructed to choose a question and try to find all relevant material on it, then repeat the process with other questions as time permitted. As with the questionnaire evaluation, the preponderance of nonlawyers meant that the system would be trained only on those aspects of the cases easily understood by laypersons (such as the facts of the case).

Each subject completed 2 to 4 questions in the hour allotted. Subjects generally issued an initial query and then two or three successive browsing probes for each question. The majority of the time was spent reading the cases to determine which ones to mark for further search. Each of the 10 questions was chosen by at least three subjects; no question was chosen by more than six. The initial beam width parameter (discussed in Section 8.3.3) was set to 10 rather than 15 to provide faster system response.

The results fall into two basic categories. First, there are specific behaviors that the system exhibited after learning which were not present before and had not been explicitly programmed in. Second, there were changes to the sets of items retrieved for various queries, and to the ordering of the response sets. The remainder of this section describes these results, and also looks at various ways to quantify them.

11.3.1   Qualitative Learning Phenomena

The most dramatic effect of learning in SCALIR was in the many linguistic operations that resulted primarily from the 274 new links created in response to user browsing.

Extension of Lexicon. Whenever users issued a query containing an unknown term, SCALIR created a node for it. Feedback then linked the term to useful responses. Subsequent users then got the benefit of the term's presence in the system. The most important example of this was the term `database`. As noted in the previous section, no cases were initially indexed by this term. After learning, however, `database` was associated with several cases and other terms, as shown in Figure 11.5. Another example was the term `interface`, which was added to the system and linked to such terms as `look` and `feel`.

"Correcting" Misspellings. Users occasionally misspelled words and then continued to use them in searches. These were treated like any other new term; a new node was created and linked to other nodes receiving positive feedback. Thus, for example, the misspelled word `correspondance` was linked to cases about letters; this would allow future misspellers to retrieve those cases. It might also allow the retrieval of documents containing the same misspelling. (This is less likely, however, because the most common spelling errors in the documents were typographical; these would not recur enough to cause term weight high enough to index the document.)

Some of the cases linked to the new node also used the correctly spelled word. This created a path from the incorrect to the correct spelling, providing future users with a kind of unobtrusive spell-checker; use of the misspelled word could cause the correct word to appear on the screen as well.

Compound Term Formation. Although SCALIR does not support phrase searching, the system did learn to associate words that are constituents of compound terms. The best example of this were the terms `fair` and `use`, which were linked to form the phrase `fair use`, a copyright law concept mentioned in the first query. Another example was the phrase `unclean hands`.

Morphological Variants. SCALIR used a very conservative stemming algorithm, only converting plural forms to singular. This was done in part to avoid overregularization. For example, *originality* is an important concept in copyright law; users interested in the requirement of originality should not retrieve documents about, say, the origin of species. However, SCALIR is capable of *learning* morphological variants when they are useful. The best example of this in the experiment was the new

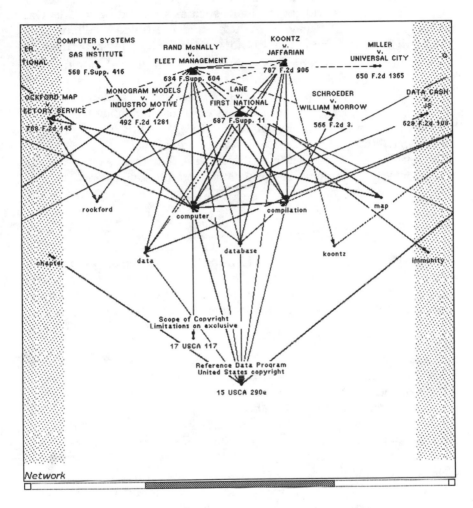

Figure 11.5: Associations of the new term database.

267

link which joined "fiction" to "fictional." Thus the system learned the functionality of WESTLAW's wild card expander; queries to "works of fiction" would equally well retrieve "fictional works."

Thesaurus Relations. Finally, SCALIR learned to cluster related terms. New links were created between items such as *form* and *chart*. This was precisely the type of behavior predicted and illustrated by Figure 11.3 (although that particular query was not used in the learning experiments).

All of these useful behaviors emerged through normal, nonintrusive interaction with users; none required explicit programming or user intervention. Whereas some of these capabilities can be added to a traditional IR system, the designer of the system must anticipate which ones are necessary and useful. By its very nature, SCALIR learns precisely those capabilities that people use. Furthermore, SCALIR supports a kind of incremental enhancement (e.g., through the dynamic incorporation of new terms) that is difficult or impossible in traditional systems.

11.3.2   Specific Improvements

To evaluate more subtle types of learning improvements, "before" and "after" response sets were examined to identify plausibly irrelevant cases whose rank was lowered and plausibly relevant cases whose rank was raised. The former were identified by their use of a mistaken association (such as "Look magazine" for "look and feel"); the latter were cases used as examples in textbooks or articles on the subject.

Decrease of Irrelevant Ranks. SCALIR seemed quite successful at lowering the ranks of cases judged irrelevant by users. For example, a case whose plaintiff was a business called "The Fair" had been mistakenly retrieved for the "fair use" question (Query 5). Initially ranked ninth, it was completely eliminated from SCALIR's response set after learning. *In other words, SCALIR learned to stop (indefinitely) retrieving a case judged irrelevant to the query.* This action stands in marked contrast to the type of fleeting change of ordinary relevance feedback.

Similar (if less dramatic) improvements were found in nearly every query. For example, the case *Gilliam v. American Broadcasting Corp.* (which dealt with an injunction prohibiting the broadcast of an edited television program) dropped from 10th to 29th position in response to the query about receiving radio broadcasts (Query 5). Because only about 20 cases are displayed on the screen (several of which are in the shaded regions at the side of the network display pane), this new ranking effectively meant that from the user's perspective, the irrelevant case was no longer retrieved.[14]

Increase of Relevant Ranks. In many cases previously unretrieved cases which were plausibly relevant were added to the response set after learning. For example, *Time Inc. v. Bernard Geis Associates* was named in one text's discussion of the fair use concept [KL82]. This case initially did not appear in response to Query 1; after learning, however, it was ranked 19th in the retrieval set. Similarly, for the "look and feel" query, the case *Atari, Inc. v. North American Philips Consumer Corp.*[15] — cited in many articles on the look-and-feel lawsuits [Bic89, Sam89] — moved from 26th place to 3rd in the retrieval ranking.

Decrease of Relevant Ranks. Unfortunately, some plausibly relevant cases also decreased in rank after learning. Often this was due to being "bumped" down or off the list of highest rated cases when user feedback caused other cases to move up or be added. For example, the case *Encyclopaedia Britannica v. Crooks*, used as a casebook example of the fair use controversy [Gol81], dropped from 26th to 37th in the response to Query 1. Note that neither position is high enough for the users to have seen the case and responded to it; the change resulted solely from the "bumping."

A more problematic phenomenon occurred when users lowered the retrieved rank of plausibly relevant cases. For example, a commonly cited [Bic89, Gol81, Sam89] "look and feel" case, *Whelan Associates v. Jaslow Laboratories*, extended copyright protection to the "structure, sequence, and organization" of computer programs. However, users did not find the case relevant, and it dropped from 13th to 23rd position. Two factors exacerbated this problem: a subject pool that was largely unfamiliar with copyright law, and an unusually high learning rate (0.005) used in the experiment to highlight changes to the network. In an actual use situation, this would be less of a problem.

Increase of Irrelevant Ranks. When users marked nodes for expansion, they occasionally caused new irrelevant items to be retrieved. For example, users liked *Koontz v. Jaffarian* as a response to the question about databases (Query 6). But *Koontz* cited another case, *Monogram Models v. Industro*, that dealt with an entirely separate issue. After learning, *Monogram* was retrieved (in 8th position). This type of behavior is not a serious problem as long as users may continue to browse and prune away irrelevant material; in legal research, the benefit of finding an unexpected relevant case outweighs the cost of having to prune an irrelevant

---

[14]Internal logging of active nodes was used in these experiments to record the ranking of items not displayed on the screen.

[15]The case dealt with the concept and appearance of a video game.

From	To	Before Learning	After Learning
fair	use	0.0	0.6689
use	fair	0.0101	0.1912
unclean	hands	0.0053	0.0076
hands	unclean	0.1066	0.2028
form	chart	0.0	0.1201
chart	form	0.0	0.0554
data	base	0.0	0.0
base	data	0.0122	0.0277
look	feel	0.0	0.0
feel	look	0.0	0.0

Table 11.4: Associative coupling for selected term nodes.

one.

11.3.3 Changes in "Associative Coupling"

Each of the 14 users was responsible for over 1,000 weight changes, not counting the additional renormalization changes. Some of these changes were as small as 10^{-9}; other very large changes were on the order of 10^{-1}. (Recall that each case has an average of 12 index terms sharing an initial total weight of 1/3; typical initial weights are thus likely to be around 0.025.) How can we assess the effect of these many small changes? One method is to measure the "associative coupling" between various pairs of nodes. This is simply how much a query consisting of just one node causes one other to become active; the number given is the activation of the second node. Learning can increase the coupling between two nodes by strengthening some or all of the paths between them, as well as by creating new links.

Table 11.4 shows the associative coupling between pairs of nodes discussed in Section 11.3.1. The terms fair and use, very weakly coupled (and only in one direction) before learning, are strongly coupled after learning. Similarly, the terms unclean and hands become more strongly associated, as do form and chart, and data and base. Interestingly, the terms look and feel remain uncoupled, even after learning. This is due to the fact that the new links that bound them to a shared set of relevant cases only occurred in one direction.

Table 11.5 shows a similar analysis of the change in coupling from query terms to cases. The query fair use, which originally retrieved the irrelevant case containing the word fair, has dropped to an asso-

From	To	Before Learning	After Learning
fair	*Vain v. The Fair*	0.0522	0.0
	Time v. Geis	0.0010	0.0070
	Brittanica v. Crooks	0.0	0.0017
use	*Vain v. The Fair*	0.0001	0.0
	Time v. Geis	0.0	0.0031
	Brittanica v. Crooks	0.0038	0.0032
look	*Atari v. Philips*	0.0	0.7021
	Whelan v. Jaslow	0.0	0.0
feel	*Atari v. Philips*	0.0	0.8756
	Whelan v. Jaslow	0.0	0.0
radio	*Gilliam v. ABC*	0.0006	0.0006
broadcast	*Gilliam v. ABC*	0.0434	0.0290

Table 11.5: Associative coupling from terms to cases.

ciative coupling of zero, as desired. Note that this simply means that the relevant weights have been sufficiently reduced to drop them below the beam width of the tapered search; this does not imply that the weights have become zero. The irrelevant cases for the different query term (*Vain* for fair use and *Gilliam* for radio broadcast) have become less retrievable. Some relevant cases (*Time* for fair use and *Atari* for look and feel) have become more retrievable. Unfortunately, as mentioned earlier, at least one relevant case — *Brittanica v. Crooks* actually decreases its coupling with its query terms, rendering it less retrievable. Interestingly, the important look and feel case *Whelan v. Jaslow*, which dropped in overall rank, was never coupled with either of these query terms; it must have been retrieved due to a connection with the other terms computer and program.

11.3.4 (In)validity of a Questionnaire Evaluation of Learning

The learning experiments planned initially included a before-and-after questionnaire similar to the one used for the SCALIR v. WESTLAW comparison. However, a draft of the questionnaire shown to two lawyers revealed several problems which resulted in the decision not to perform the experiment. First, the overlap between the "before" and "after" retrieval sets was extremely high in many cases, as shown in Table 11.6. This meant that the systems were being compared on the basis of cases they both considered relatively irrelevant. Looking at the responses to Query 3 (after the top 21 cases had been discarded due to overlap), one

Query	Overlap
1	5
2	3
3	21
4	25
5	4
6	3
7	26
8	9
9	5
10	30
Mean	13.1

Table 11.6: Overlap in SCALIR retrieval sets before and after learning.

lawyer examining the results reported that no remaining cases were relevant.

The high overlap does not imply that there was little change due to learning. As the previous sections demonstrated, the actual responses in fact show substantial reordering. However, the type of questionnaire used for the SCALIR v. WESTLAW comparison is ill-suited for evaluating this reordering. In the previous comparison, the question was essentially "Looking at the (different) best cases retrieved by each system, which set did users prefer?" The question for the learning task is (primarily) "How did the ranking of the best cases improve or worsen?" To measure this, overlapping cases would have to included in the survey but given weighted scores dependent on their ranks. This type of evaluation merits further study.

However, there was an additional problem which cast doubt on the existing questionnaire methodology. As evidenced by the results of the SCALIR v. WESTLAW study, the questionnaire was too long to be completed by most subjects. At the same time, however, the case excerpts were often too short for subjects to be able to make relevance judgments. In the SCALIR v. WESTLAW comparison, a lawyer prescreening the questionnaire approved of the format and believed it would be possible to judge relevance in most cases. But for the learning comparison, where differences were often more subtle (due to the increased overlap), the (different) lawyer consulted believed this was not possible. Further evidence resulted from the sample responses of the two lawyers: In one instance, a case marked "totally irrelevant" by one was judged "vitally relevant" by the other.

11.4   Evaluating the Evaluation

The SCALIR evaluation experiments provide some initial evidence that the approach is promising. The system exhibited in practice the advantages hypothetically described before its construction. It demonstrated several capabilities superior to a traditional CALR system, and performed at least as well when restricted to a subset of its functionality. Its learning mechanisms resulted in qualitative improvements in many retrievals as well as several new capabilities not explicitly programmed.

These results are not conclusive, however. The evaluation of interactive and adaptive IR systems is a major research project in itself, one that cannot be resolved by a single experiment. The SCALIR experience demonstrates the problem of evaluating IR systems: If real users are to be involved — as they should be — the process is difficult, costly, and time-consuming.

Earlier, some of the problems with SCALIR's questionnaire methodology were discussed. Is this technique worth pursuing for future studies, perhaps with more experienced subjects paid to spend more time? Although this is again an empirical question, it appears that subjects need to have more of the text available in order to judge the relevance of a case.

When subjects were tested actually using SCALIR, they generally read the synopsis of the case or the first paragraph of the judge's opinion in order to assess its relevance. Thus they probably read as little text as appeared on the questionnaires most of the time. But when the relevance of the case was not apparent, subjects were able to scroll through the document, skimming the text until they understood enough of its content. This ability to choose how much of the case to look at apparently allowed users to make much more sophisticated relevance judgments than those filling out the questionnaire.

This suggests one possible way to improve future evaluations: Present a version of the questionnaire on-line. Each case would be presented as a scrollable text window; subjects could browse through the text and then mark it with their relevance score.

An additional difficulty in evaluating systems such as SCALIR is the lack of availability of qualified subjects. Subjects' relative ignorance of the domain adds yet another source of variation that increases the difficulty of getting significant results. For this reason further study of the evaluation methodology might best be performed on a more well-understood domain where a large qualified subject pool could be found.

As soon as any IR systems add new capabilities, they become harder and harder to evaluate. This discourages resesarch on such systems, and makes it hard to demonstrate their real value. Despite these difficulties, we should continue to stretch the boundaries of IR with systems like SCALIR; the potential reward is too great to ignore.

Chapter 12

Discussion

The work presented in the previous chapters represents a fabric of inter-twined concepts drawn from various sources and combined in various ways. This breadth and complexity is both a strength and a weakness of the SCALIR approach. It is a strength in that it demonstrates how sharing of ideas between disciplines or paradigms can produce results unavailable to those who restrict themselves to the constraints of a given approach. It is a weakness in that it results in tensions and tradeoffs between the approaches, and makes evaluation more difficult.

This chapter is an attempt to summarize the SCALIR research and assess what conclusions, if any, may be drawn from it.

12.1   The Research Goals, Revisited

Chapter 1 described the three goals outlined when the research was ini-tially undertaken. It is illuminating to return to these goals and assess how well they were satisfied.

12.1.1   Improving Legal Information Retrieval

Does SCALIR represent an improvement to existing legal information retrieval techniques? Certainly it represents a new alternative. Existing computer-assisted legal research systems feature (among other things) inverted file full-text indexing, Boolean and proximity connectives, and wild card term expansion. WESTLAW in particular adds the ability to search for manually assigned index terms (the West key number topics used in case headnotes). Shepard's provides an additional on-line citation searching capability. These systems also operate in a text-oriented command-line mode.

SCALIR, in contrast, uses statistical analysis of text to assign initial index terms (like many IR research systems). Its retrieval mechanism relies on the gradual combination of evidence from multiple sources of knowledge, implemented as spreading activation through a hybrid network. Citations are one of several knowledge sources available during a retrieval. SCALIR is designed to encourage browsing and direct manipulation; users point to items they want to pursue or prune and get immediate graphical feedback from their actions. SCALIR uses this browsing information further, to improve its representation of documents and terms.

As we have seen in chapters 4 and 5, existing CALR systems have many shortcomings. Their retrievals are extremely brittle, often resulting in important cases being missed (as in the VCR/VTR example) surprisingly often (as the Blair and Maron study [BM85] suggests), as well as in totally irrelevant cases being retrieved (as in the second amendment /*Roe v. Wade*) example. Furthermore, users have difficulty with the Boolean query method required by these systems.

There is little doubt that SCALIR addresses all of these problems. Because SCALIR's decision to retrieve or not retrieve a case is based on a continuous rather than a binary function, its searches are less brittle. Because cases can be retrieved through a variety of associations, it is less subject to the vocabulary problem that lowers recall. And because it learns what its users consider relevant, it is able to gradually improve its precision.

Legal research with SCALIR also has a fundamentally different character. The "map" of associations continually visible to users provides a perspective on the document not found in pure text-based interfaces, showing cases in their conceptual and precedential context. Thus SCALIR may be characterized as the dual of a hypertext system, as discussed in chapter 10.

For all these benefits, however, SCALIR has some drawbacks. Most important, perhaps, is the lack of exactness[1] of the sort found in Boolean systems. For example, when a Boolean query asks for documents containing both terms A and B, it will not "accidentally" retrieve those containing only A. It may be that exactness and brittleness are two sides of the same coin, and that by reducing brittleness we lose exactness as well. SCALIR's symbolic component alleviates this problem to some degree

---

[1] Unfortunately, *precision* is a "reserved word" in IR.

(by restricting certain types of activity propagation), but not completely, as the results presented in chapter 11 demonstrate. In any case, this lack of exactness results in SCALIR's frequent retrieval of irrelevant cases that were strongly associated to one constituent of a compound term such as fair use. If absolute relevance judgments were available, it appears likely that SCALIR would score higher on recall, but lower on precision, than a Boolean system. On the other hand, we do not know yet how much legal research could be improved by the capabilities unique to SCALIR, such as learning.

Given these tradeoffs, has SCALIR "improved" legal IR? I believe it has advanced the state of the art. Although it may turn out that not all of SCALIR's mechanisms are ultimately practical for legal IR, or that not all of existing CALR techniques should be discarded, SCALIR has clearly demonstrated that there are ways to overcome existing problems and to provide a broader notion of what it means to do computer-assisted legal research. In the future, a SCALIR-like system may complement traditional CALR systems.

12.1.2 Feasibility of Hybrid AI Systems

The second research goal was to demonstrate the feasibility of hybrid AI systems. This goal provided the impetus for the analysis of knowledge representation approaches in chapter 3, and the symbolic/sub-symbolic framework proposed in chapter 6.

Does SCALIR in fact demonstrate the feasibility of hybrid AI? On the one hand, SCALIR is a kind of existence proof that it is possible to combine the approaches in a fine-grained, "tightly coupled" way. SCALIR's hybrid methodology consists of two primary features, the hybrid activity propagation mechanism and the hybrid learning rule.

SCALIR represents activity as a vector of "colored" activations, and treats the different labeled link types as differed colored filters. This allows the system to respond to both gradual combinations of evidence (as in sub-symbolic systems) and explicit symbolic labels. These two types of processing can be combined when it is convenient and separated when it is useful.

The hybrid learning rule (or learning rules) is a direct consequence of the representation of activity. As shown in chapter 9, SCALIR's learning rule allows the benefits of connectionist learning procedures to be reaped by labeled links. This prevents unwanted crosstalk, but again, allows it when it is useful. Furthermore, SCALIR is able to apportion credit between the symbolic and sub-symbolic components of the system by allowing C-links and H-links to compete for the same scarce resource (outgoing weight from a node).

Although hybrid systems are becoming more popular in AI, few of these have provided the tight coupling necessary to support useful interactions between the two mechanisms. Furthermore, hybrid systems have generally avoided the issue of learning, and particularly credit assignment.

On the other hand, SCALIR's results in actual usage situations were inconclusive in this respect. Although there were individual retrievals which benefited from the presence of symbolic associations, it is not clear that these results could not have been obtained from a connectionist network with weights initialized in the same manner as H-links (i.e., from preexisting knowledge of the domain). In other words, the role of the *separation* between the symbolic and sub-symbolic components has not been demonstrated. Although this issue clearly merits further study, it should first be conducted on a smaller scale system under tightly controlled conditions. There are simply too many factors in SCALIR — not least of which is the differing goals of the users — to use it as a testbed for studying this problem.

12.1.3   IR for Natural Language

The third goal was to show how an adaptive information retrieval system might provide an "end run" around the natural language problem. As noted in chapter 1, the focus of the project shifted somewhat, so that there were no specific experiments designed to demonstrate this concept.

Nevertheless, this idea motivated the analysis of symbol grounding in artificial systems, presented in chapter 3. This argument was based on two important ideas: the (obvious) critical role of language in communication, and a Wittgensteinian view of meaning as use. Because IR systems are the intermediaries between authors and researchers (and in the case of globally adaptive IR systems, between researchers and other researchers), they participate in a communication across space and, especially in law, time. Because their representations are based on how words are used in text and how they are used by people retrieving text, they can develop a use-based meaning. Finally, because all representations are the result of interactions with actual users who participate in full perceptual experience with the world, the systems' uses of language are properly grounded.

This should not be interpreted as a claim that SCALIR "understands" natural language. For one thing, saying that the meaning of a word lies in how it is used in the language does *not* mean that it can be found in a simple list — or even a complex web — of associations based on word frequency statistics. Nevertheless, *some* information about a word's meaning is undoubtedly conveyed by data about the company it keeps. The quality of these data improve tremendously when they are informed by the judgments of actual humans who interact with the world. Furthermore, it is not unreasonable to say that SCALIR comes to learn what people "have in mind" when they use a word in a query. Similarly, one might argue that frequency data and usage statistics tell SCALIR what documents are "about."

Most importantly, however, it should be noted that IR is not being proposed as a *solution* to the natural language understanding problem, but rather as a way to *bypass* the problem. At one time it was common in AI to claim that with a few more improvements to natural language processing systems, we could all soon converse with our computers as we do with our fellow humans, albeit through a keyboard and screen. It was never completely clear exactly why we would want to do this; why should I type "open the file for the latest draft of chapter 12 of my book" when I can simply point to it and press a button?[2] It quickly became clear that the importance of natural language processing lay in its ability to digest large amounts of text. It is for these text-based applications that an adaptive IR system provides a powerful alternative.

12.2 Other Considerations

In addition to the issues raised by the three initial goals, there are several additional considerations that have arisen as a result of the SCALIR research.

12.2.1 SCALIR and IR Research

Section 12.1.1 discussed whether SCALIR represented an improvement over existing computer-assisted legal research techniques. However, commercial CALR systems do not capture the range of existing IR techniques, especially experimental research systems. How does SCALIR compare to these more sophisticated systems?

As noted in chapter 4, SCALIR shares many similarities with some experimental IR techniques. Term weighting, relevance feedback, dynamic document representation, retrieval by higher order associations, spreading activation, and use of multiple sources of association, can each

---

[2]This is a caricature, of course. There may well be many important uses for NLP in computer interfaces — just not all the ones that used to be bandied about.

be found in one or more of the systems mentioned in chapter 4. Some of these features (such as dynamic document representation) are rare enough that it is unusual even to include them, whereas others (such as term weighting) have become standard components of IR systems. What differentiates SCALIR is the particular combination of all of these features into a single system.

Once again, the question ultimately is whether this particular combination of mechanisms provides any advantage. The answer would be easier to determine if the system features combined in a linear fashion. Then we could test each feature in isolation against some baseline (perhaps a standard vector model) and add up the costs and benefits of each. Unfortunately, such linearity does not apply. For one thing, some of the features (such as learning) make no sense without others being present (relevance feedback). For another, there may be interactions between the effects of different features. Finally, as long as real users are involved in relevance judgements (either while using the system or evaluating its responses off-line), their reactions will depend on their prior experiences and expectations, and on the overall context of what other responses the system is giving and has given in the past.

How can this dilemma be avoided? One way might be to use a stepwise-regression-style model: Measure the performance of the entire system, drop some component, and measure the performance again. Then the difference due to that component can be determined. This will not prevent all interaction effects, and some tests will still not be possible (e.g., learning without feedback). Nevertheless, it provides a better approximation of one component's contribution than could be obtained by testing it in isolation.

12.2.2   Scaling and Incremental Modification

SCALIR's database contains all federal cases in a particular, relatively small area of law. How might it be scaled up to collections of the size used by WESTLAW and LEXIS? For one thing, those collections themselves are divided up topically. The existing SCALIR techniques seem robust enough to scale up to the topical database size. For example, WESTLAW's intellectual property database is only about five times larger than SCALIR's copyright-only database. As long as connectivity is controlled (by limiting the number of terms used to index cases) and propagation fan-out is restricted (by the tapered search mechanism), such a system seems feasible with the existing SCALIR approach.[3] Approximately the same number of nodes would be visited in the scaled-up system as in the existing system, and searches would take about the same amount of time.

If a SCALIR-type system could be built for several topical legal databases, this would already have tremendous value. Even so, such a system would fail to capture the interactions between the topical areas. For instance, it would be unable to follow a citation from intellectual property to constitutional law, unless the same case appeared in both databases. This suggests that some mechanism is needed for linking the subsystems, though it is not clear what this would be.

Another issue is the incremental modification of the SCALIR database. As new cases are decided, there should be a way to incorporate them into the database. This is relatively painless in SCALIR; new nodes can be created for the new documents, and these can be linked in to the existing network without destroying any existing structure, learned weights in particular. The only difficulty lies in the textual analysis required to choose the index terms, and the weights on the new document-to-term links. The term weighting formula described in chapter 7 includes a "global" term — the *document frequency* — that depends on statistics about the entire corpus. Adding a few documents will not make much difference to an already large corpus, so existing global statistics could still be used. As the cumulative number of new documents increases, however, these statistics become increasingly less valid. In order to alleviate this problem, it may be necessary to update the global weighting term as each new document is entered (or in batch mode once enough new items have accumulated). This is not difficult with document frequency, though it does require that this data be kept around for the life of the system.

12.2.3 SCALIR, Learning, and the Law Firm

Lawyers who see SCALIR demonstrated are often impressed by many of its capabilities, but are hostile to the notion of an adaptive system. The idea that research results are variable is frightening; users want to be able to always find the same items using the same query. In part, it seems plausible that this objection will weaken if the system consistently improves. Furthermore, it is often pointed out that reference librarians continually adapt in response to their previous experiences; no one would

---

[3]Such a system might require more efficient file storage and access mechanisms, however.

want a librarian who suggested the same book you said you hated last time you talked to him or her.

Despite the potential benefits of learning, there is a sense in which *forcing* the users to use the adaptive mechanism is as mistaken as forcing them to use "fully automated" systems. It may be that learning simply takes too much control away from the user.

It would certainly be possible to make learning conditional on some action by the user. For instance, one can imagine an extension of the feedback mechanism that allows users to indicate *optionally* whether the system should "remember" and respond to the user's action. In fact, if used effectively, this feature might improve the accuracy of learning. Currently, a user might prune a document from a search because he or she has already read it. SCALIR treats this negative feedback as an indication that the document is not relevant, and decreases its likelihood of future retrieval. This may prevent future users from finding the useful document. By omitting the proposed "optional learning signal," however, the user could indicate that no permanent changes should be made.

Another variant of the conditional learning idea is to have the learning rate set differently depending on the experience or authority of the user. For instance, legal experts might cause large changes to the system, whereas novices caused small changes, or none at all.

The prospect of controlling when and how much to learn raises the additional question of the size of the user community contributing to the system's learning. There are arguments to be made for combining the feedback from the largest possible collection of users; the large population would be more statistically robust, thus the system's representation would not have as many noise-induced peculiarities. On the other hand, there are benefits to a "personal" system that adapts only to individuals.

SCALIR is viewed as falling in the middle. Its intended user community is a single law firm. This would allow members of the community to benefit from each others' knowledge — a proprietary quantity in the legal profession — without sharing it with their potential legal adversaries. Furthermore, it could result in the formation of in-house research traditions (i.e., the system would learn to interpret search terms in ways that previous people in the firm have found useful).

12.2.4   User Satisfaction and System Performance

In the previous section it was noted that learning may be viewed as taking control away from users. If this makes them unwilling to use the system, then it may not be worth including. However, the opposite problem is also a possibility. One system may be eminently preferred by users while actually performing a less useful task, or the same task less well, than another, less usable system.

This tradeoff between usability and usefulness may be particularly acute in the law. When demonstrating SCALIR, I often pointed out that legal research is performed by the most junior members of the law firm — paralegals and associates. A common response (given by lawyers as well as others) was, "That's true, but lawyers might do the research themselves if they had a system like this to use."

Let us suppose for the sake of argument that SCALIR actually does a terrible job of finding relevant documents, but that it is so enthralling to use that lawyers prefer it over LEXIS and WESTLAW by a wide margin. If the system's performance in terms of recall or precision were bad enough, the users would certainly notice and would abandon it as an ineffective legal research tool. But if it were only somewhat bad, the Blair and Maron results suggest that users *would not know*.

Fortunately, SCALIR does not do the "terrible job" of this hypothetical situation. Nevertheless, it is important to keep this factor in mind when designing a user-oriented system. Should the goal be to make it possible for users to "do what they want," on the grounds that an unused system is a useless system? Or is it to focus on their ultimate aim, "doing what is best for them"? Carried to their logical extreme, both of these approaches spell disaster. The answer presumably lies somewhere in between — hopefully where SCALIR is situated — but the exact balance almost certainly depends on the nature of the task and the costs of error in that particular domain.

12.3 Future Directions

There are many ways in which the SCALIR research might be pursued further. This section describes two possibilities: "broadening" the research by generalizing it to domains other than law, and "deepening" it by extending its role in law.

12.3.1 Generalizing to Other Domains

Many of the arguments presented in chapter 5 suggest that the SCALIR approach is particularly well suited to the legal research task. There are several reasons for this, including the known problems of existing CALR systems, the important role of text in the law, and the way in which the law can be viewed as possessing both symbolic and sub-symbolic characteristics. Indeed, the design of SCALIR was informed by these attributes.

How, then, might similar techniques be applied to other domains? (By "similar techniques," I mean primarily the use of the hybrid connectionist/symbolic representations and retrieval algorithms.) It is true that many other domains rely less heavily on text, and thus might be less amenable to a text-based approach. It is also true that many other domains do not have such a clear duality, and might therefore benefit less from a hybrid model.

Despite these differences, I believe there are ways to generalize the SCALIR approach. Although other domains may not have artifacts like the West key number taxonomy or Shepard's citations to describe the "architecture" of their world, that architecture often exists nonetheless. In chemistry, for example, researchers often look up information by molecular structure. It is easy to imagine a system whose symbolic component represents a priori knowledge about these structures. There might be taxonomic branches for, say, ketones and aldehydes, cross-references between structures capable of bonding together, and so on. Each of these represents a structural aspect of the chemical world. In medicine, the "architecture of the world" might be the various subsystems of the human body. A document might be retrieved because there is a strong interaction between its subsystem and the one explicitly being searched by the medical researcher or physician. One can even imagine this being an effective way to flag side-effects of drugs, for example.

Generalizing to other domains would also involve an understanding of the relationship of documents to the structural relations described previously; this relationship will seldom be as explicit as it is in law. Furthermore, the role of research in these domains must be considered. If the documents are sources of "raw data" in the domain, such as medical records or software problem reports, the user's task — and the system's — will be different than if the documents are journal articles or newspaper stories.

Clearly, the details of these other applications would need to be worked out, and many aspects of the system — including the way it interacts with users — might require modification. Nevertheless, these do not seem to be insurmountable problems.

12.3.2 Analogy and Legal Reasoning

Analogy is among the central processes involved of legal reasoning, at least in a common law system [Mur82]. A judge must determine which past decisions are sufficiently analogous to the current situation to serve as precedents. Similarly, attorneys try to anticipate the set of possible precedents, and convince the judge that the analogy they select is the correct one. There are many other uses of analogy in law — Ashley, for example, identifies eight [Ash85]. In the AI and law community, analogy has emerged as a central tenet of the case-based (or exemplar-based) reasoning approach. Examples of this approach are Ashley and Rissland's Hypo [Ash90, RA87] (described in chapter 5) and Branting's GREBE [Bra89] systems.

When a judge or lawyer thinks of a potential precedent, this can be viewed as an example of the problem of selecting a potential analogue to the current situation. Clearly, judges do not exhaustively search all cases in memory to select precedents. Nor should our legal information retrieval systems need exhaustive search to assist this task. The legal researcher should be able to describe some features of a case, or simply mention a previously decided case, and have the system return all the other cases it was "reminded" of which might be relevant. This is precisely the problem that SCALIR is designed to address. By using spreading activation in a network of microfeatures, the need for exhaustive search is eliminated.

Thus the SCALIR approach to legal analogy may be viewed as *complementary* to that of the case-based reasoning community. Although there are many potential difficulties (primarily our different representations), there appears to be promise in combining the two approaches. A future system might then be able to take a set of issues from a user, select potentially relevant sources from a large database, evaluate their suitability, and suggest promising precedents. Thus SCALIR could play a role not just in the legal research task, but as the "back end" of a future legal reasoning system.

In fact, the techniques used in SCALIR for locating relevant documents in a large corpus might be applied to the problem of reminding and analogy more generally. Analogy is a difficult phenomenon. Two situations can be superficially dissimilar yet strongly analogous. Gentner [Gen83] illustrated this with a typical example, "an electric battery is like a reservoir"; she pointed out that the strength of the analogy is independent of whether batteries and reservoirs have the same shape, size, and so on. Rather, it is some kind of underlying structure that gives the analogy its force.

The problem of analogy has been studied and modeled by psychologists ([Gen83], [GH80]) and AI researchers ([Car83], [HMF87], [Win80]). The basic premise of analogical reasoning is that a previously solved or understood situation — usually known as the *source* or *base* — can be used to help understand a new problem or situation — usually known as the *target*. Most researchers divide the analogy task into at least three parts:

- *selecting* one or more appropriate sources;

- *mapping* relevant features or structures of the target onto the corresponding components of the source(s);

- *transferring* the additional parts of the source(s) to their corresponding components of the target.

This last step, of course, is what makes the process useful; missing pieces of the target problem can be filled in with previously known information from the source.

The majority of AI models of analogy have focused almost exclusively on the mapping task. Given two situations, systems such as Winston's attempt to find correspondences between them. Because many of the representations used are structured, they can be viewed (and are often implemented) as semantic networks. The mapping problem then turns out to be a question of finding a subgraph isomorphism between the two representations. The difficulty is in knowing what subgraph to consider — in other words, knowing what features are relevant. Once this is accomplished, the transfer problem is fairly trivial.

Less research[4] has been done on the selection problem: Where do the sources come from in the first place? In traditional AI, one version of this problem might be stated as "given a particular situation, how do we know what frame/script/schema should become activated?" Some researchers seem to view this as a sort of implementation detail, whereas others have solved it by using exhaustive search of a small number of candidates. Although this is acceptable in certain limited domains, it fails to capture the "reminding" sorts of phenomena described, for example, by Schank [Sch82]. Why is it that when watching *West Side Story* we say, "Hey, this is just like *Romeo and Juliet*"? Surely it is not that we have searched a database for every potentially analogous play or movie.

Chapter 3 discussed the need for "deep" knowledge representation schemes that avoided explicit encoding of predetermined features. As noted earlier, text itself has many of the desired characteristics. This suggests a broader research program than the legal application described previously: A text-based intelligent system as a general mechanism for the selection problem in analogy. This is clearly a speculative proposal, but one that calls out for further investigation.

---

[4]See, for example, the survey by [Hal88] of computational approaches to analogy.

12.4 Conclusion

The research that has been described in this book involves aspects of information retrieval, human-computer interaction, law, and artificial intelligence. It includes conceptual hypotheses as well as algorithm specification; conversations with users as well as analyses of weight changes. What unites all of these investigations is a real-world problem — retrieving relevant documents on copyright law — using the complete set of data in that domain.

Real-world problems are not always well-behaved, and SCALIR's is no exception. In particular, the need for skilled users — and the variability of those users once they are found — makes evaluation of the system extremely difficult. Yet I believe that these difficulties are a worthwhile price to pay for a better understanding of a complex task, and a system to help perform it.

Artificial Intelligence has often been accused of focusing on "toy" problems, with the implication that it has little to offer by way of practical solutions to actual problems. The SCALIR system demonstrates that this need not be the case.

References

[ANS80]   American national standard guidelines for thesaurus structure, construction, and use. American National Standards Institute, Inc., 1980. (Z39.19).

[AS85]   Layman Allen and Charles Saxon. Computer-aided normalization and unpacking: Some interesting machine-processable transformations of legal rules. In Charles Walter, editor, *Computing Power and Legal Reasoning*, chapter 20, pages 495–572. West Publishing Co., St. Paul, MN, 1985.

[AS87]   Layman E. Allen and Charles S. Saxon. Some problems in designing expert systems to aid legal reasoning. In *Proceedings of the First International Conference on Artificial Intelligence and Law*, pages 94–103, May 1987.

[Ash85]   Kevin D. Ashley. Reasoning by analogy: A survey of selected AI research with implications for legal expert systems. In Charles Walter, editor, *Computing Power and Legal Reasoning*, chapter 6, pages 105–127. West Publishing Co., St. Paul, MN, 1985.

[Ash90]   Kevin D. Ashley. *Modeling Legal Argument: Reasoning with Cases and Hypotheticals*. MIT Press, 1990.

[BA85]   A. G. Barto and P. Anandan. Pattern recognizing stochastic learning automata. *IEEE Transactions on Systems, Man and Cybernetics*, 15:360–375, 1985.

[Bat79a] Marcia J. Bates. Idea tactics. *Journal of the American Society for Information Science*, pages 280–289, September 1979.

[Bat79b] Marcia J. Bates. Information search tactics. *Journal of the American Society for Information Science*, pages 205–214, July 1979.

[Bat90]   Marcia J. Bates. Where should the person stop and the information search interface start? *Information Processing and Management*, 26(5):575–591, 1990.

[Bat91]   Marcia J. Bates. The berrypicking search: User interface design. In Martin Dillon, editor, *Interfaces for Information Retrieval*. Greenwood Press, Westport, CT, 1991.

[BC91]   Brian T. Bartell and Garrison W. Cottrell. A model of symbol ground-
           ing in a temporal environment. In *Proceedings of the International Joint
           Conference on Neural Networks*, 1991. To appear.

[Bel86]   Richard K. Belew. *Adaptive Information Retrieval: Machine Learning in
           Associative Networks*. PhD thesis, University of Michigan, 1986.

[Bel89]   Richard K. Belew. Adaptive information retrieval: Using a connec-
           tionist representation to retrieve and learn about documents. In N. J.
           Belkin and C. J. van Rijsbergen, editors, *Proceedings of the 12th Inter-
           national Conference on Research and Development in Information Retrieval*,
           pages 11–20, Cambridge, MA, June 1989.

[Ber73]   H. J. Berliner. Some necessary conditions for a master chess program.
           In *IJCAI 3*, pages 77–85, 1973.

[Ber89]   Donald H. Berman. Cutting legal loops. In *Proceedings of the Second
           International Conference on Artificial Intelligence and Law*, pages 251–258,
           Vancouver, Canada, June 1989.

[BF81]   Avron Barr and Edward A. Feigenbaum, editors. *The Handbook of
           Artificial Intelligence*, volume 1. William Kaufmann, Los Altos, CA,
           1981.

[BF88]   Richard K. Belew and Stephanie Forrest. Learning and programming
           in the classifier system. *Machine Learning*, 3(2):193–223, 1988.

[BFL85]   Ronald J. Brachman, Richard E. Fikes, and Hector J. Levesque.
           KRYPTON: A functional approach to knowledge representation. In
           Ronald J. Brachman and Hector J. Levesque, editors, *Readings in
           Knowledge Representation*, pages 411–429. Morgan Kaufmann Publish-
           ers, Inc., Los Altos, CA, 1985.

[BH88]   Donald Berman and Carole Hafner. Obstacles to the developments
           of logic-based models of legal reasoning. In Charles Walter, editor,
           Computer Power and Legal Language, pages 183–214. Quorum Books,
           New York, 1988.

[Bic89]   Riva Wenig Bickel. Self-assessment procedure XIX: A self-assessment
           procedure on the application of copyright law to computer programs.
           Comunications of the ACM, 32(4):472–479, April 1989.

[Bin84]   Jon Bing, editor. *Handbook of Legal Information Retrieval*. Elsevier Sci-
           ence Publishers, Amsterdam, 1984.

[Bin87a]   Jon Bing. Designing text retrieval systems for "conceptual searching".
           In *Proceedings of the First International Conference on Artificial Intelligence
           and Law*, pages 43–51, May 1987.

[Bin87b]   Jon Bing. Performance of legal text retrieval systems: The curse of
           Boole. *Law Library Journal*, 79(2):187–202, Spring 1987.

[Bin88]   Jon Bing. The text retrieval system as a conversation factor. In Charles
           Walter, editor, *Computer Power and Legal Language*, pages 119–134. Quo-
           rum Books, New York, 1988.

[BL85]   Ronald J. Brachman and Hector J. Levesque, editors. *Readings In Knowledge Representation*. Morgan Kaufmann Publishers, Inc., Los Altos, CA, 1985.

[Bla90]   David C. Blair. *Language and Representation in Information Retrieval*. Elsevier, New York, 1990.

[BM85]   David C. Blair and M. E. Maron. An evaluation of retrieval effectiveness for a full-text document-retrieval system. *CACM*, 28(3):289 299, March 1985.

[BM88]   Ronald J. Brachman and Deborah L. McGuinness. Knowledge representation, connectionism, and conceptual retrieval. In *Proceedings of the 11th International Conference on Research and Development in Information Retrieval*, 1988.

[BM90]   David C. Blair and M. E. Maron. Full-text information retrieval: Further analysis and clarification. *Information Processing and Management*, 26(3):437–447, 1990.

[BOB82]   N. J. Belkin, R. N. Oddy, and H. M. Brooks. ASK for information retrieval: Part I. background and theory. *Journal of Documentation*, 38(2):61–71, June 1982.

[Bod77]   Margaret A. Boden. *Artificial Intelligence and Natural Man*. Basic Books, New York, 1977.

[Bor86a]   C. L. Borgman. Why are online catalogs hard to use? Lessons learned from information-retrieval studies. *Journal of the American Society for Information Science*, 37:387–400, 1986.

[Bor86b]   Christine L. Borgman. The user's mental model of an information retrieval system: An experiment on a prototype online catalog. *International Journal of Man-Machine Studies*, 24:47–64, 1986.

[BR88]   Richard K. Belew and Daniel E. Rose. Learning semantics from word use. Unpublished, 1988.

[Bra71]   T. L. Brauen. Document vector modfication. In Gerard Salton, editor, *The SMART Retrieval System — Experiments in Automatic Document Processing*, chapter 24. Prentice-Hall, Inc., Englewood Cliffs, NJ, 1971.

[Bra83]   Ronald J. Brachman. What IS-A is and isn't: An analysis of taxonomic links in semantic networks. *IEEE Computer*, pages 30–36, October 1983.

[Bra85]   Ronald J. Brachman. On the epistemological status of semantic networks. In Ronald J. Brachman and Hector J. Levesque, editors, *Readings in Knowledge Representation*, pages 191–215. Morgan Kaufmann Publishers, Inc., Los Altos, CA, 1985.

[Bra89]   Karl L. Branting. Representing and reusing explanations of legal precedents. In *Proceedings of the Second International Conference on Artificial Intelligence and Law*, pages 103–110, Vancouver, Canada, June 1989.

[Bre90]   Susan E. Brennan. Conversation as direct manipulation: An iconoclastic view. In Brenda Laurel, editor, *The Art of Human-Computer Interface Design*, pages 393–405. Addison-Wesley, Reading, MA, 1990.

[BS85]   R. J. Brachman and J. Schmolze. An overview of the KL-ONE knowledge representation system. *Cognitive Science*, 9(2):171–216, 1985.

[Bus45]   Vannevar Bush. As we may think. *Atlantic Monthly*, pages 101–108, July 1945.

[Car83]   Jaime Carbonell. Learning by analogy: Formulating and generalizing plans from past experience. In R. Michalski, J. Carbonell, and T. Mitchell, editors, *Machine Learning: An Artificial Intelligence Approach*. Tioga Press, Palo Alto, CA, 1983.

[CBH90]   Garrison W. Cottrell, Brian Bartell, and Christopher Haupt. Grounding meaning in perception. In *14th German Workshop on Artificial Intelligence*, pages 307–321. Springer-Verlag, 1990.

[CK87]   Paul R. Cohen and Rick Kjeldsen. Information retrieval by constrained spreading activation in semantic networks. *Information Processing and Management*, 23(4):255–268, 1987.

[CM85]   Eugene Charniak and Drew McDermott. *Introduction to Artificial Intelligence*. Addison-Wesley, Reading, MA, 1985.

[CMN83]   Stuart K. Card, Thomas P. Moran, and Allen Newell. *The Psychology of Human-Computer Interaction*. Lawrence Erlbaum Associates, Hillsdale, NJ, 1983.

[CMZ87]   G. W. Cottrell, P. Munro, and D. Zipser. Learning internal representations from gray-scale images: An example of extensional programming. In *Proceedings of the Ninth Annual Conference of the Cognitive Science Society*, pages 461–473, Seattle, WA, 1987.

[Con87]   Jeff Conklin. Hypertext: An introduction and survey. *IEEE Computer*, pages 17–41, September 1987.

[Coo68]   W. S. Cooper. Expected search length: A single measure of retrieval effectiveness based on weak ordering action of retrieval systems. *Journal of the American Society for Information Science*, 19:30–41, 1968.

[Coo71]   William S. Cooper. A definition of relevance for information retrieval. *Information Storage and Retrieval*, 7:19–37, 1971.

[Cro84]   W. Bruce Croft. The role of context and adaptation in user interfaces. *International Journal of Man-Machine Studies*, 21:283–292, 1984.

[CT87]   W. B. Croft and R. H. Thompson. I^3R: A new approach to the design of document retrieval systems. *Journal of the American Society for Information Science*, 38:389–404, November 1987.

[CW88]   J. F. Cove and B. C. Walsh. Online text retrieval via browsing. *Information Processing and Management*, 24(1):31–37, 1988.

[DBS77]   Randall Davis, Bruce Buchanan, and Edward Shortliffe. Production rules as a representation for a knowledge-based consultation program. *Artificial Intelligence*, 8:15–45, 1977.

[DDF+90]   Scott Deerwester, Susan T. Dumais, George W. Furnas, Thomas K. Landauer, and Richard Harshman. Indexing by latent semantic analysis. *Journal of the American Society for Information Science*, 41(6):391–407, 1990.

[DeJ79]   Gerald DeJong. Prediction and substantiation: A new approach to natural language processing. *Cognitive Science*, 3:251–273, 1979.

[Der90]   Mark A. Derthick. Mundane reasoning by settling on a plausible model. *Artificial Intelligence*, 46(1–2):107–157, November 1990.

[DFL+88]   Susan T. Dumais, George W. Furnas, Thomas K. Landauer, Scott Deerwester, and Richard Harshman. Using latent semantic analysis to improve access to textual information. In *Human Factors In Computing Systems: CHI '88 Conference Proceedings*, pages 281–285, 1988.

[Dic87]   Judith P. Dick. Conceptual retrieval and case law. In *Proceedings of the First International Conference on Artificial Intelligence and Law*, pages 106–114, May 1987.

[DP86]   Mark Derthick and David C. Plaut. Is distributed connectionism compatible with the physical symbol system hypothesis? In *Proceedings of the Eighth Annual Conference of the Cognitive Science Society*, pages 639–644, 1986.

[Dre79]   Hubert L. Dreyfus. *What Computers Can't Do: The Limits of Artificial Intelligence*. Harper & Row, New York, revised edition, 1979.

[DRL90]   Tamas E. Doszkocs, James Reggia, and Xia Lin. Connectionist models and information retrieval. *Annual Review of Information Science and Technology*, 25, 1990.

[DS89]   Charles P. Dolan and Paul Smolensky. Tensor product production system: a modular archictecture and representation. *Connection Science*, 1(1):53–68, 1989.

[DW87]   R. Durbin and D. Willshaw. The elastic net method: An analogue approach to the traveling salesman problem. *Nature*, 326:689–691, 1987.

[Dye91]   Michael G. Dyer. Symbolic neuroengineering for natural language processing: A multilevel research approach. In J. Barnden and J. Pollack, editors, *Advances in Connectionist and Neural Computation Theory. Volume 1: High-Level Connectionist Models*, pages 32–86. Ablex, Norwood, NJ, 1991.

[Elm89]   Jeffrey L. Elman. Representation and structure in connectionist models. Technical Report CRL-8903, Center for Research in Language, UCSD, La Jolla, CA, 1989.

[ER85]   David W. Etherington and Raymond Reiter. On inheritance hierarchies with exceptions. In Ronald J. Brachman and Hector J. Levesque, editors, *Readings in Knowledge Representation*, pages 329–334. Morgan Kaufmann Publishers, Inc., Los Altos, CA, 1985.

[FB82]   J. A. Feldman and D. H. Ballard. Connectionist models and their properties. *Cognitive Science*, 6:205–254, 1982.

[Fil68]   Charles J. Fillmore. The case for case. In E. Bach and R. T. Harms, editors, *Universals in Linguistic Theory*, pages 1–88. Holt, Rinehart, and Winston, New York, 1968.

[FLGD87]   G. W. Furnas, T. K. Landauer, L. M. Gomez, and S. T. Dumais. The vocabulary problem in human-system communication. *Communications of the ACM*, 30(11):964–971, November 1987.

[FP88]   Jerry A. Fodor and Zenon W. Pylyshyn. Connectionism and cognitive architecture: A critical analysis. *Cognition*, 28:3–71, 1988.

[Fra63]   Jerome Frank. *Law and the Modern Mind*. Anchor Books, Garden City, NY, 1963.

[Fre87]   Robert French. Romano-germanic and common law traditions and their analogy with expert-systems and emergent, evolutionary approaches to artificial intelligence. Unpublished, 1987.

[Gal88]   S. I. Gallant. Connectionist expert systems. *Communications of the ACM*, 31:152–169, 1988.

[Gar87]   Anne von der Lieth Gardner. *An Artificial Intelligence Approach to Legal Reasoning*. MIT Press, Cambridge, MA, 1987.

[GEC67]   R. D. Greenblatt, D. E. Eastlake, and S. D. Crocker. The Greenblatt chess program. In *AFIPS Conference Proceedings, Fall Joint Computer Conference*, pages 801–810, Washington, D.C., 1967. Thompson.

[Gen83]   Dedre L. Gentner. Structure-mapping: A theoretical framework for analogy. *Cognitive Science*, 7(2), 1983.

[GH80]   M. L. Gick and K. J. Holyoak. Analogical problem solving. *Cognitive Psychology*, 12:306–355, 1980.

[GKP86]   Paul Goldstein, Edmund W. Kitch, and Harvey S. Perlman, editors. *Selected Statutes and International Agreements on Unfair Competition, Trademark, Copyright and Patent*. Foundation Press, Mineola, NY, 1987 edition, 1986.

[GL90]   R. V. Guha and Douglas B. Lenat. Cyc: A midterm report. *AI Magazine*, 11(3):32–59, Fall 1990.

[Gol81]   Paul Goldstein. *Copyright, Patent, Trademark and Related State Doctrines: Cases and Materials on the Law of Intellectual Property*. The Foundation Press, Inc., Mineola, NY, second edition, 1981.

[Gol89]   David E. Goldberg. *Genetic Algorithms in Search, Optimization, and Machine Learning*. Addison-Wesley, Reading, MA, 1989.

[Gor88]   Michael Gordon. Probabilistic and genetic algorithms in document retrieval. *Communications of the ACM*, 31(10), October 1988.

[Gou88]   Stephen Jay Gould. Robert C. Elliott Memorial Lecture. La Jolla, CA, February 18, 1988.

[Gri75]   H. P. Grice. Logic and conversation. In P. Cole and J. Morgan, editors, *Syntax and Semantics 3: Speech Acts*, pages 41–58. Academic Press, New York, 1975.

[Gro80]   S. Grossberg. How does the brain build a cognitive code? *Psychological Review*, 87:1–51, 1980.

[Haf81]   Carole D. Hafner. *An Information Retrieval System Based on a Computer Model of Legal Knowledge*. UMI Research Press, Ann Arbor, Michigan, 1981.

[Hal88]   Rogers P. Hall. Computational approaches to analogical reasoning: A comparative analysis. *Artificial Intelligence*, 1988.

[Har61]   H. L. A. Hart. *The Concept of Law*. Clarendon Press, Oxford, 1961.

[Har85]   William G. Harrington. A brief history of computer-assisted legal research. *Law Library Journal*, 77:543–556, 1985.

[Har87]   Stevan Harnad. Category induction and representation. In Stevan Harnad, editor, *Categorical Perception*. Cambridge University Press, New York, 1987.

[Hau85]   John Haugeland. *Artificial Intelligence: The Very Idea*. MIT Press, Cambridge, MA, 1985.

[Heb49]   Donald O. Hebb. *The Organization of Behavior*. Wiley, New York, 1949.

[Hen87]   James A. Hendler. *Integrating Marker-passing and Problem Solving: A Spreading Activation Approach to Improved Choice in Planning*. Lawrence Erlbaum Associates, Hillsdale, NJ, 1987.

[Hen89a] James A. Hendler. The design and implementation of marker-passing systems. *Connection Science*, 1(1):17–40, 1989.

[Hen89b] James A. Hendler. Editorial: On the need for hybrid systems. *Connection Science*, 1(3):227–229, 1989.

[Hen89c] James A. Hendler. Marker-passing over microfeatures. *Cognitive Science*, 13(1):79–106, 1989.

[HHN86]   Edwin L. Hutchins, James D. Hollan, and Donald A. Norman. Direct manipulation interfaces. In Donald A. Norman and Stephen W. Draper, editors, *User Centered System Design: New Perspectives on Human-Computer Interaction*. Lawrence Erlbaum Associates, Hillsdale, NJ, 1986.

[HHNT86] John H. Holland, Keith J. Holyoak, Richard E. Nisbitt, and Paul Thagard. *Induction: Processes of Learning, Inference and Discovery*. Bradford Books, Cambridge, MA, 1986.

[Hil83]   C. R. Hildreth. To Boolean or not to Boolean. *Information Technology and Libraries*, 2:235–237, 1983.

[Hil85]   D. Hillis. *The Connection Machine*. MIT Press, Cambridge, MA, 1985.

[Hin89]   Geoffrey E. Hinton. Connectionist learning procedures. *Artificial Intelligence*, 40, 1989.

[HMF87]   Douglas R. Hofstadter, Melanie Mitchell, and Robert M. French. Fluid concepts and creative analogies: A theory and its computer implementation. Technical Report 87-1, Fluid Analogies Research Group, University of Michigan, Ann Arbor, MI, March 1987.

[HMR86]   Geoffrey E. Hinton, James L. McClelland, and David E. Rumelhart. Distributed representations. In David E. Rumelhart and James L. McClelland, editors, *Parallel Distributed Processing: Explorations in the Microstructure of Cognition. Volume 1: Foundations*, pages 77–109. MIT Press, Cambridge, MA, 1986.

[Hof79]   Douglas R. Hofstadter. *Gödel, Escher, Bach: An Eternal Golden Braid*. Basic Books, New York, 1979.

[Hof82]   Douglas R. Hofstadter. Artificial intelligence: Subcognition as computation. Technical report, Computer Science Dept., Indiana University, Bloomington, IN, 1982.

[Hol75]   John H. Holland. *Adaptation in Natural and Artificial Systems*. University of Michigan Press, Ann Arbor, MI, 1975.

[Hop82]   John J. Hopfield. Neural networks and physical systems with emergent collective computational abilities. *Proceedings of the National Academy of Sciences*, 79:2554–2558, 1982.

[Hop84]   John J. Hopfield. Neurons with graded response have collective computational properties like those of two-state neurons. *Proceedings of the National Academy of Sciences*, 81:3088–3092, 1984.

[HW90]   John B. Hampshire and Alex Waibel. Connectionist architectures for multi-speaker phoneme recognition. In David S. Touretzky, editor, *Advances in Neural Information Processing Systems 2*, pages 203–210. Morgan Kaufmann, San Mateo, CA, 1990.

[Ide71]   E. Ide. New experiments in relevance feedback. In Gerard Salton, editor, *The SMART Retrieval System — Experiments in Automatic Document Processing*, chapter 16. Prentice-Hall, Inc., Englewood Cliffs, NJ, 1971.

[JF87]   W. P. Jones and G. W. Furnas. Pictures of relevance — a geometric analysis of similarity measures. *Journal of the American Society for Information Science*, 38(6):420–442, 1987.

[JH76]   Elmer D. Johnson and Michael D. Harris. *History of Libraries in the Western World*. The Scarecrow Press, Inc., Metuchen, NJ, third edition, 1976.

[Jon86]   William P. Jones. The memory extender personal filing system. In *Human Factors In Computing Systems: CHI '86 Conference Proceedings*, pages 298–305, 1986.

[JR88]   P. S. Jacobs and L. F. Rau. Natural language techniques for intelligent information retrieval. In Y. Chiaramella, editor, *Proceedings of the 11th International Conference on Research and Development in Information Retrieval*, pages 85–99, Grenoble, France, June 1988.

[Kim73]   Chai Kim. Theoretical foundations of thesaurus-construction and some methodological considerations for thesaurus-updating. *Journal of the American Society for Information Science*, pages 148–156, March-April 1973.

[KL82]   Earl W. Kintner and Jack Lahr. *An Intellectual Property Law Primer: A Survey of the Law of Patents, Trade Secrets, Trademarks, Franchises, Copyrights, and Personality and Entertainment Rights*. Clark Boardman Company, Ltd., New York, second edition, 1982.

[Kla80]   Roberta L. Klatzky. *Human Memory: Structures and Processes*. W. H. Freeman and Company, New York, 2nd edition, 1980.

[Koh82]   Teuvo Kohonen. Self-organized formation of topologically correct feature maps. *Biological Cybernetics*, 43:59–69, 1982.

[Kwo89]   K. L. Kwok. A neural network for probabilistic information retrieval. In N. J. Belkin and C. J. van Rijsbergen, editors, *Proceedings of the 12th International Conference on Research and Development in Information Retrieval*, pages 21–30, Cambridge, MA, June 1989.

[Lam85]   Sydney Lamb. Information and its representation in english texts. In Charles Walter, editor, *Computing Power and Legal Reasoning*, pages 145–155. West Publishing Co., St. Paul, MN, 1985.

[Lan87]   Christopher C. Langdell. *Law Quarterly Review*, 3, 1887.

[Lau86]   Brenda K. Laurel. Interface as mimesis. In Donald A. Norman and Stephen W. Draper, editors, *User Centered System Design: New Perspectives on Human-Computer Interaction*. Lawrence Erlbaum Associates, Hillsdale, NJ, 1986.

[LB84]   D. B. Lenat and J. S. Brown. Why AM and EURISKO appear to work. *Artificial Intelligence*, 23(3):269–294, 1984.

[LD89]   Trent E. Lange and Michael G. Dyer. Frame selection in a connectionist model of high-level inferencing. In *Proceedings of the Eleventh Annual Conference of the Cognitive Science Society*, Ann Arbor, MI, August 1989.

[Len83]   Douglas B. Lenat. The role of heuristics in learning by discovery: Three case studies. In Ryszard S. Michalski, Jaime G. Carbonell, and Tom M. Mitchell, editors, *Machine Learning: An Artificial Intelligence Approach*, pages 243–306. Tioga Publishing Company, Palo Alto, CA, 1983.

[Lew46]   C. I. Lewis. *An Analysis of Knowledge and Valuation*. Open Court Publishing Co., La Salle, IL, 1946.

[Lin88]   Peter Linzer. Precise meaning and open texture in legal writing and meaning. In Charles Walter, editor, *Computer Power and Legal Language*, chapter 2, pages 6–12. Quorum Books, New York, 1988.

[Lle30]   Karl N. Llewellyn. *The Bramble Bush: On Our Law and Its Study*. Oceana, New York, 1930.

[Lle62]   Karl N. Llewellyn. *Jurisprudence: Realism in Theory and Practice*. University of Chicago Press, Chicago, 1962.

[LNR87]   John E. Laird, Allen Newell, and Paul S. Rosenbloom. SOAR: An architecture for general intelligence. *Artificial Intelligence*, 33:1–64, 1987.

[LOD90]   Brenda Laurel, Tim Oren, and Abbe Don. Issues in multimedia interface design: Media integration and interface agents. In *Human Factors In Computing Systems: CHI '90 Conference Proceedings*, pages 133–139, 1990.

[Mac77]   Ejan Mackaay. Designing DATUM II: Why not and how? *Datenverarbeitung im Recht*, pages 47–81, March 1977.

[Mar89]   Catherine C. Marshall. Representing the structure of a legal argument. In *Proceedings of the Second International Conference on Artificial Intelligence and Law*, pages 121–127, Vancouver, Canada, June 1989.

[Mau86]   Michael L. Mauldin. Retrieving information with a text skimming parser. In *Eastern States Conference on Linguistics*, October 1986.

[McC89]   James L. McClelland. Parallel distributed processing: Implications for cognition and development. In R. G. M. Morris, editor, *Parallel Distributed Processing: Implications for Psychology and Neurobiology*. Clarendon Press, Oxford, 1989.

[McD81]   Drew McDermott. Artificial intelligence meets natural stupidity. In John Haugeland, editor, *Mind Design: Philosophy, Psychology, Artificial Intelligence*, pages 143–160. MIT Press, Cambridge, MA, 1981.

[MCT87]   Michael Mauldin, Jaime Carbonell, and Richard Thomason. Beyond the keyword barrier: Knowledge-based information retrieval. In *Proceedings of the 29th Annual Conference of the National Federation of Abstracting and Information Services*. Elsevier Press, 1987.

[Mel82]   David Mellinkoff. *Legal Writing: Sense and Nonsense*. Charles Scribner's Sons, 1982.

[Min63]   Marvin L. Minsky. Steps toward artificial intelligence. In E. A. Feigenbaum and J. Feldman, editors, *Computers and thought*, pages 406–450. McGraw-Hill, Inc., New York, 1963.

[Min68]   Marvin L. Minsky, editor. *Semantic Information Processing*. MIT Press, Cambridge, MA, 1968.

[Min75] Marvin L. Minsky. A framework for representing knowledge. In Patrick H. Winston, editor, *The Psychology of Computer Vision*. McGraw-Hill, New York, 1975.

[Mit77] T. M. Mitchell. Version spaces: a candidate elimination approach to rule learning. In *IJCAI 5*, pages 305–310, 1977.

[MK60] M. E. Maron and J. L. Kuhns. On relevance, probabilistic indexing and information retrieval. *Journal of the ACM*, 7:216–244, 1960.

[Moz84] Michael C. Mozer. Inductive information retrieval using parallel distributed computation. Technical Report 8406, Institute for Cognitive Science, UCSD, La Jolla, CA, May 1984.

[MP43] Warren S. McCulloch and Walter Pitts. A logical calculus of the ideas immanent in nervous activity. *Bulletin of Mathematical Biophysics*, 5:115–133, 1943.

[MPRV87] R. J. McEliece, E. C. Posner, E. R. Rodemich, and S. S. Venkatesh. The capacity of the Hopfield associative memory. *IEEE Transactions on Information Theory*, 33:461–482, 1987.

[MR81] James L. McClelland and David E. Rumelhart. An interactive activation model of context effects in letter perception: Part 1. An account of basic findings. *Psychological Review*, 88:375–407, 1981.

[Mur82] James L. Murray. The role of analogy in legal reasoning. *UCLA Law Review*, 29:833–871, 1982.

[NB79] D. A. Norman and D. G. Bobrow. Descriptions: An intermediate stage in memory retrieval. *Cognitive Psychology*, 11:107–123, 1979.

[NC83] Joseph R. Nolan and M. J. Connolly. *Black's Law Dictionary*. West Publishing Co., St. Paul, MN, abridged fifth edition, 1983.

[New80] Allen Newell. Physical symbol systems. *Cognitive Science*, 2, 1980.

[Nil80] Nils J. Nilsson. *Principles of Artificial Intelligence*. Tioga Publishing Co., Palo Alto, CA, 1980.

[NN86] Melville B. Nimmer and David Nimmer. *Nimmer on Copyright: A Treatise on the Law of Literary, Musical and Artistic Property, and the Protection of Ideas*. Matthew Bender & Co., Inc., New York, 1978 edition, 1986.

[Nor86] Donald A. Norman. Reflections on cognition and parallel distributed processing. In James L. McClelland and David E. Rumelhart, editors, *Parallel Distributed Processing: Explorations in the microstructure of cognition. Volume 2: Psychological and Biological Models*, pages 531–546. MIT Press, Cambridge, MA, 1986.

[Nor91] Donald A. Norman. Cognitive artifacts. In John M. Carroll, editor, *Designing Interaction: Psychology at the Human-Computer Interface*. Cambridge University Press, New York, 1991.

[NR81]   A. Newell and P. S. Rosenbloom. Mechanisms of skill acquisition and the law of practice. In J. R. Anderson, editor, *Cognitive Skills and Their Acquisition*. Lawrence Erlbaum Associates, Hillsdale, NJ, 1981.

[OSKD90] Tim Oren, Gitta Salomon, Kristee Kreitman, and Abbe Don. Guides: Characterizing the interface. In Brenda Laurel, editor, *The Art of Human-Computer Interface Design*, pages 367–381. Addison-Wesley, Reading, MA, 1990.

[Pej89]   Annelise Mark Pejtersen. A library system for information retrieval based on a cognitive task analysis and supported by an icon-based interface. In *Proceedings of the 12th International Conference on Research and Development in Information Retrieval*, Cambridge, MA, June 1989.

[Pol90]   Jordan B. Pollack. Recursive distributed representation. *Artificial Intelligence*, 46(1–2):77–105, November 1990.

[Qui85]   M. Ross Quillian. Word concepts: A theory and simulation of some basic semantic capabilities. In Ronald J. Brachman and Hector J. Levesque, editors, *Readings in Knowledge Representation*, pages 97–118. Morgan Kaufmann Publishers, Inc., Los Altos, CA, 1985.

[RA87]   Edwina L. Rissland and Kevin D. Ashley. A case-based system for trade secrets law. In *Proceedings of the First International Conference on Artificial Intelligence and Law*, pages 60–66, May 1987.

[Rau87]   Lisa F. Rau. Information retrieval from never-ending stories. In *Proceedings AAAI-87*, pages 317–321. American Association for Artificial Intelligence, July 1987.

[RB89]   Daniel E. Rose and Richard K. Belew. Legal information retrieval: A hybrid approach. In *Proceedings of the Second International Conference on Artificial Intelligence and Law*, pages 138–146, Vancouver, Canada, June 1989.

[RB91a]   Daniel E. Rose and Richard K. Belew. A connectionist and symbolic hybrid for improving legal research. *International Journal of Man-Machine Studies*, 35:1–33, 1991.

[RB91b]   Daniel E. Rose and Richard K. Belew. Toward a direct-manipulation interface for conceptual information retrieval systems. In Martin Dillon, editor, *Interfaces for Information Retrieval and Online Systems: The State of the Art*, pages 39–54. Greenwood Press, Westport, CT, 1991.

[RHM86]   David E. Rumelhart, Geoffrey E. Hinton, and James L. McClelland. A general framework for parallel distributed processing. In David E. Rumelhart and James L. McClelland, editors, *Parallel Distributed Processing: Explorations in the microstructure of cognition. Volume 1: Foundations*, pages 45–76. MIT Press, Cambridge, MA, 1986.

[RHW86]   David E. Rumelhart, Geoffrey E. Hinton, and Ronald J. Williams. Learning internal representations by error propagation. In David E.

Rumelhart and James L. McClelland, editors, *Parallel Distributed Processing: Explorations in the microstructure of cognition. Volume 1: Foundations*, pages 318–362. MIT Press, Cambridge, MA, 1986.

[Ric83]   Elaine Rich. *Artificial Intelligence*. McGraw-Hill, New York, 1983.

[Ris84]   Edwina L. Rissland. Ingredients of intelligent user interfaces. *International Journal of Man-Machine Studies*, 21:377–388, 1984.

[RK91]   Elaine Rich and Kevin Knight. *Artificial Intelligence*. McGraw-Hill, New York, second edition, 1991.

[RM82]   David E. Rumelhart and James L. McClelland. An interactive activation model of context effects in letter perception: Part 2. The contextual enhancement effect and some tests and extensions of the model. *Psychological Review*, 89:60–94, 1982.

[RN78]   David E. Rumelhart and Donald A. Norman. Accretion, tuning, and restructuring: Three modes of learning. In J. W. Cotton and R. Klatzky, editors, *Semantic Factors in Cognition*, pages 37–53. Lawrence Erlbaum Associates, Hillsdale, NJ, 1978.

[Rob77]   S. E. Robertson. The probability ranking principle in IR. *Journal of Documentation*, 33:294–304, 1977.

[Roc71]   J. J. Rocchio, Jr. Relevance feedback in information retrieval. In Gerard Salton, editor, *The SMART Retrieval System — Experiments in Automatic Document Processing*, chapter 14. Prentice-Hall, Inc., Englewood Cliffs, NJ, 1971.

[Ros58]   F. Rosenblatt. The perceptron: A probabilistic model for information storage and organization in the brain. *Psychological Review*, 65:386–408, 1958.

[Ros90]   Daniel E. Rose. Appropriate uses of hybrid systems. In D. S. Touretzky, J. L. Elman, T. J. Sejnowski, and G. E. Hinton, editors, *Connectionist Models: Proceedings of the 1990 Summer School*, pages 277–286, San Mateo, CA, 1990. Morgan Kaufmann.

[RS76]   S. E. Robertson and K. Sparck Jones. Relevance weighting of search terms. *Journal of the American Society for Information Science*, 27:129–146, 1976.

[Rum75]   David E. Rumelhart. Notes on a schema for stories. In Daniel G. Bobrow and Alan M. Collins, editors, *Representation and Understanding: Studies in Cognitive Science*, pages 211–236. Academic Press, New York, 1975.

[RZ85]   D. E. Rumelhart and D. Zipser. Competitive learning. *Cognitive Science*, 9:75–112, 1985.

[SA77]   R. C. Schank and R. Abelson. *Scripts, Plans, Goals, and Understanding*. Lawrence Erlbaum Associates, Hillsdale, NJ, 1977.

[SA90]   Lokendra Shastri and Venkat Ajjanagadde. From simple associations
           to systematic reasoning: A connectionist representation of rules, vari-
           ables, and dynamic bindings. Technical Report MS-CIS-90-05, Com-
           puter and Information Science Department, University of Pennsylva-
           nia, 1990.

[Sal68]   Gerard Salton. *Automatic Information Organization and Retrieval.*
           McGraw-Hill, Inc., New York, NY, 1968.

[Sam63]   Arthur L. Samuel. Some studies in machine learning using the game
           of checkers. In E. A. Feigenbaum and J. Feldman, editors, *Computers
           and thought*, pages 71–105. McGraw-Hill, Inc., New York, 1963.

[Sam89]   Pamela Samuelson. Why the look and feel of software user interfaces
           should not be protected by copyright law. *Comunications of the ACM*,
           32(5):563–572, May 1989.

[Sar76]   Tefko Saracevic. Relevance: A review of the literature and a frame-
           work for thinking on the notion in information science. In Melvin J.
           Voight and Michael H. Harris, editors, *Advances in Librarianship*, vol-
           ume 6, pages 79–138. Academic Press, New York, 1976.

[SB88a]   Gerard Salton and Chris Buckley. Parallel text search methods. *Com-
           munications of the ACM*, 31(2):202–215, February 1988.

[SB88b]   Gerard Salton and Christopher Buckley. Term-weighting approaches
           in automatic text retrieval. *Information Processing and Management*,
           24(5):513–523, 1988.

[Sch82]   Roger C. Schank. *Dynamic Memory: A Theory of Learning in Computers
           and People.* Cambridge University Press, Cambridge, 1982.

[Sea78]   John R. Searle. Minds, brains, and programs. *Behavioral and Brain
           Sciences*, 1:215–226, 1978.

[SFW83]   Gerard Salton, Edward A. Fox, and Harry Wu. Extended boolean
           information retrieval. *Communications of the ACM*, 26(12):1022–1036,
           December 1983.

[Sha88]   Lokendra Shastri. *Semantic Networks: An Evidential Formalization and
           its Connectionist Realization.* Pitman Publishing, London, 1988.

[Shn87]   Ben Shneiderman. *Designing the User Interface: Strategies for Effective
           Human-Computer Interaction.* Addison-Wesley, Reading, MA, 1987.

[Sim81]   Herbert A. Simon. 1980 Procter Award Lecture. *The American Scientist*,
           1981.

[Sim83]   Herbert A. Simon. Why should machines learn? In Ryszard S. Michal-
           ski, Jaime G. Carbonell, and Tom M. Mitchell, editors, *Machine Learn-
           ing: An Artificial Intelligence Approach*, pages 25–37. Tioga Publishing
           Company, Palo Alto, CA, 1983.

[SJT84]   K. Sparck Jones and J. I. Tait. Automatic search term variant genera-
           tion. *Journal of Documentation*, 40(1):50–66, March 1984.

[SK86]   Craig Stanfill and Brewster Kahle. Parallel free-text search on the connection machine system. *Communications of the ACM*, 29(12), December 1986.

[SL71]   G. Salton and M. E. Lesk. Information analysis and dictionary construction. In Gerard Salton, editor, *The SMART Retrieval System — Experiments in Automatic Document Processing*, chapter 6. Prentice-Hall, Inc., Englewood Cliffs, NJ, 1971.

[SM83]   Gerard Salton and Michael J. McGill. *Introduction to Modern Information Retrieval*. McGraw-Hill, Inc., New York, 1983.

[Smo88]   Paul Smolensky. On the proper treatment of connectionism. *Behavioral and Brain Sciences*, 11(1), March 1988.

[Smo90]   Paul Smolensky. Tensor product variable binding and the representation of symbolic structures in connectionist systems. *Artificial Intelligence*, 46(1–2):159–216, November 1990.

[Spa71]   Karen Sparck Jones. *Automatic Keyword Classification for Information Retrieval*. Butterworths, London, 1971.

[SR74]   Roger C. Schank and Charles J. Rieger III. Inference and the computer understanding of natural language. *Artificial Intelligence*, 5:373–412, 1974.

[SS89]   Gerard Salton and Maria Smith. On the application of syntactic methodologies in automatic text analysis. In N. J. Belkin and C. J. van Rijsbergen, editors, *Proceedings of the 12th International Conference on Research and Development in Information Retrieval*, pages 137–150, Cambridge, MA, June 1989.

[Sta88]   Craig Stanfill. Parallel computing for information retrieval: Recent developments. Technical Report DR88-1, Thinking Machines Corporation, 1988.

[Sta90]   Craig Stanfill. Partitioned posting files: A parallel inverted file structure for information retrieval. In Jean-Luc Vidick, editor, *Proceedings of the 13th International Conference on Research and Development in Information Retrieval*, pages 413–428, Brussels, September 1990.

[Sto87]   H. S. Stone. Parallel querying of large databases: A case study. *IEEE Computer*, pages 11–21, October 1987.

[Str88]   Gilbert Strang. *Linear Algebra and its Applications*. Harcourt Brace Jovanovich, San Diego, third edition, 1988.

[STW89]   Craig Stanfill, Robert Thau, and David Waltz. A parallel indexed algorithm for information retrieval. In N. J. Belkin and C. J. van Rijsbergen, editors, *Proceedings of the 12th International Conference on Research and Development in Information Retrieval*, pages 88–97, Cambridge, MA, June 1989.

[Tap73]   Colin Tapper, editor. *Computers and the Law*. Weidenfeld and Nicholson, London, 1973.

[Tap80]   Colin Tapper. Citations as a tool for searching the law by computer. In Bryan Niblett, editor, *Computer Science and Law*. Cambridge University Press, Cambridge, England, 1980.

[TC89]   R. H. Thompson and W. B. Croft. Support for browsing in an intelligent text retrieval system. *International Journal of Man-Machine Studies*, 30:639–668, 1989.

[Ten90]   Edward Tenner. From slip to chip: How evolving techniques of information storage and retrieval have shaped the way we do mental work. *Harvard Magazine*, 93(2):52–57, November–December 1990.

[TH87]   David W. Tank and John J. Hopfield. Collective computation in neuronlike circuits. *Scientific American*, 6(257), December 1987.

[TH88]   David S. Touretzky and Geoffrey E. Hinton. A distributed connectionist production system. *Cognitive Science*, 12:423–466, 1988.

[TK74]   A. Tversky and D. Kahneman. Judgments under uncertainty: Heuristics and biases. *Science*, 185:1124–1131, 1974.

[TM81]   W. Teitelman and L. Masinter. The interlisp programming environment. *IEEE Computer*, pages 25–33, April 1981.

[Tou58]   Stephen Toulmin. *The Uses of Argument*. Cambridge University Press, Cambridge, 1958.

[Tou90]   David S. Touretzky. BoltzCONS: Dynamic symbol structures in a connectionist network. *Artificial Intelligence*, 46(1–2):5–46, November 1990.

[Ull82]   Jeffrey D. Ullman. *Principles of Database Systems*. Computer Science Press, Rockville, MD, 2nd edition, 1982.

[Ung83]   Roberto M. Unger. *The Critical Legal Studies Movement*. Harvard University Press, Cambridge, MA, 1983.

[Val84]   L. G. Valiant. A theory of the learnable. *Communications of the ACM*, 27(11):1134–1142, November 1984.

[vG89]   Timothy J. van Gelder. *Distributed Representation*. PhD thesis, University of Pittsburgh, 1989.

[Vil77]   Claude A. Villee. *Biology*. W. B. Saunders Co., Philadelphia, PA, 1977.

[vMG77]   Arthur Taylor von Mehren and James Russell Gordley. *The Civil Law System: An Introduction to the Comparative Study of Law*. Little, Brown and Company, Boston, second edition, 1977.

[vN58]   John von Neumann. *The Computer and the Brain*. Yale University Press, New Haven, 1958.

[vR79]   C. J. van Rijsbergen. *Information Retrieval*. Butterworths, London, second edition, 1979.

[WB45]   Paul Weiss and Arthur Burks. Peirce's sixty-six signs. *Journal of Philosophy*, 42:383–388, 1945.

[Wes89]   *WESTLAW Reference Manual*. West Publishing Company, St. Paul, MN, 3rd edition, 1989.

[Wey89]   Stephen A. Weyer. Questing for the "dao": Dowquest and intelligent text retrieval. *Online*, 13(5):39–48, September 1989.

[WF86]   Terry Winograd and Fernando Flores. *Understanding Computers and Cognition*. Ablex Publishing, Norwood, NJ, 1986.

[WH60]   Bernard Widrow and Marcian E. Hoff. Adaptive switching circuits. In *IRE WESCON Convention Record*, pages 96–104, New York, 1960. IRE.

[WH81]   M. D. Williams and J. D. Hollan. The process of retrieval from very long term memory. *Cognitive Science*, 5:87–119, 1981.

[Wil84]   Michael David Williams. What makes RABBIT run? *International Journal of Man-Machine Studies*, 21:333–352, 1984.

[Win71]   B. J. Winer. *Statistical Principles in Experimental Design*. McGraw-Hill, New York, second edition, 1971.

[Win75]   Patrick H. Winston. Learning structural descriptions from examples. In Patrick H. Winston, editor, *The Psychology of Computer Vision*. McGraw-Hill, New York, 1975.

[Win77]   Patrick Henry Winston. *Artificial Intelligence*. Addison-Wesley, Reading, MA, 1977.

[Win80]   Patrick H. Winston. Learning and reasoning by analogy. *Communications of the ACM*, 23:689–703, 1980.

[Wit58]   Ludwig Wittgenstein. *Philosophical Investigations*. Macmillan Publishing Co., Inc., New York, third edition, 1958. Translated by G. E. M. Anscombe.

[Woo75]   William A. Woods. What's in a link: Foundations for semantic networks. In Daniel G. Bobrow and Alan M. Collins, editors, *Representation and Understanding: Studies in Cognitive Science*, pages 35–82. Academic Press, New York, 1975.

[WW83]   Christopher G. Wren and Jill Robinson Wren. *The Legal Research Manual: A Game Plan for Legal Research and Analysis*. A-R Editions, Inc., Madison, WI, 1983.

[WZ89]   Ronald J. Williams and David Zipser. A learning algorithm for continually running fully recurrent neural networks. *Neural Computation*, 1:270–280, 1989.

[Zlo75]   Moshé M. Zloof. Query by example. In *Proceedings of the 1975 National Computer Conference*, pages 431–437, Montvale, NJ, 1975. AFIPS Press.

Author Index

Subject Index

R

RABBIT, 25–26
realism, 96–97
recall (evaluation measure), 71, 75–76, 209
 normalized, 71
recall (memory), 27, 73, 118
recognition, 27, 73, 118
reinforcement learning, 202–203
relational algebra, 22
relevance, 60–61, 65, 75
 conveyed by shading, 234
 relativity of, 61, 209
 subjectivity of, 61
relevance feedback, 30, 61, 80–82, 86
 for learning, 204
 in SCALIR, 234
 simulation of user, 208–209
reminding, 27, 285, 286
reporter (common law), 103–104
retention constant (ρ), 180
retrieval
 conceptual, 109–116
 errors, 68–69
retrieval by example, 26, 35, 248
retrieval by reformulation, 22, 25–26
ROBIN, 134
Roget's thesaurus, 77
rule-based system, 42, 98

S

S-link, 156, 158–162
 as colored filter, 189
 for dependency, 159
 taxonomic, 159
 weighting of, 161
Samuel's checkers program, 44, 204
scaling, 42, 51, 165, 280–281
SCALIR
 "map" of associations in, 276
 activation function, 185–186
 approach of, 6–9
 associative retrieval in, 252–253
 browsing in, 234–236
 comparison with WESTLAW, 255–265
 connectionist network in, 156
 credit assignment in, 204–205
 description of, 2
 documents in, 150, 151
 evaluation of, 251–274
 evaluation of learning, 265–272
 generalizing, 283–284

hybrid nature of, 143–145
hypertext as dual, 243–244
interaction attributes, 245–246
learning rule in, 212–217
menu commands, 225–227
network statistics, 165–168
overview of, 150
propagation, 178–199
relevance feedback in, 234
retrieval algorithm, 186–188
retrieval in, 171–172
retrieval parameters, 183
semantic network in, 158
single descriptors in, 241–242
specifying symbolic relationships, 230–232
symbolic retrieval in, 254–255
terms used in, 152–154
user interface, 225–236
user testing of, 236–244
vector representation of activity, 190
Science Citation Index, 101
SCISOR, 79
search terms
 adding, 242
Second Amendment example, 68
selective dissemination of information (SDI), 29
semantic network, 46–50, 126, 130, 134–137, 158
 definition of, 48–49
 for law, 101
 in SCALIR, 118
settling network, 173
 capacity of, 174
 for IR, 174
shading for relevance, 234
Shepard's Citations, 20, 101, 104, 118, 140, 149, 158, 276
 as source of H-links, 164–165
 treatment phrases in, 101, 162
shepardizing, 106
signature files, 85
significance threshold (θ_s), 180–182
significance threshold in AIR, 177
similarity measures, 66
singular value decomposition (SVD), 87
SMART, 77, 80–82
SOAR, 142
Sony v. Universal, 69, 154, 252–254
spelling correction, 266
spreading activation, 7, 28, 47, 89–91

SQL, 23
STAIRS/TLS, 72–74
star paging, 164
stare decisis, 94
statute nodes, 154–155
statutory law, 94, 98, 103
    cross-references in, 101, 159
stop list, 64, 152
sub-symbolic processing, 126–133, 137
    benefits of, 139–140
sub-symbolic system, 40, 123
    definition of, 129
    SCALIR as, 143–145
supervised learning, 201–203
Supreme Court Reporter, 104
symbol grounding, 52–58, 123
    by communication, 55–58
    by observation, 54–55
symbolic AI, 4, 40
symbolic problem characteristics, 140
symbolic processing, 124–126, 137
    benefits of, 140–141
symbolic query, 196–199
symbolic system, 123
    definition of, 125
    SCALIR as, 145
Symbolics Common Lisp, 155
synonymy, 73, 76, 103, 117

T

tapered search, 183
taxonomy, 13, 47, 99–101
    of copyright law, 154
temporal integration, 177
term frequency, 152
term node, 154, 165
term weighting, 66, 152
    in query, 66
    length normalization, 152
term-document matrix, 66
text as knowledge representation, 57–58
text-based intelligent system, 4
    law as, 95
text-skimming, 79
thesaurus construction, 76–78, 268
Toulmin structures, 114
trail, 20–21
transitivity of links, 197–198
traveling salesperson problem, 129
treatment citation, 104, 161

U

unbounded depth, 37, 45–46, 52
undo, 242
United States Code, 103
United States Reports, 104
unsupervised learning, 202–203
user effort
    evaluation of, 76
user interface, 11, 30–32, 225–236
user testing, 236–244

V

variable binding, 135, 142
VCR example, *see* Betamax example
vector model, 65–67, 86, 87
version space, 140
vocabulary problem, 74–76, 87

W

weight
    adjustment of, 158
    constraint on sum, 156
    damping of, 215
    normalization of, 157, 215
West key number system, 99, 104, 110, 140, 149, 154, 157, 161–162, 275
WESTLAW, 15–19, 68, 69, 107, 110, 238, 241–244, 252, 275
    comparison with SCALIR, 255–265
Widrow-Hoff rule, 202
wild card, 65, 242